IMAGES
of America

FOREST ACRES

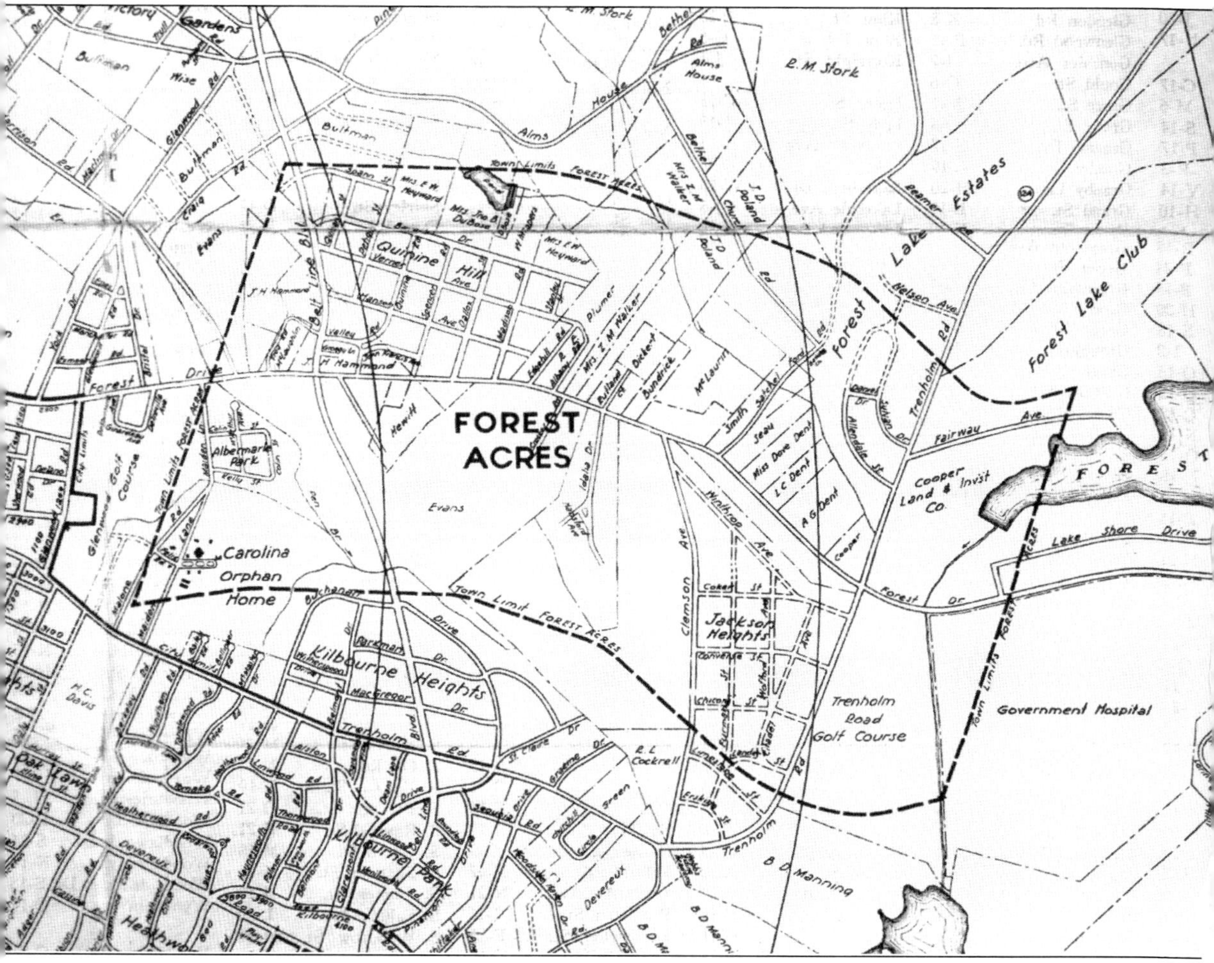

This 1945 map shows the original boundaries of Forest Acres. The city consisted of 2 square miles along Forest Drive. (Courtesy of the City of Forest Acres.)

On the Cover: S. W. Dent established a general merchandise store in the late 1800s on the Old Camden Road (now Forest Drive). Boykin T. and Fannie Davis took over the store in 1909 and operated it as B. T. Davis Groceries. It was the first store between Columbia and Camden to have a gasoline pump. After 1935, elections and city council meetings were held in the store. The Davis store closed in 1938, but the building continued to serve as Lake View voting precinct. The building was demolished in the late 1980s. (Courtesy of Hammond Edwards III.)

IMAGES
of America

FOREST ACRES

Warner M. Montgomery, Ph.D.

ARCADIA
PUBLISHING

ISBN 978-0-7385-8618-2

Published by Arcadia Publishing
Charleston, South Carolina

Printed in the United States of America

Library of Congress Control Number: 2010922163

For all general information contact Arcadia Publishing at:
Telephone 843-853-2070
Fax 843-853-0044
E-mail sales@arcadiapublishing.com
For customer service and orders:
Toll-Free 1-888-313-2665

Visit us on the Internet at www.arcadiapublishing.com

Charles Fetner's family tamed the forests and tilled the soil of Forest Acres for 200 years. Charlie has served on the city council since 1977.

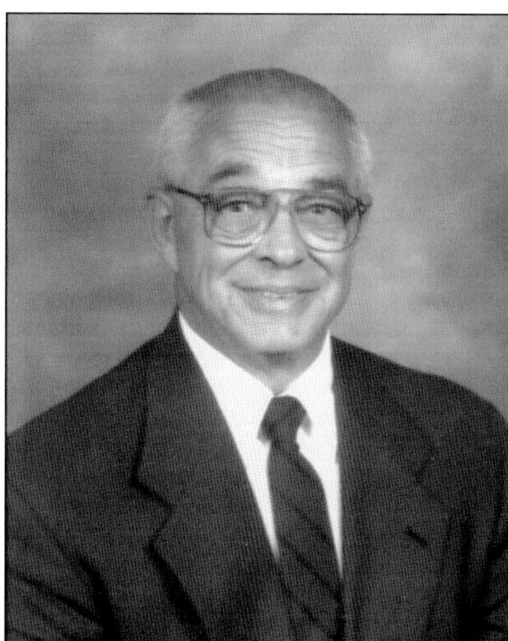

Contents

Acknowledgments

I would like to thank the many kind and generous people who had a part in the publication of this book. The idea of a history of Forest Acres sprang from a course I taught at the Shepherds Center on the history of Columbia. Chris Powell, a former incorrigible student of mine at A. C. Flora High (now successfully retired), suggested I follow it up with a course on his beloved Forest Acres. I did, and in poured the stories and photographs. Of special importance was the *History of Forest Acres* written by Carol Cook Dugan in 1997. Forest Acres councilman Charles Fetner provided the political background. City administrator Mark Williams, police chief Marion "Gene" Sealey, and administrative assistant Tera Webster guided me through the records at city hall.

Information and photographs were provided by Liz Hazlehurst Cantey, Edwin Cooper Jr., Pete and Mary Dent, Cal Dent, Wilhelmina and Hammond Edwards, Ron and Karen Galloway, Frankie Garrick and Jane Garrick Dyke, former police chief Charles McLean, Adele Jeffords Pope, Jesse T. Reese III, Ellen Verner Scoville, Dr. Edmund Taylor, Harry Taylor, Legrand Cooper, Debbie Richardson Fletcher, Chuck Gerald, Margaret McCrory Hicks, Mark Lynn, George McCutchen Jr., S. Rhea Preston, John Sherrer, and Rodger and Martha Stroup. Additional support and photographs were provided by the Historic Columbia Foundation. And of course, my wonderful wife, Linda Sosbee, provided me sustenance and critiques along the way.

INTRODUCTION

Forest Acres was incorporated as a city in 1935 largely due to the efforts of Sen. James H. Hammond, who had created the "town" of Quinine Hill, and John Hughes Cooper, who had developed the Forest Lake subdivision. The city grew from a community of a few hundred hardworking people living in 2 square miles to an upscale community of over 10,000 in three times the area.

The land that is now Forest Acres is made up of a series of sandhill ridges drained by Gills Creek and its tributaries, Eightmile Branch and Pen Branch. The beautiful manmade lakes are all fed by these creeks. The highest point is Quinine Hill (253 feet in altitude) in the west. The lowest is Gills Creek, 2 miles to the east.

The early Native Americans walked a path among the pine barrens between villages of the Congarees and the Waterees. During colonial days, the Native American path became a rutted wagon road connecting the towns of Saxe Gotha on the Congaree River and Pine Tree Hill on the Wateree River.

During the American Revolution, Saxe Gotha and Pine Tree Hill were renamed Granby and Camden and were the sites of major battles. The Taylor brothers—Thomas, John, and James—and Wade Hampton I fought with Gen. Thomas Sumter, "the Gamecock," defending the Granby-Camden Road.

In 1785, Thomas Taylor (1743–1833), Wade Hampton I (c. 1751–1835), and Timothy Rives (1748–1821) purchased 18,500 acres on both sides of Gills (Jackson's) Creek from north of the Old Camden Road (now Forest Drive) to the Congaree River. Taylor and Hampton bought out Rives and divided their land at Gills Creek, Taylor taking the west side and Hampton the east side. When the South Carolina Legislature decided in 1786 to build the new state capital on the flood-safe side of the Congaree River opposite Granby, Taylor sold his property on the designated capital plat back to the state.

Both Taylor and Hampton had a strong sense of duty to their state and country. Taylor served in the South Carolina Convention that ratified the U.S. Constitution, was appointed as one of the commissioners to plan the city of Columbia, and was elected to the South Carolina Legislature. Thomas and Anne Taylor's eldest son, John (1770–1832), was elected Columbia's first intendant (mayor) and was later elected to the U.S. Congress, South Carolina Senate, and as South Carolina governor.

Wade Hampton I was elected to the South Carolina Legislature, U.S. Congress, and served as a commander in the War of 1812. He purchased land in Alabama, Mississippi, and Louisiana and became the wealthiest planter in the United States. He hosted Pres. George Washington in his Columbia home (now called the Hampton-Preston Mansion) in 1791. Hampton and Taylor were members of the small delegation that escorted President Washington from Augusta to Columbia and then on to Camden.

Thomas Harwell (d. 1808) purchased a 640-acre tract in 1784 on the western side of Gills Creek south of the Old Camden Road for the 2007 equivalent of $1,381 and established a homestead.

Harwell accidently shot and killed his sister and buried her body near his home at what is now the Kelly Cemetery. The Harwell property fell to his daughters, Sarah Harwell Kelly and Mary Harwell Dooley. Sarah's son, James Kelly, inherited the property and built a home near what became known as Kelly Hill (now the site of the Kelly Cemetery at 1500 Kathwood Road).

In 1796, Taylor built a gristmill at the junction of the Old Camden Road and Gills Creek. Samuel Boatwright was the superintendent. Taylor later sold the mill to John and Edward Fisher, who turned it into a cotton mill known as Fisher's Mill. The Fishers ran the mill until they bought the much larger Saluda Factory from Abram Blanding and moved their operations to the Saluda River.

Hampton turned his land east of Gills Creek into two prosperous plantations, Woodlands and Millwood. These plantations joined at Hampton Hill overlooking Columbia. It was from the Taylor and Hampton land that Forest Acres was created 135 years later by farmers, entrepreneurs, developers, and finally suburbanites.

One

The Beginning at Quinine Hill

The highest point on the Taylor property on the Old Camden Road had a spring flowing from its sandy soil. In those days, a malaria medicine called quinine was being made from the bark of the South American cinchona tree. Since there was no standing water and few mosquitoes on the hill, Dr. James Madison Taylor (1812–1845), a nephew of Thomas Taylor, named it Quinine Hill to promote its healthy qualities.

John Francis Dalloz (first spelled Doloz) (1788–1831) was probably the first settler on Quinine Hill. He served with Napoleon, was wounded at the Battle of Waterloo in 1815, and soon thereafter immigrated to South Carolina, where he was employed by the Hamptons as a gardener.

Dalloz purchased a few acres on the Old Camden Road at Quinine Hill from Dr. James Madison Taylor, where he planted vineyards and produced wine in the French style. His son, John Francis Dalloz Jr. (1826–1898), inherited his father's farm. The Dalloz women were seamstresses to the wealthy women of Columbia. The legacy of this hardy French family lies in the names of two streets on Quinine Hill, John Francis Court and Dalloz Road.

Key portions of Quinine Hill were sold in 1834 by Dr. J. M. Taylor to Dr. James Davis, who had been instrumental in the establishment of the State Lunatic Asylum (later South Carolina State Mental Health Hospital) in 1828. His property remained in his family for almost a hundred years.

Dr. Abner Landrum (1785–1859) established the Pottersville Kiln in 1810 in Edgefield County, South Carolina, to produce unique stoneware using an alkaline glaze he had developed. Landrum's pottery became the basis for the much-desired Edgefield pottery. In violation of the established laws against educating slaves, Landrum taught his slave, Dave, to read, write, and set type, and together they published the *Edgefield Hive*, a pro-Union newspaper.

Seeking a wider audience for his liberal views, in 1830 Dr. Landrum moved to Columbia, where he published the *Columbia Free Press* and *Hive* newspaper for two years. It was succeeded by the *Columbia Hive* and was published until 1837. His son, Pressley Landrum (1801–1886), continued in the printing business until the Civil War.

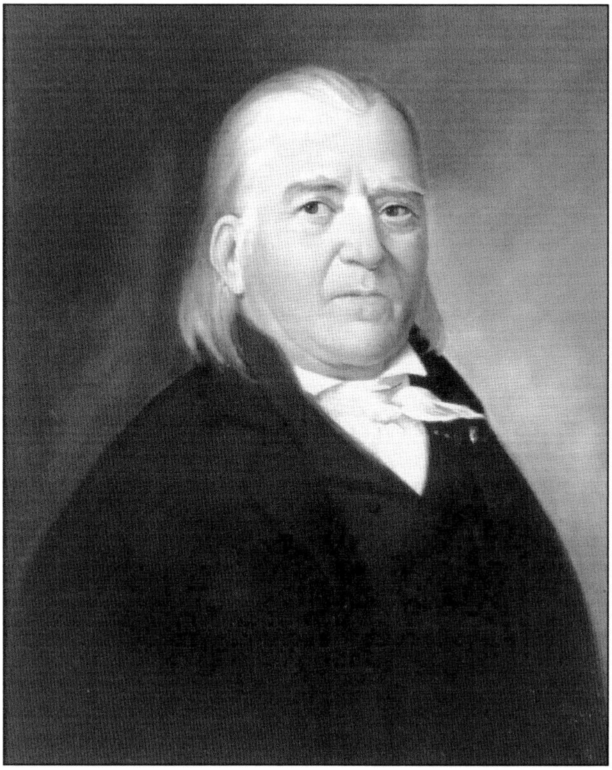

Col. Thomas Taylor (1743–1833) purchased land along the Old Camden Road (now Forest Drive) soon after the American Revolution. His property west of Gills Creek became the center of Forest Acres in 1935. (Courtesy of Dr. Edmund R. Taylor.)

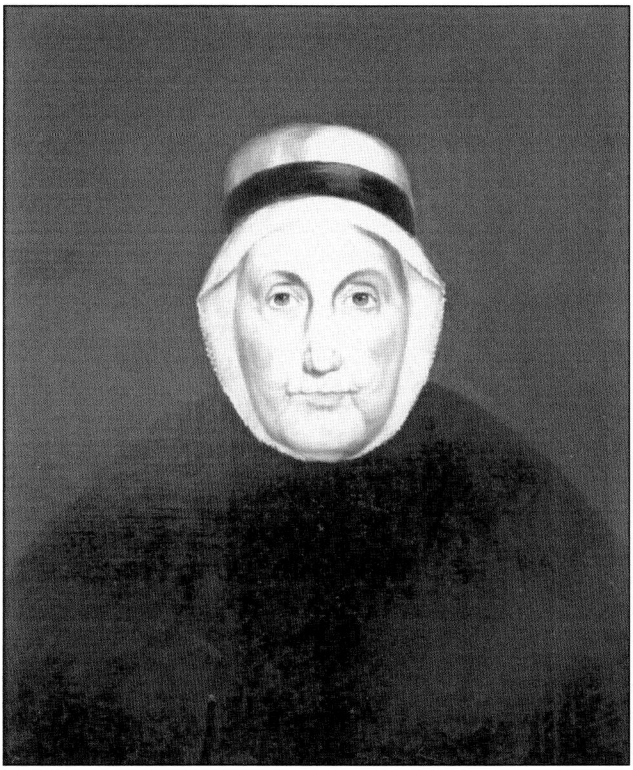

Thomas and Anne Taylor and their 12 children maintained a home in Columbia on Richland Street. In addition to his home, at his death Taylor owned 18 blocks in the city, 248 slaves, and hundreds of acres on both sides of the Congaree River, including approximately 2 square miles along the Old Camden Road known as "Taylor Town." (Courtesy of Dr. Edmund R. Taylor.)

Gen. Wade Hampton I (1754–1833) owned land east of Gills Creek. Portions of his property became parts of Fort Jackson in 1917 and Forest Acres in 1935. His Millwood and Woodlands Plantations are still in the Hampton family today. (Courtesy of the South Caroliniana Library.)

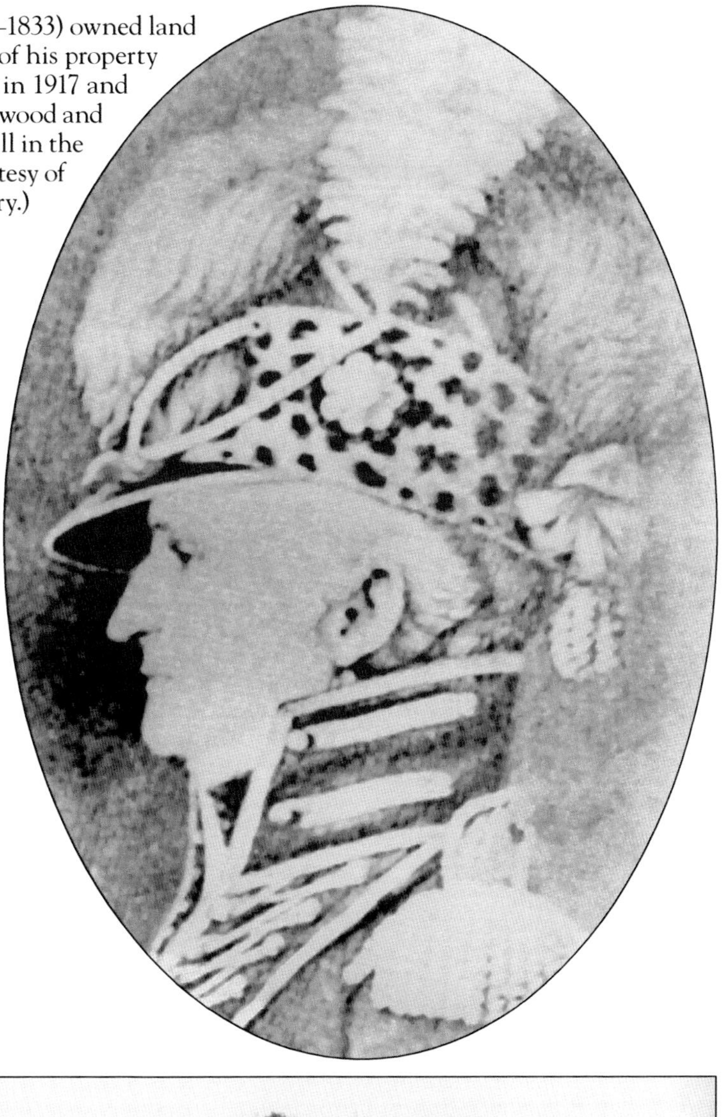

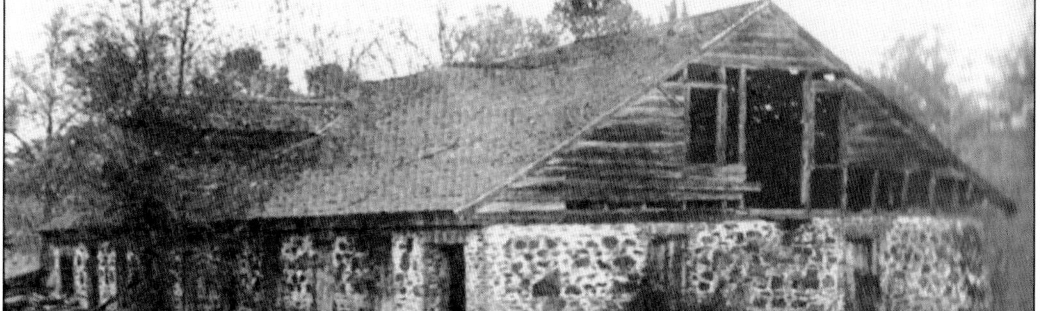

Col. Thomas Taylor erected a gristmill on Gills Creek in 1796. Pictured here are the remains as they appeared in 1935. (Courtesy of the South Caroliniana Library.)

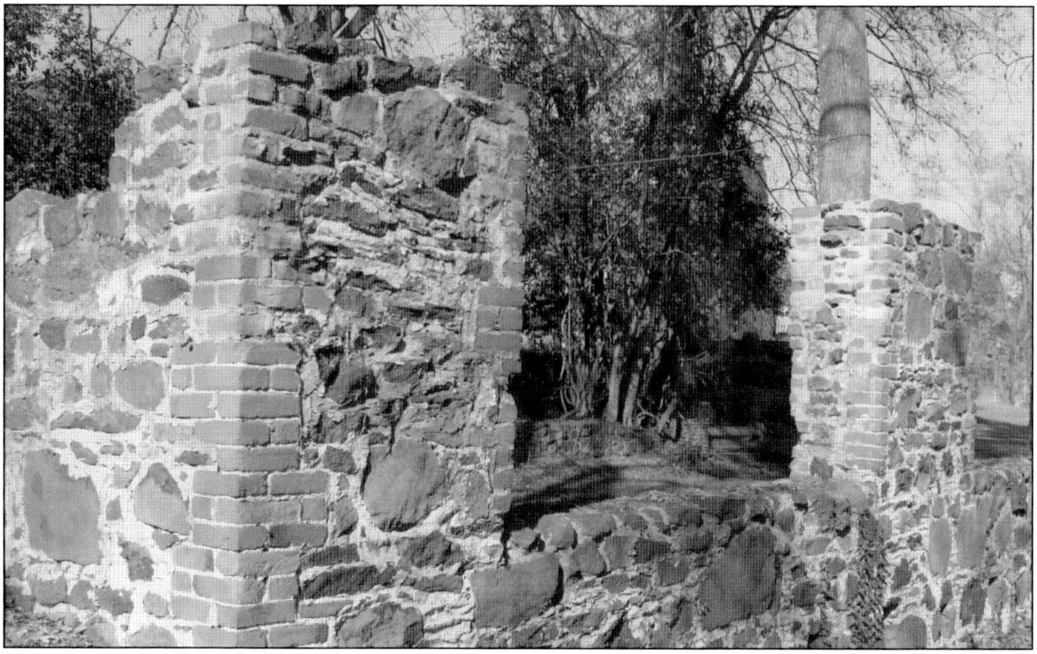

Taylor's Old Mill, now a private park on Old Mill Circle, became one of the earliest spinning mills in Richland County under the ownership of John and Edward Fisher. (Photograph by Warner M. Montgomery.)

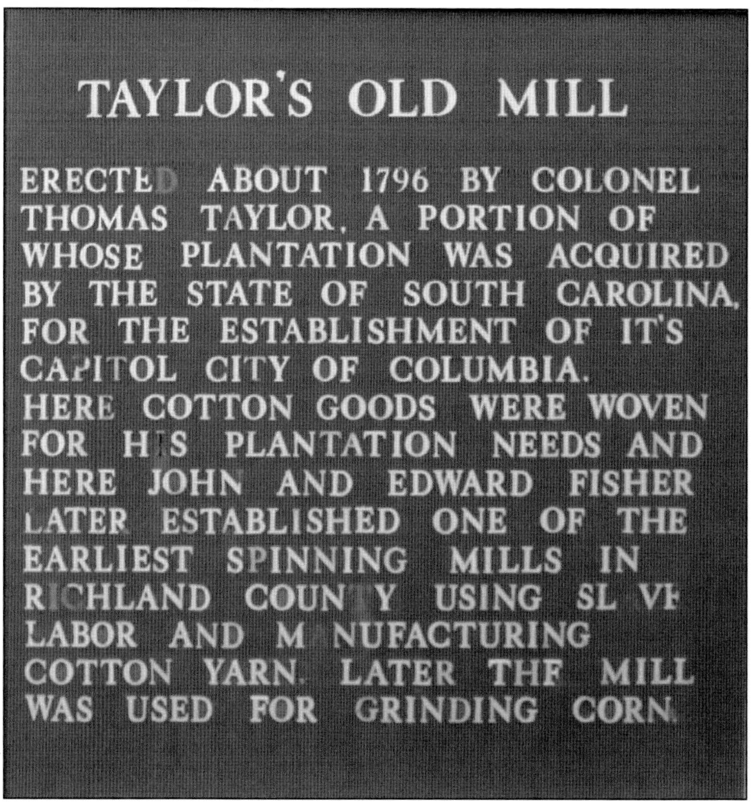

This sign marks Taylor's Old Mill. Dr. Benjamin Franklin Taylor (1791–1852), the 11th child of Thomas and Anne, inherited over 400 acres. He married Sally Coles and built a home he called Edgehill at the corner of what is now Cherry Laurel and Verner Streets. Taylor graduated from Princeton and served in the state legislature, but he spent most of his time farming and raising horses. Daniel Webster visited Taylor's plantation when he was investigating slavery for Sen. John C. Calhoun. (Photograph by Warner M. Montgomery.)

The names Old Mill and Lake View are still used today. (Photograph by Warner M. Montgomery.)

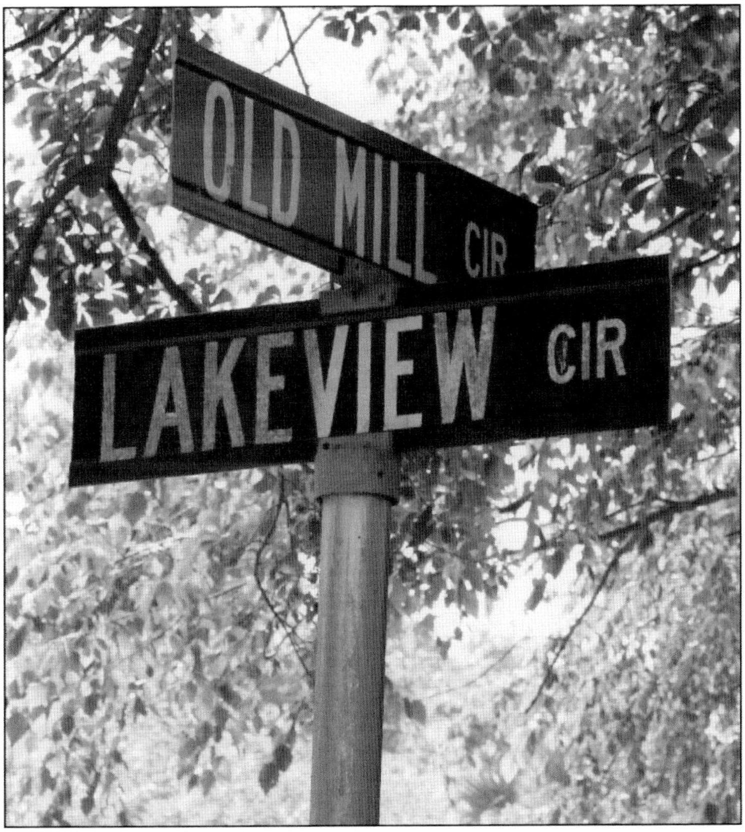

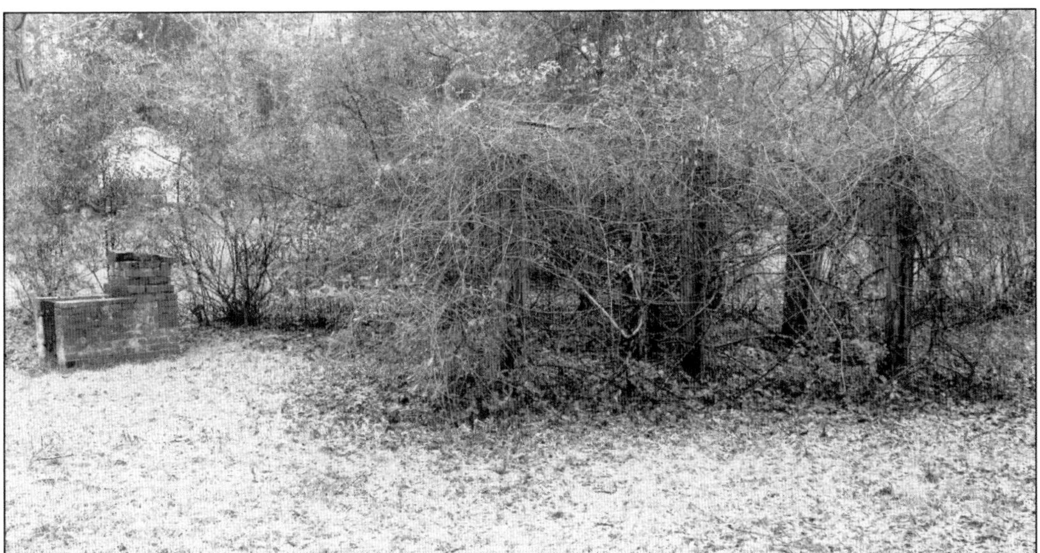

These grapevines on John Francis Court on Quinine Hill were planted by John Francis Dalloz almost 200 years ago, and they still yield grapes each year. Dalloz may have received viticulture information from Nicholas Herbemont (1771–1839), a fellow Frenchman who taught at South Carolina College. Herbemont had an 8-acre vineyard, Palmyra, on Eightmile Branch, a mile east of Quinine Hill. (Photograph by Warner M. Montgomery.)

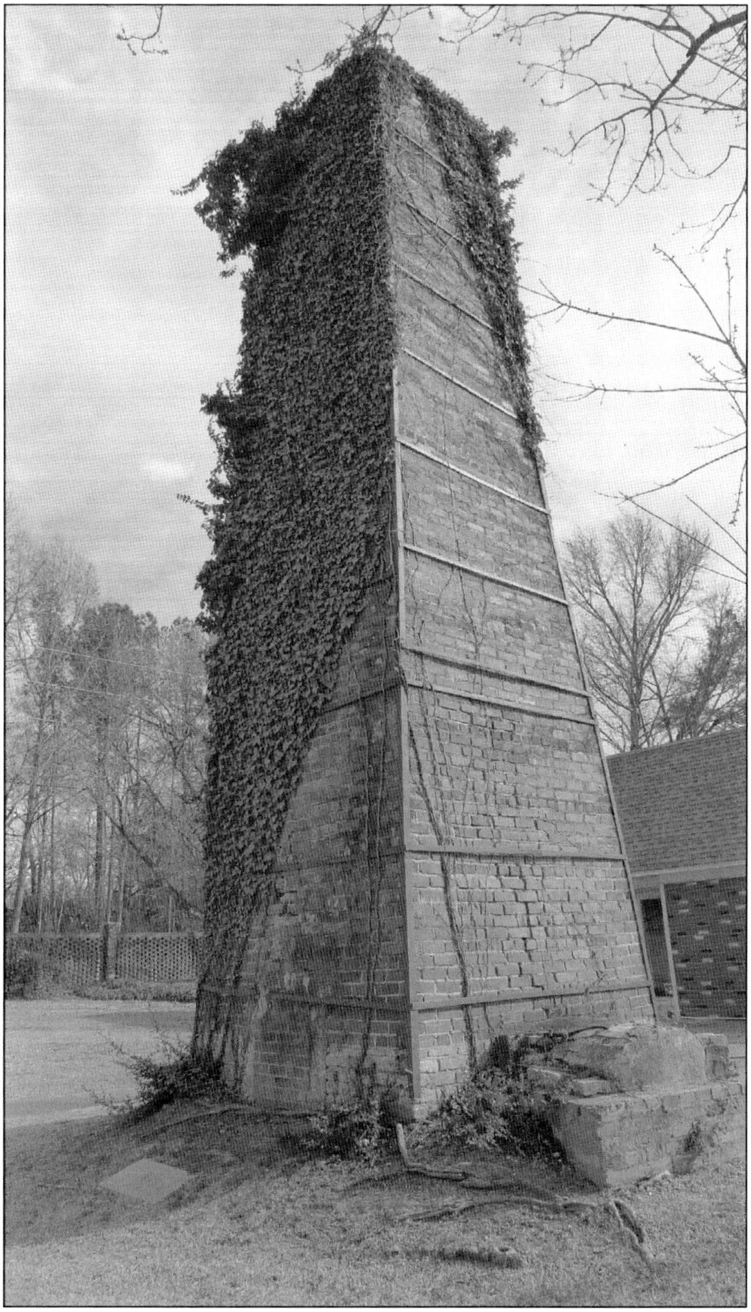

Dr. Abner Landrum built a home (4712 Bethel Church Road) and a brick factory on Eightmile Branch. Using the native sand, clay, and creek water, Landrum's factory produced strong fireplace bricks for the new homes being built in the growing Columbia area. Landrum purchased additional acreage toward Gills Creek. By 1880, the Landrum Brickworks was producing quality bricks and pottery. The families of Lineous Landrum (1829–1891) and John Stork worked closely together in the business. The original brickyard chimney erected in the 1800s by Landrum was encased in this chimney in 1935. The old Landrum-Stork Brickyard is now a residential development. (Photograph by Warner M. Montgomery.)

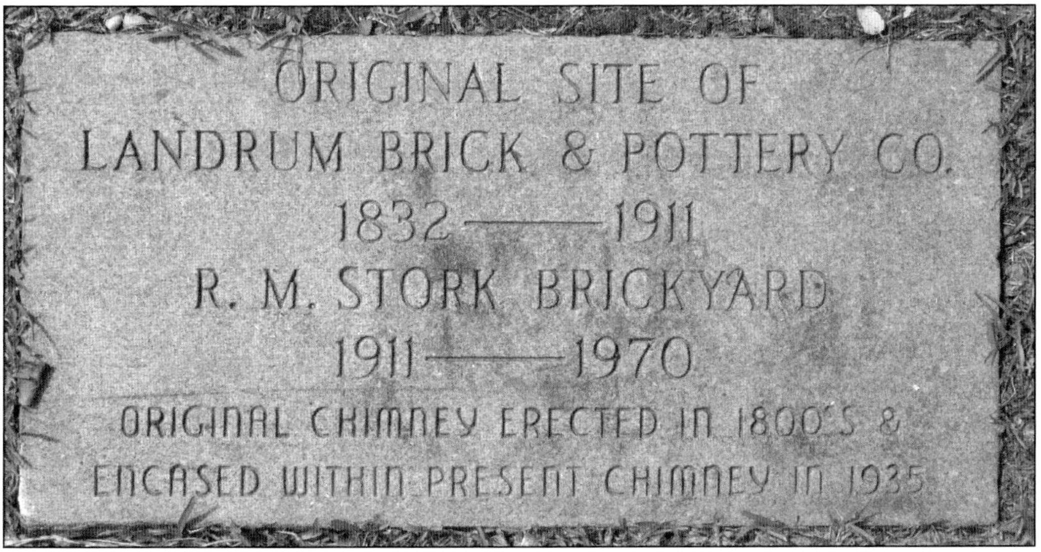

The Landrum Brick and Pottery Company operated until 1911, when Dr. Landrum's granddaughter, Julia (1847–1887), and her husband, R. M. Stork (1873–1954), took over and renamed it the Stork Brickyard. The Stork family operated it until 1970, when the property was sold and developed as Brickyard Condominiums. The original chimney from the 1800s is encased within another chimney built in 1935 on the grounds of the Brickyard Condominiums. This plaque marks the original site of the Landrum-Stork Brickyard. (Photograph by Warner M. Montgomery.)

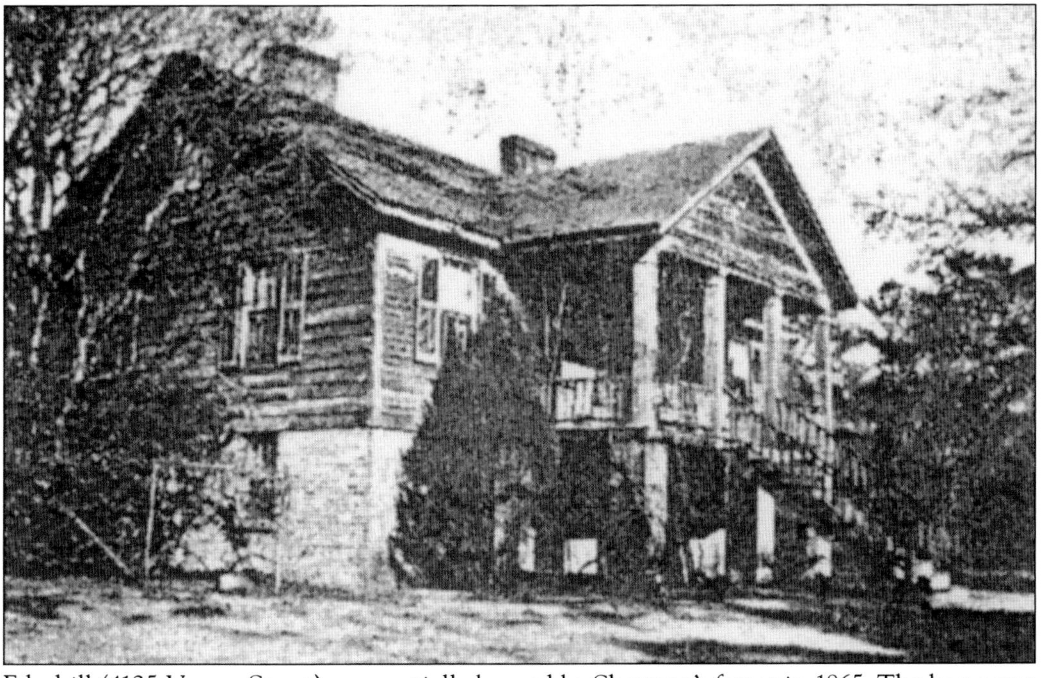

Edgehill (4125 Verner Street) was partially burned by Sherman's forces in 1865. The home was restored by R. E. Plumer, who married Sarah Taylor. Their son Robert (1853–1938) married Adelaide Dalloz (1854–1899), daughter of John Francis Dalloz Jr. Robert and Adelaide's daughter, Sally Roof, lived in the home until her death in 1978. The home is shown here in 1943. (Courtesy of Frankie Garrick.)

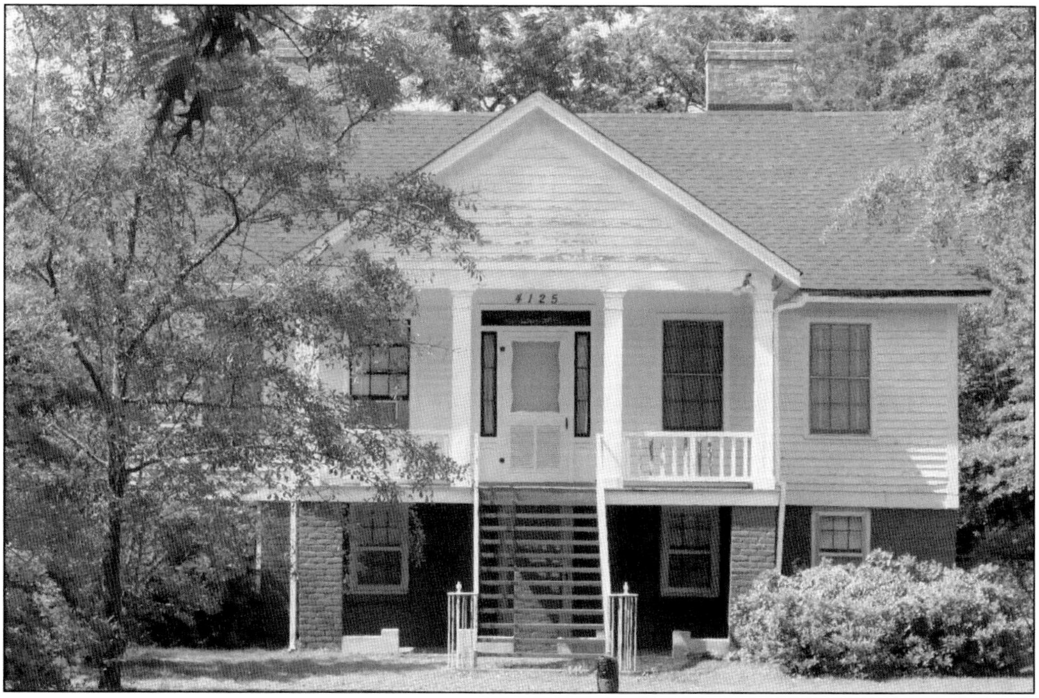

The Taylor-Dalloz-Plumer House, built before the Civil War, has been restored many times. (Photograph by Warner M. Montgomery.)

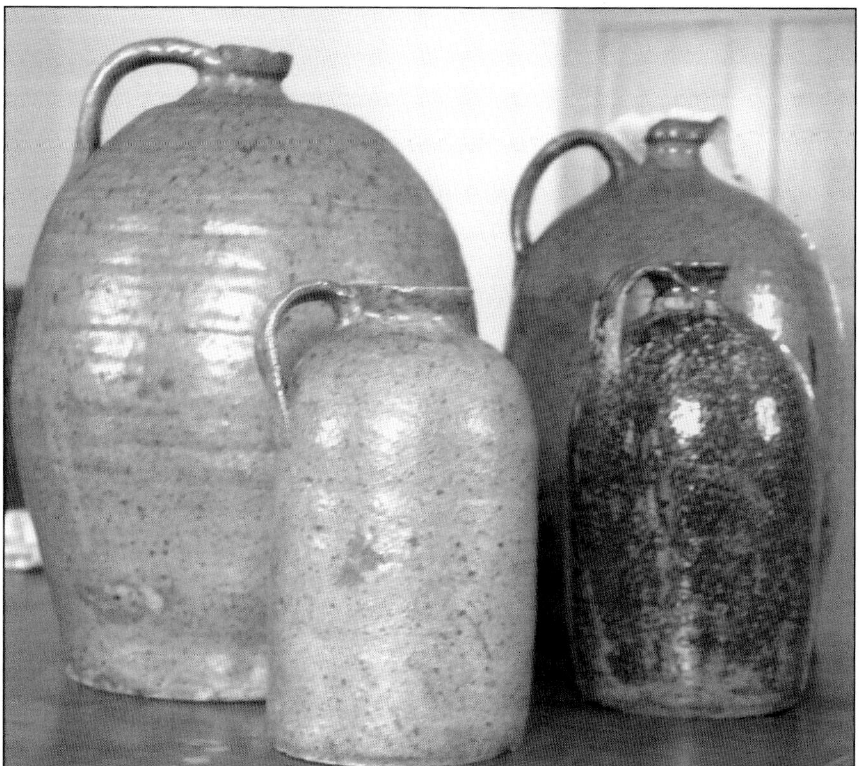

These pottery pitchers made in the Stork Brickyard are now in the South Carolina State Museum. (Courtesy of the South Carolina State Museum.)

Bricks made until 1950 in the Landrum-Stork Brickyard were used in many of the homes in Columbia and Forest Acres. (Courtesy of Martha Stroup.)

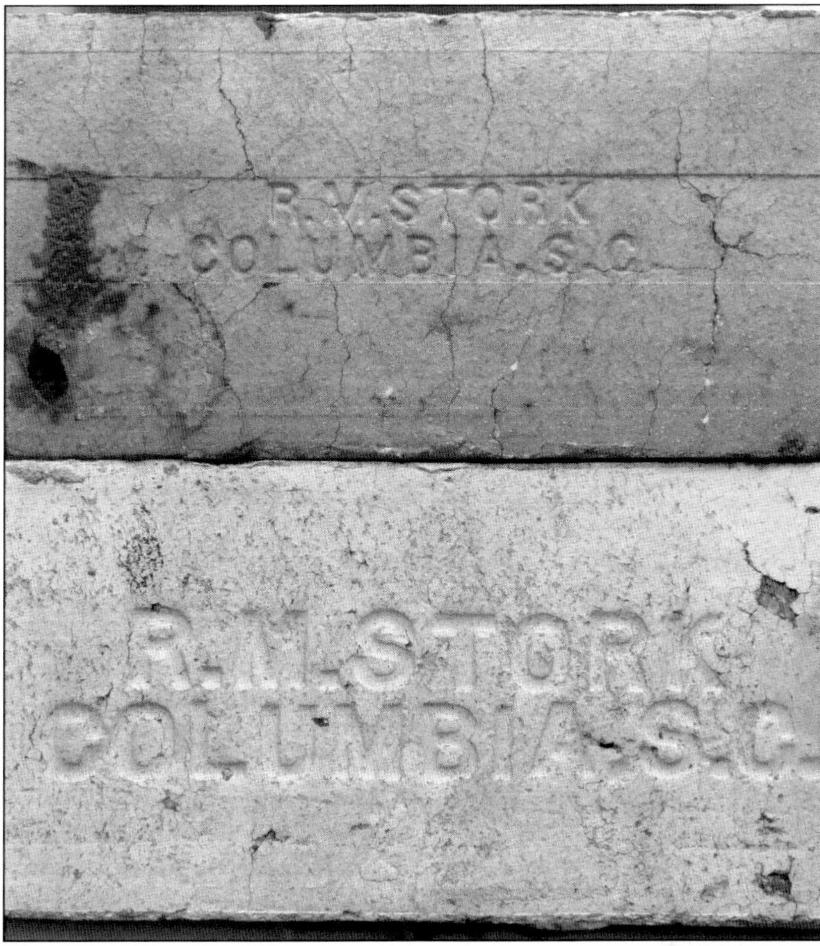

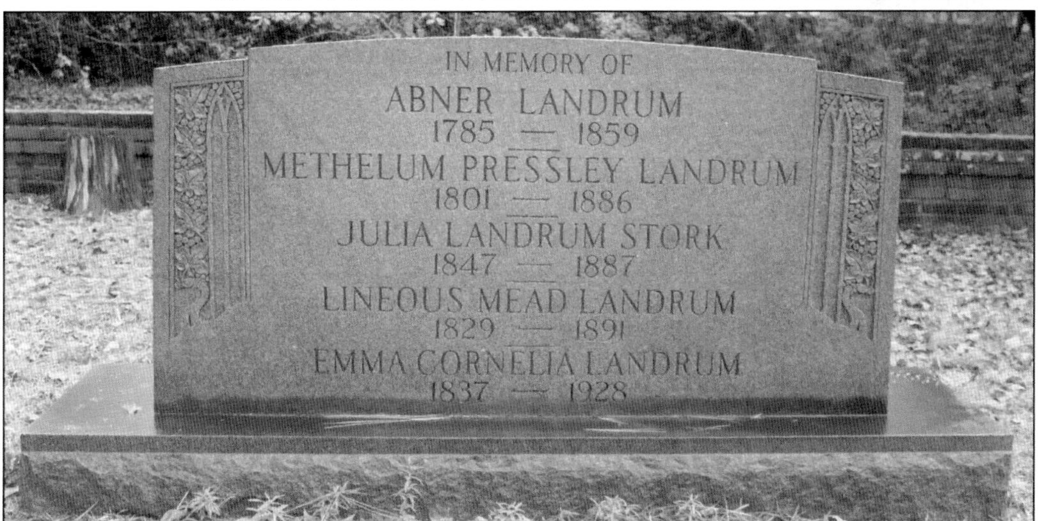

The Landrum-Stork family cemetery is located on Briarfield Road near Satchel Ford Elementary School. (Photograph by Warner M. Montgomery.)

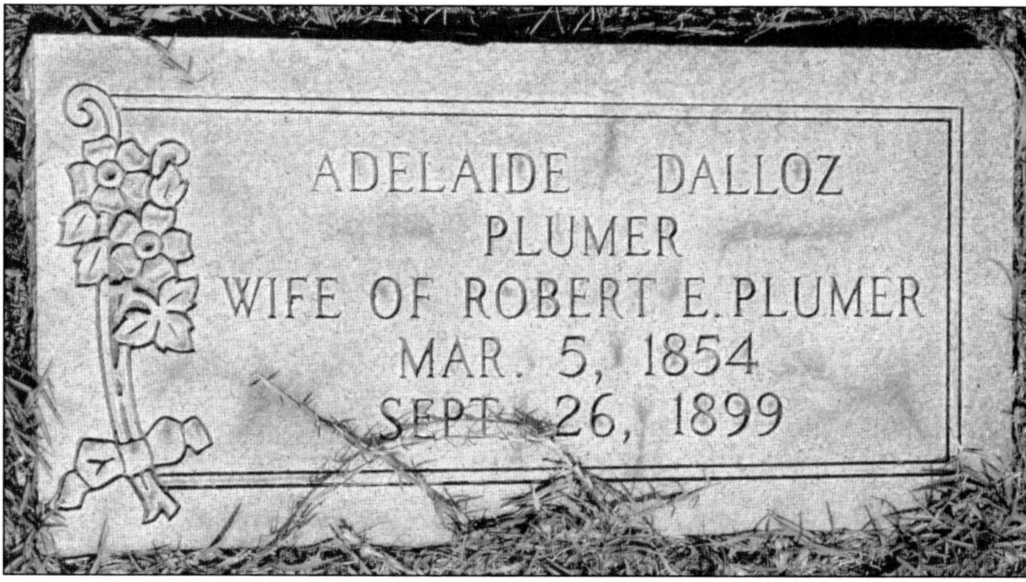

Adelaide Plumer was the daughter-in-law of John Francis Dalloz, who was born in St. Guade, France, in 1788 and came to America shortly after the fall of Napoleon in 1815. Mrs. Wade Hampton employed Dalloz to beautify the gardens at her home, the Hampton-Preston Mansion bounded by Blanding, Henderson, Laurel, and Pickens Streets in Columbia. The grave of Adelaide Dalloz Plumer is in the Landrum-Stork cemetery in Forest Acres. (Photograph by Warner M. Montgomery.)

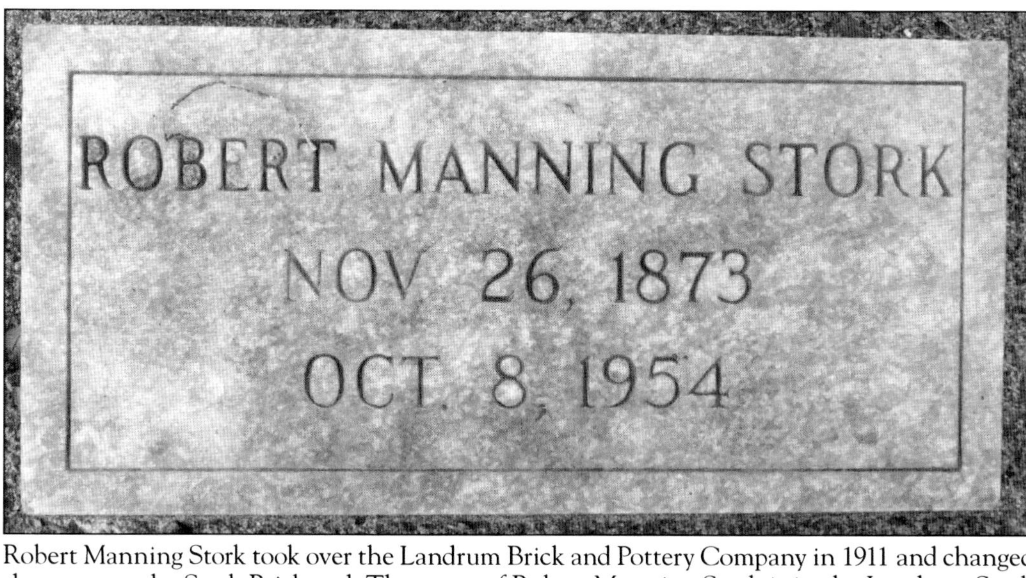

Robert Manning Stork took over the Landrum Brick and Pottery Company in 1911 and changed the name to the Stork Brickyard. The grave of Robert Manning Stork is in the Landrum-Stork cemetery. (Photograph by Warner M. Montgomery.)

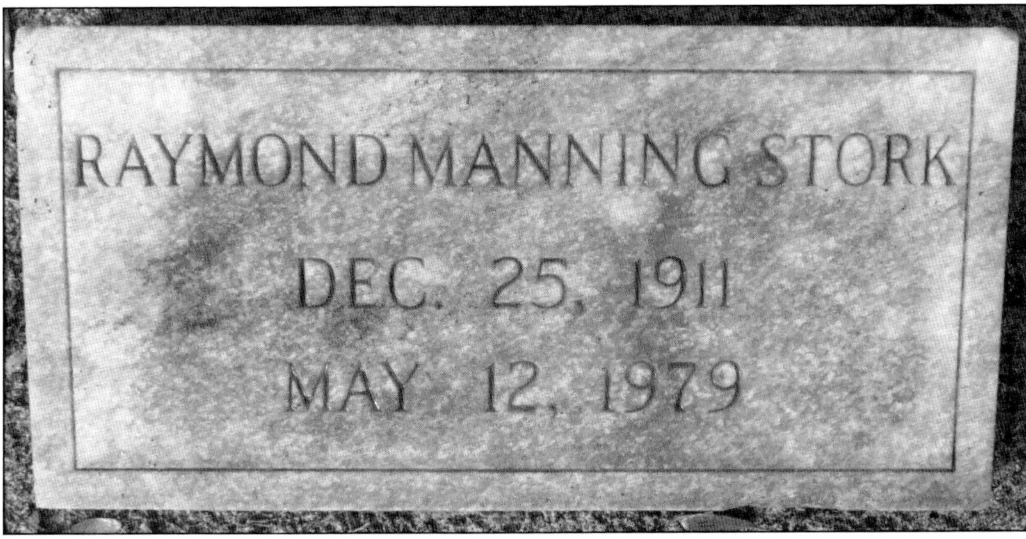

The grave of Raymond Manning Stork is in the Landrum-Stork cemetery. (Photograph by Warner M. Montgomery.)

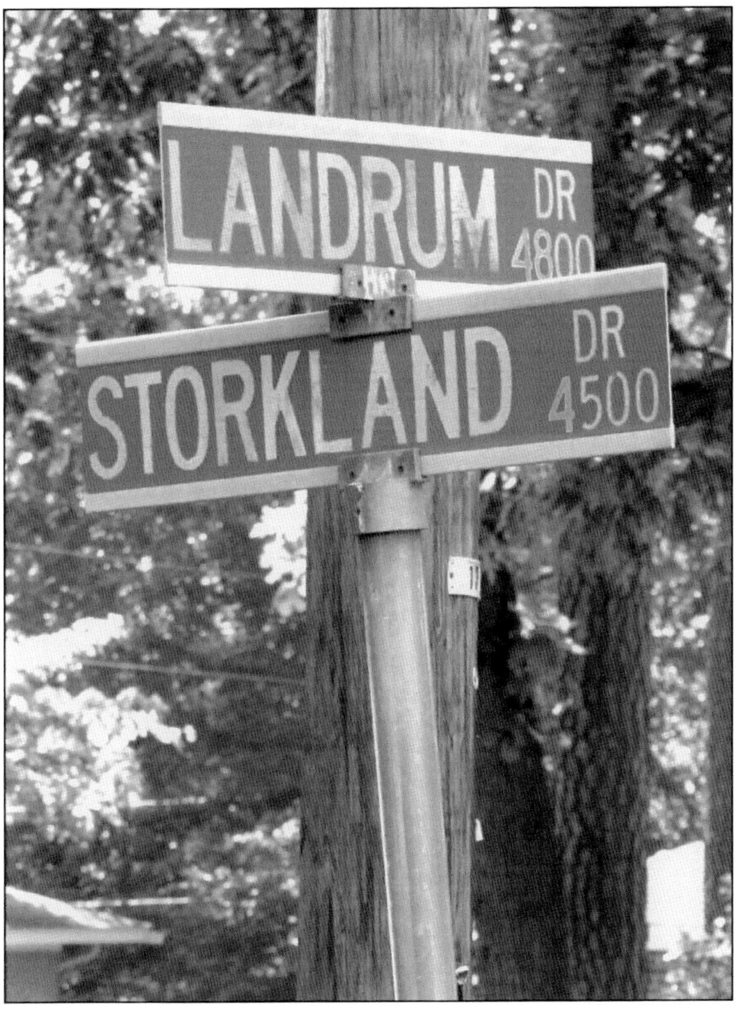

Streets surrounding the old brickyard keep the Landrum and Stork names. (Photograph by Warner M. Montgomery.)

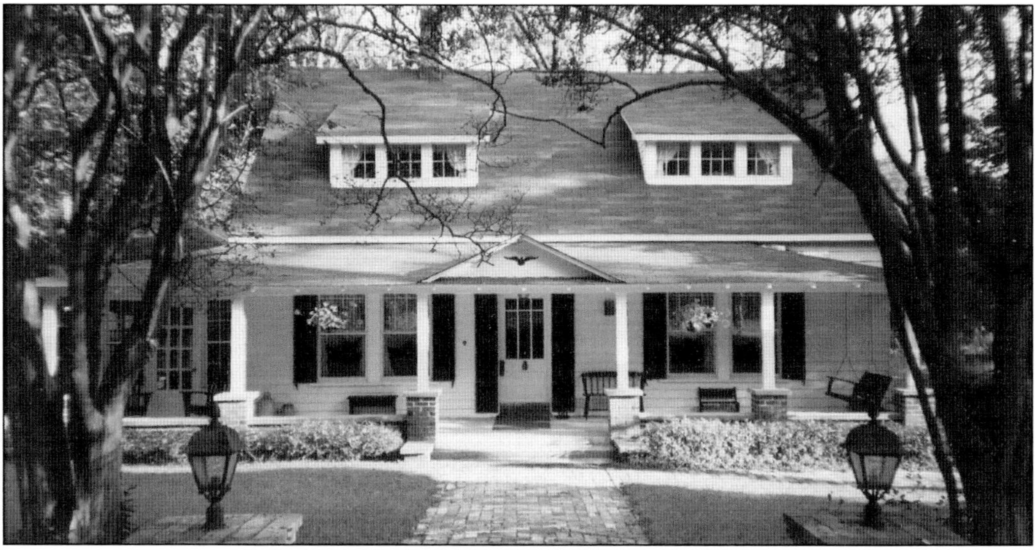

The Landrum-Stork Home at 4712 Bethel Church Road was built by Dr. Abner Landrum prior to the Civil War and has been renovated many times. This photograph was taken in 1970. (Courtesy of Legrand Cooper.)

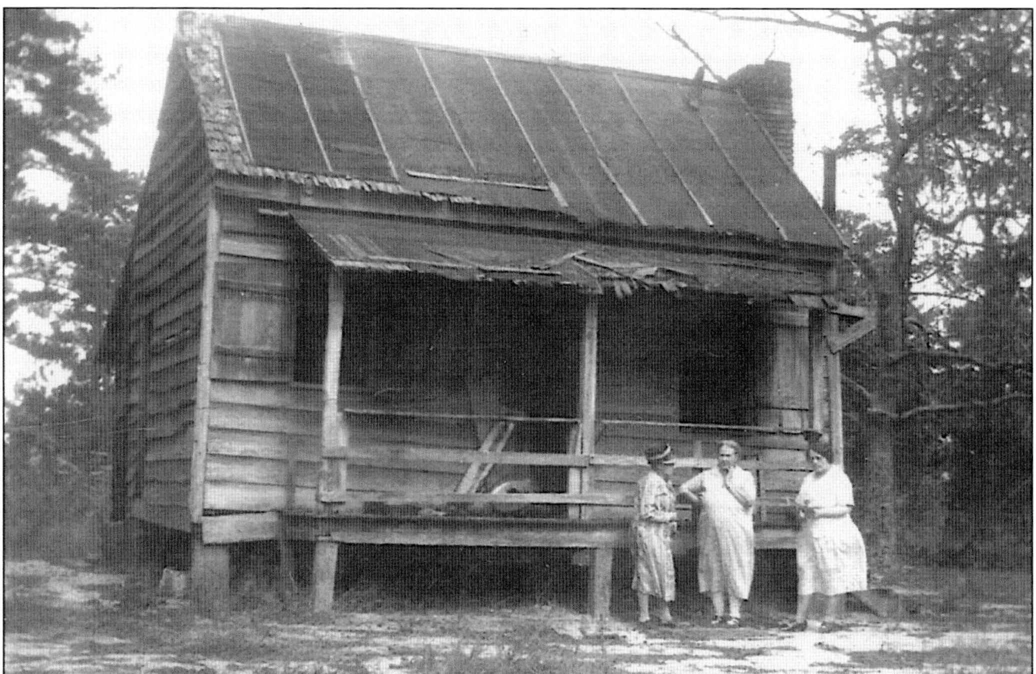

The Kelly homestead was located on Gills Creek in the early 1800s. It was abandoned in 1928 just before this photograph was taken. Mary Colgan (left), who left the home in 1877, is visiting her daughter Sophia Colgan (right) and Lola Kelly Daniels (center). (Courtesy of Mark Lynn.)

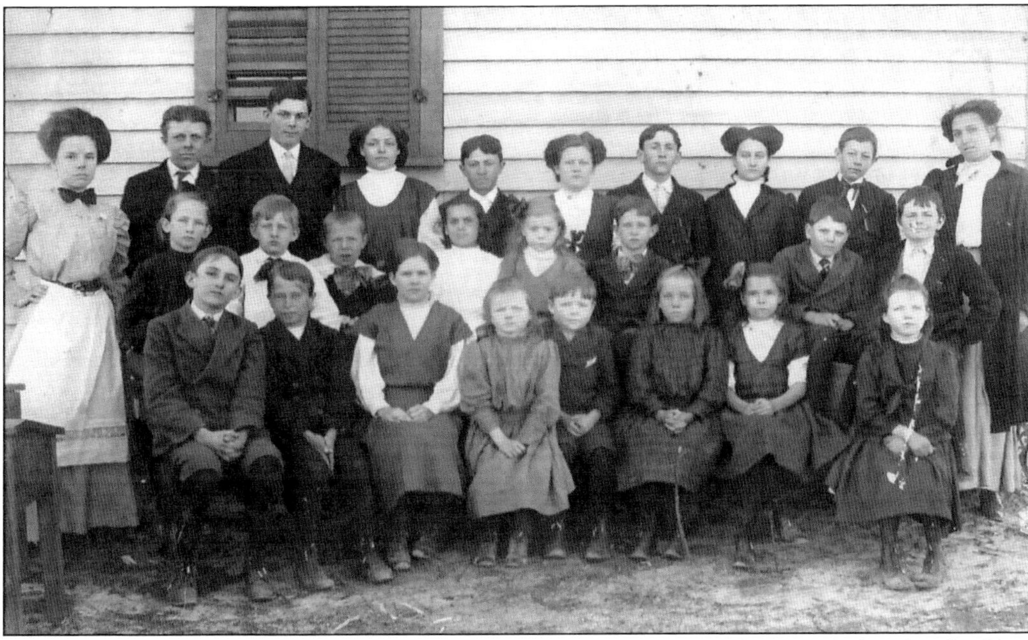

The Kelly family gathered for this photograph in 1908. Joe W. Hipp (1900–1978) is the third boy on the second row from the left. Hipp, the grandfather of Mark Lynn of Lexington, is buried in the Kelly Cemetery on Kathwood Road above Lake Katherine. (Courtesy of Mark Lynn.)

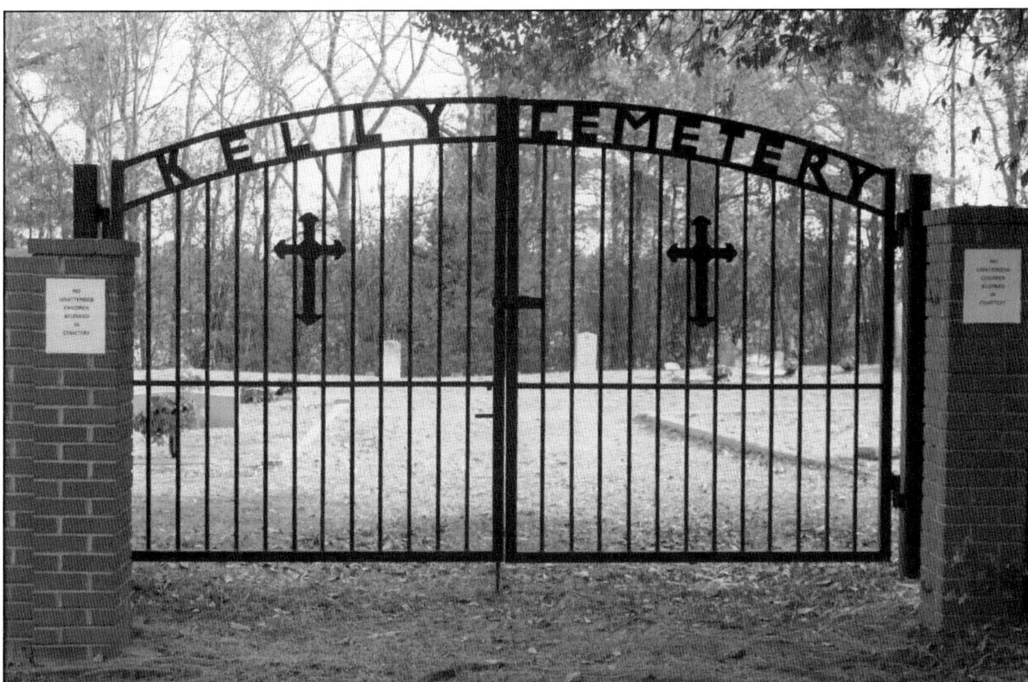

The Kelly Cemetery is located at 1500 Kathwood Road, Columbia, South Carolina. (Photograph by Warner M. Montgomery.)

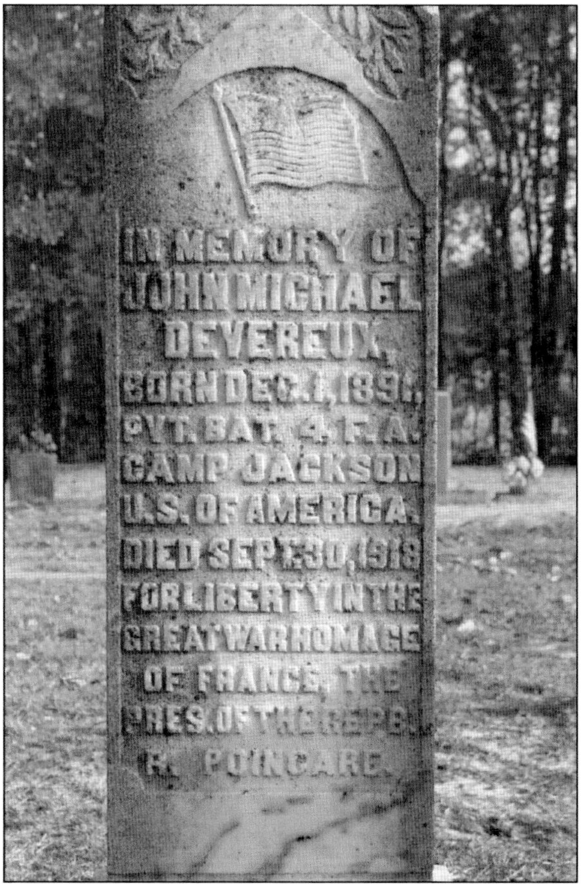

John Michael Devereaux (b. 1891), who served at Camp Jackson and died in France in 1918, is buried in the Kelly Cemetery. (Photograph by Warner M. Montgomery.)

John Bowers, who helped operate Bowers Beach, is buried in the Kelly Cemetery. (Photograph by Warner M. Montgomery.)

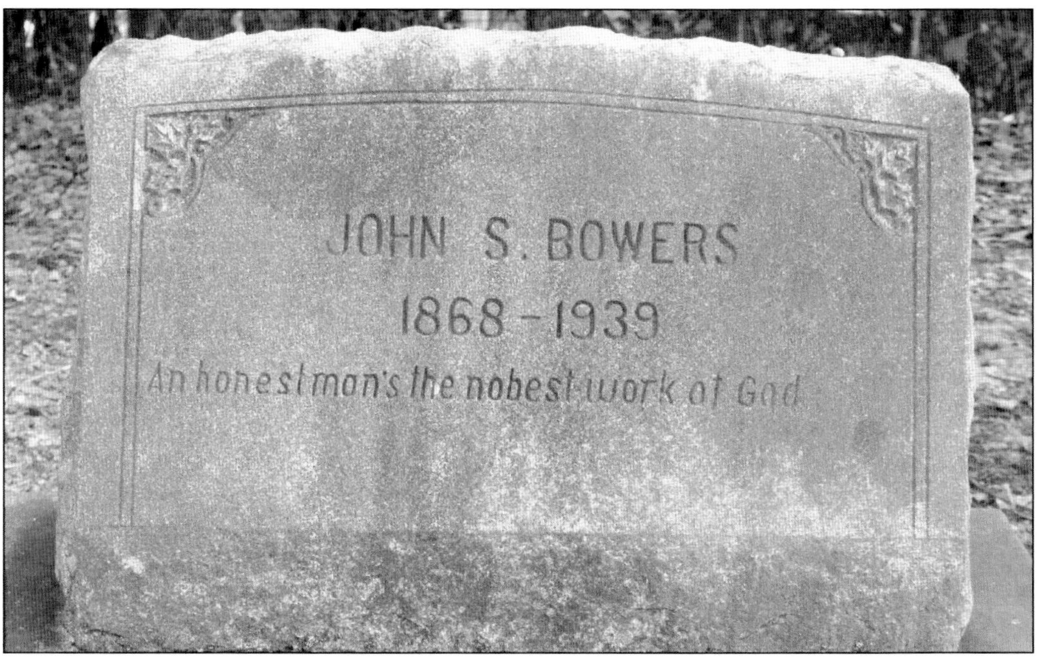

Two

THE GILLS CREEK SETTLEMENT

The Taylor property on Gills Creek also underwent settlement and change. By 1810, Hezekiah Dent (1775–1833) was engaged in farming and logging along Two Notch Road, the northern route to Camden.

Samuel Dent (1810–1879), one of Hezekiah's many children, managed Thomas Taylor's eastern timberland, farmed 1,800 acres along Gills Creek he had purchased from Taylor in 1858, and operated a rope factory. Dent dammed Gills Creek, forming Dent's Pond (now Forest Lake), which provided waterpower for a sawmill. He built a home on the pond (now 104 Country Club Drive). Samuel was also a planter but did not own any slaves. According to the 1850 census, he had a taxable worth of $10,000, making him a wealthy man.

Samuel and his wife, Alice (1816–1884), had at least 12 children, many of whom spent their lives in the surrounding area logging, farming, and producing turpentine, pitch, and tar for the shipbuilding industry. The community along Gills Creek between Two Notch Road and the Old Camden Road became known as Dents.

By 1870, the railroad ran along Two Notch Road. During World War I when Camp Jackson was being constructed, a Seaboard Air Line Railroad station and switch was installed at Dents at the request of Quartermaster Lt. Col. William Cooper to handle labor trains. In the 1930s, a post office named Dentsville was established near the train station at the junction of Two Notch Road, North Trenholm Road, and Decker Boulevard.

Bethel Methodist Church was established in 1835. Thomas Taylor donated land for the church near Eightmile Branch on Satchel Ford Road, the main road at that time between the Old Camden Road and Two Notch Road. Adjacent property was owned by Samuel Dent and Abner Landrum. Samuel Dent cut the lumber and directed construction of the church building (4600 Daniel Drive).

Samuel Dunwoody, John N. Davis, Ebenezer LeGette, Bartlett Thomason, Robert J. Limehouse, Edward L. King, and 18 other ministers served the Bethel Methodist Church before the building was destroyed by fire in 1867. Rev. Richard R. Dagnall led the construction of a new "little church in the wildwood" a year later. Samuel Henry Dent (1853–1933) supervised the remodeling of the sanctuary.

A masonry sanctuary, the church's third, was completed in 1948 under the leadership of Rev. Henry J. Bennett. The fourth sanctuary, which seats 528, was constructed by J. A. Metze and Sons, Inc. in 1964 after a two-year fund-raising campaign led by Dr. A. W. Lowe.

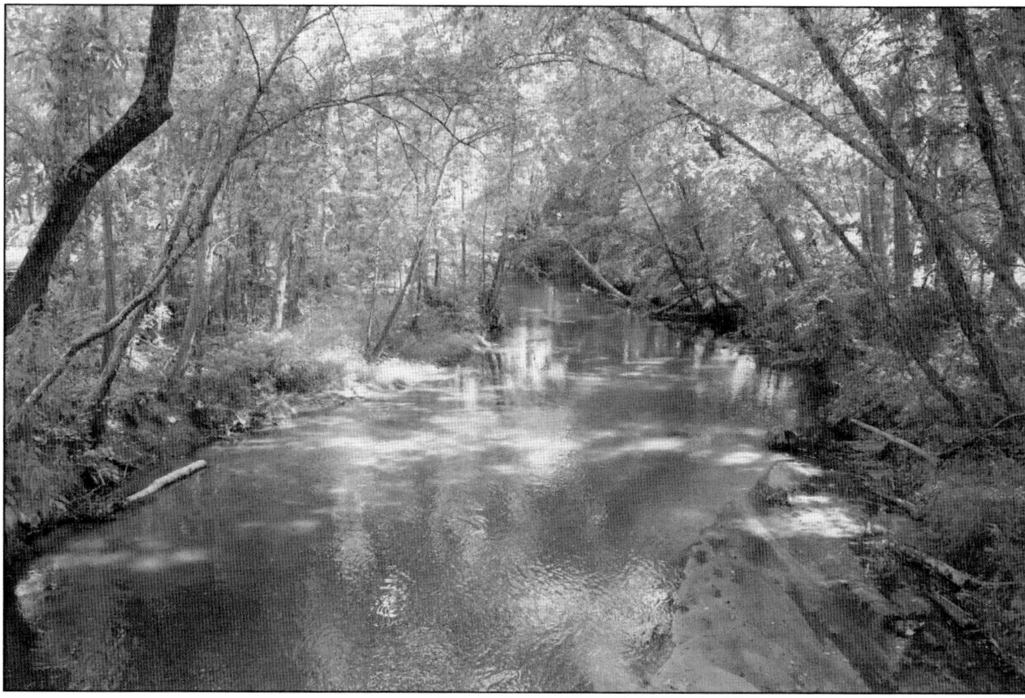

Gills Creek is the major waterway in Forest Acres. It drains into the Congaree River and was the mode of transportation and source of water for the early settlers. (Photograph by Warner M. Montgomery.)

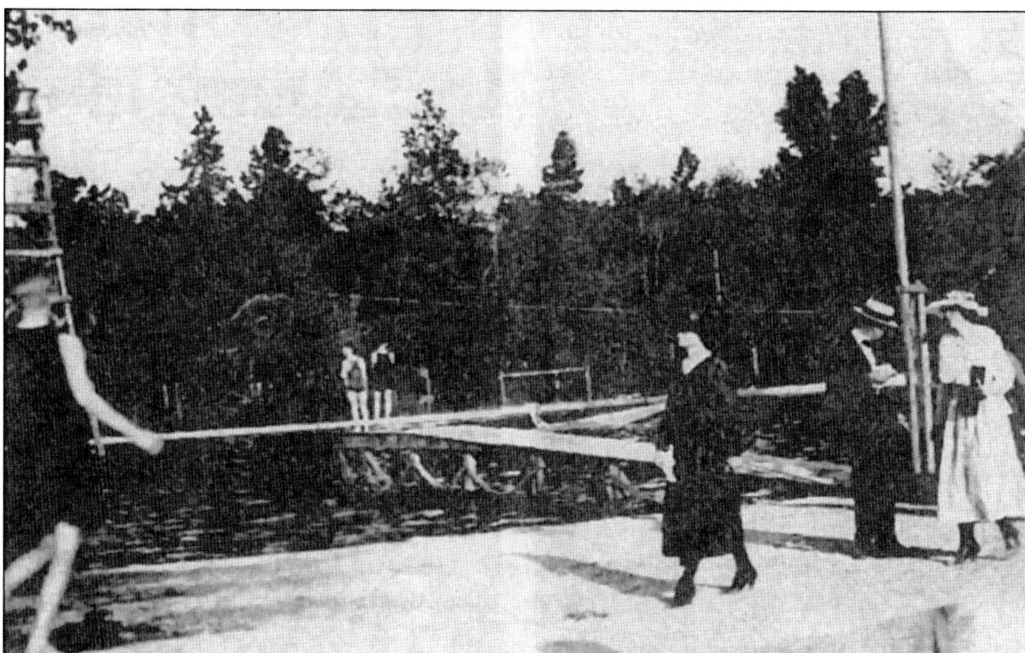

Dent's Pond was created by Samuel Dent prior to the Civil War for waterpower for a sawmill. By 1910, when this photograph was taken, the pond was a public swimming and recreational area. It is now part of Forest Lake. (Courtesy of Richland County Public Library.)

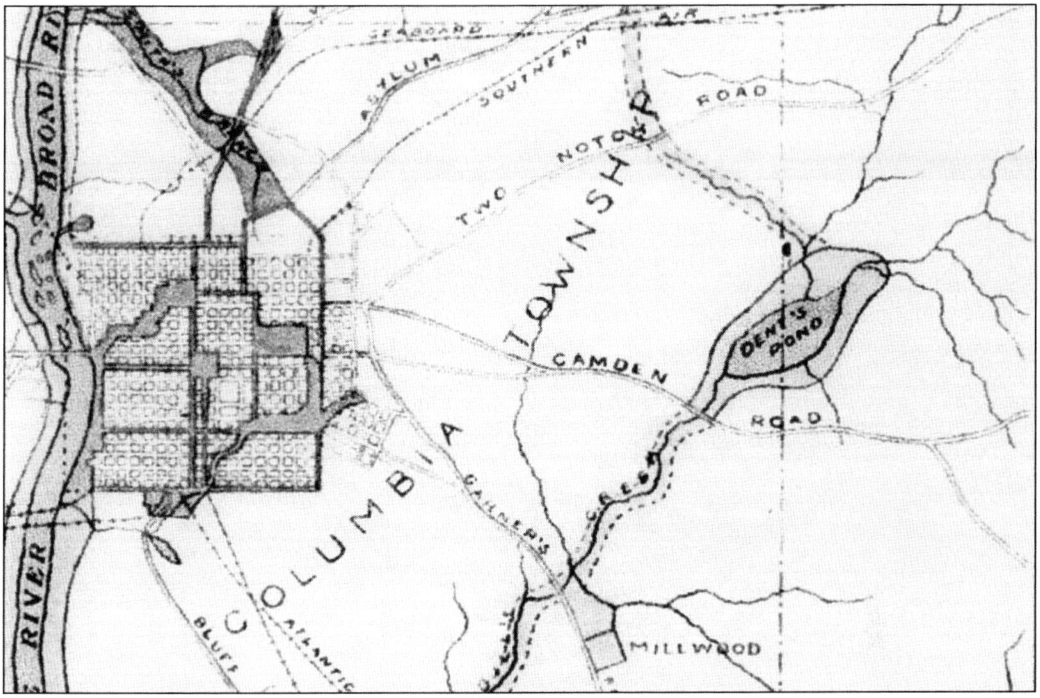

This 1905 map shows Dent's Pond and Millwood on Gills Creek. (Courtesy of Historic Columbia Foundation.)

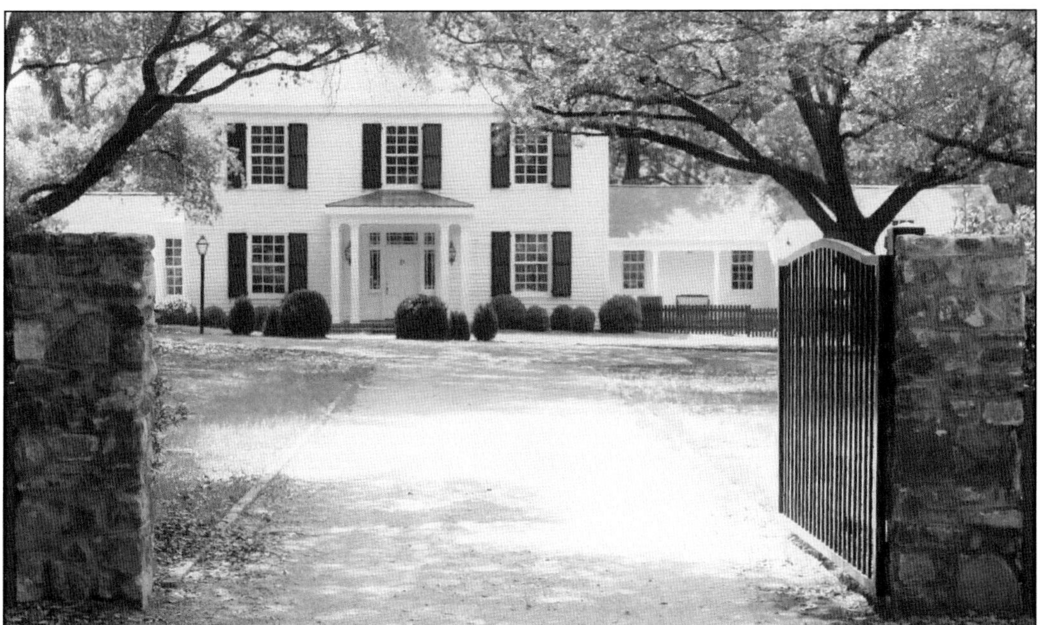
Samuel Dent built a home on Dent's Pond prior to the Civil War. John Hughes Cooper moved into the home after he bought the property in 1920. He renamed the pond Forest Lake and the home Forest Lake Gardens. It is now the home of Edwin Cooper Jr., nephew of John Hughes Cooper. (Photograph by Warner M. Montgomery.)

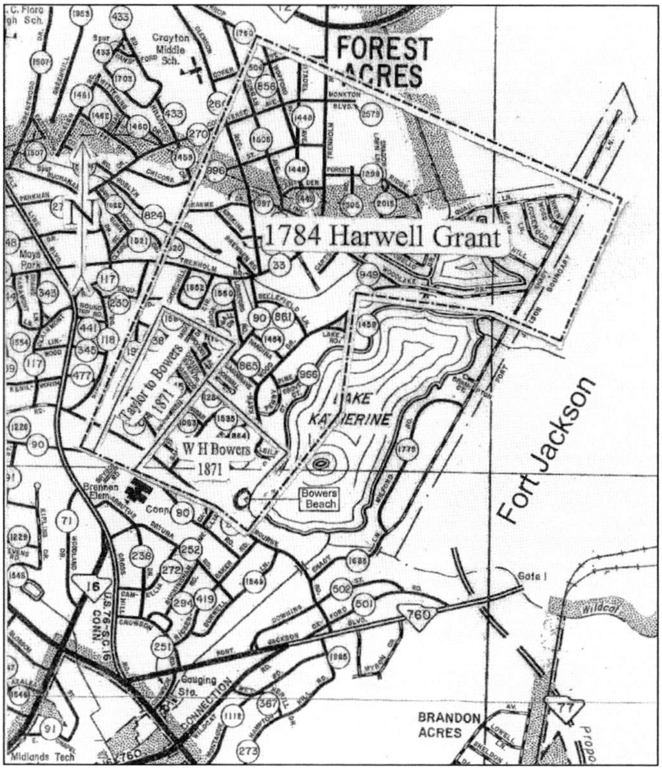

In 1784, Thomas Harwell received a state grant for a 640-acre tract of land on the west side of Gills Creek south of the Old Camden Road. When he died in 1808, his daughters, Sarah Kelly and Mary Dooley, inherited the land. The Harwell-Kelly property fell to Sarah's grandson, William Henry Bowers (1824–1895), in 1843. In 1871, Bowers bought another 50 acres from Benjamin F. Taylor, bringing his holdings to 110 acres. He and his wife had six children. They farmed the land and sold produce at the Columbia Farmers Market. (Courtesy of the Bowers family.)

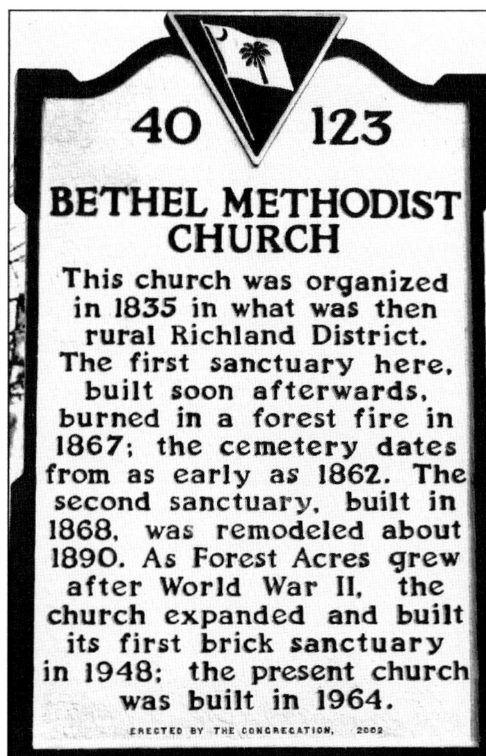

Bethel Methodist Church was the first church established in Forest Acres. (Photograph by Warner M. Montgomery.)

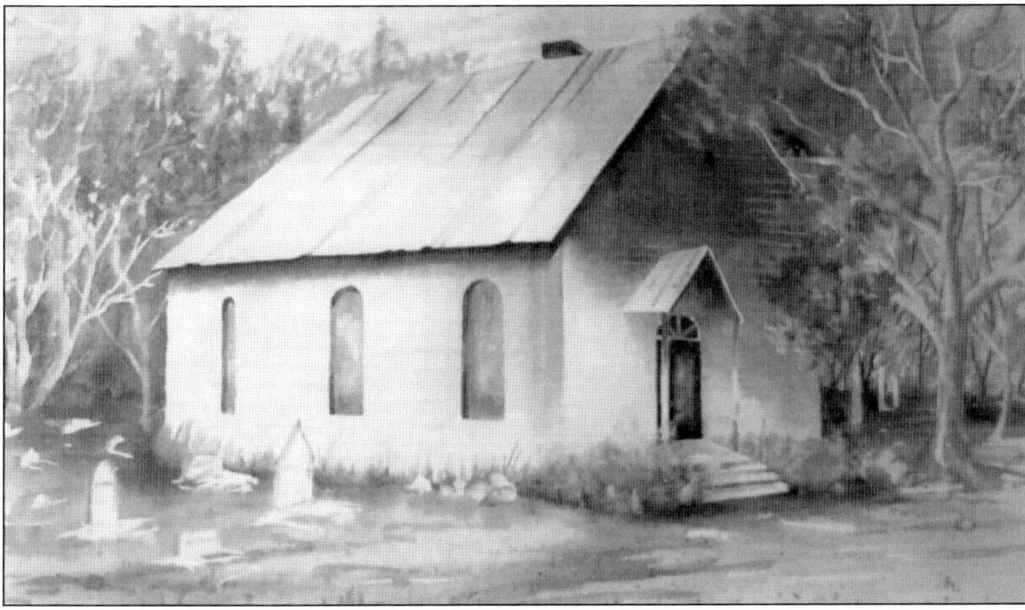

In the early 1800s, the families that had settled between Quinine Hill and Gills Creek organized a Methodist congregation. Some of these families were the Dents, Plumers, Romanstines, Landrums, Dallozes, Fetners, Richbourgs, Geigers, Riels, Wages, and Storks. Rev. John Tarrant and Rev. Payton G. Bowman, two Methodist circuit riders based in Columbia, began serving the faithful in 1830. This drawing by Nelle Dyar depicts the church constructed soon after 1835. (Courtesy of Bethel Methodist Church.)

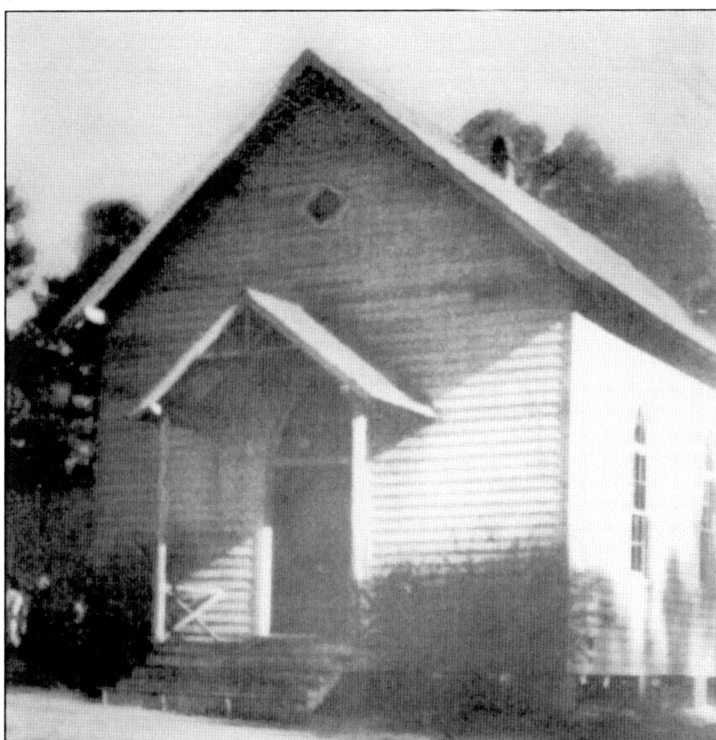

After Bethel Methodist Church was destroyed by fire in 1867, this building was constructed under the leadership of Rev. Henry J. Bennett. (Courtesy of Bethel Methodist Church.)

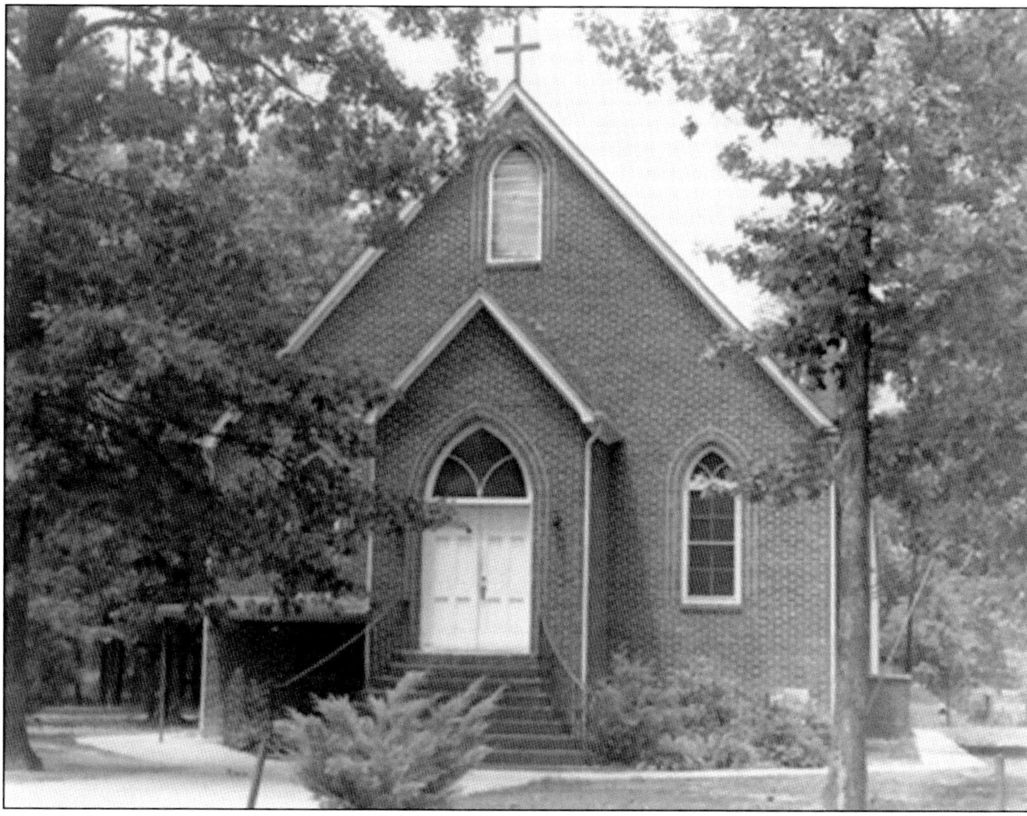

The third Bethel Methodist Church sanctuary was completed in 1948. (Courtesy of Bethel Methodist Church.)

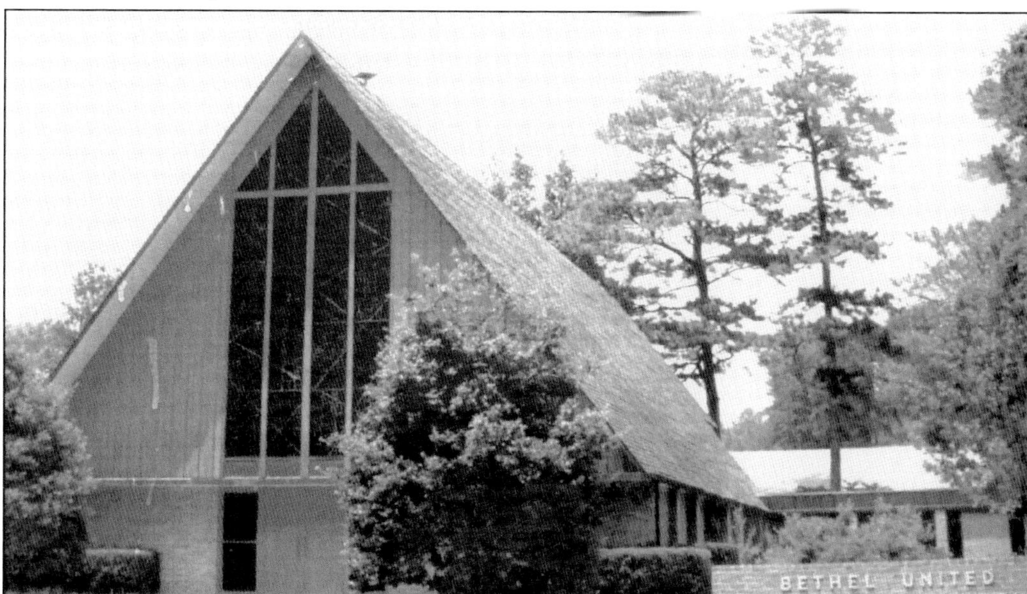

The fourth Bethel Methodist Church sanctuary was constructed in 1964 and remains in use in 2010. (Courtesy of Bethel Methodist Church.)

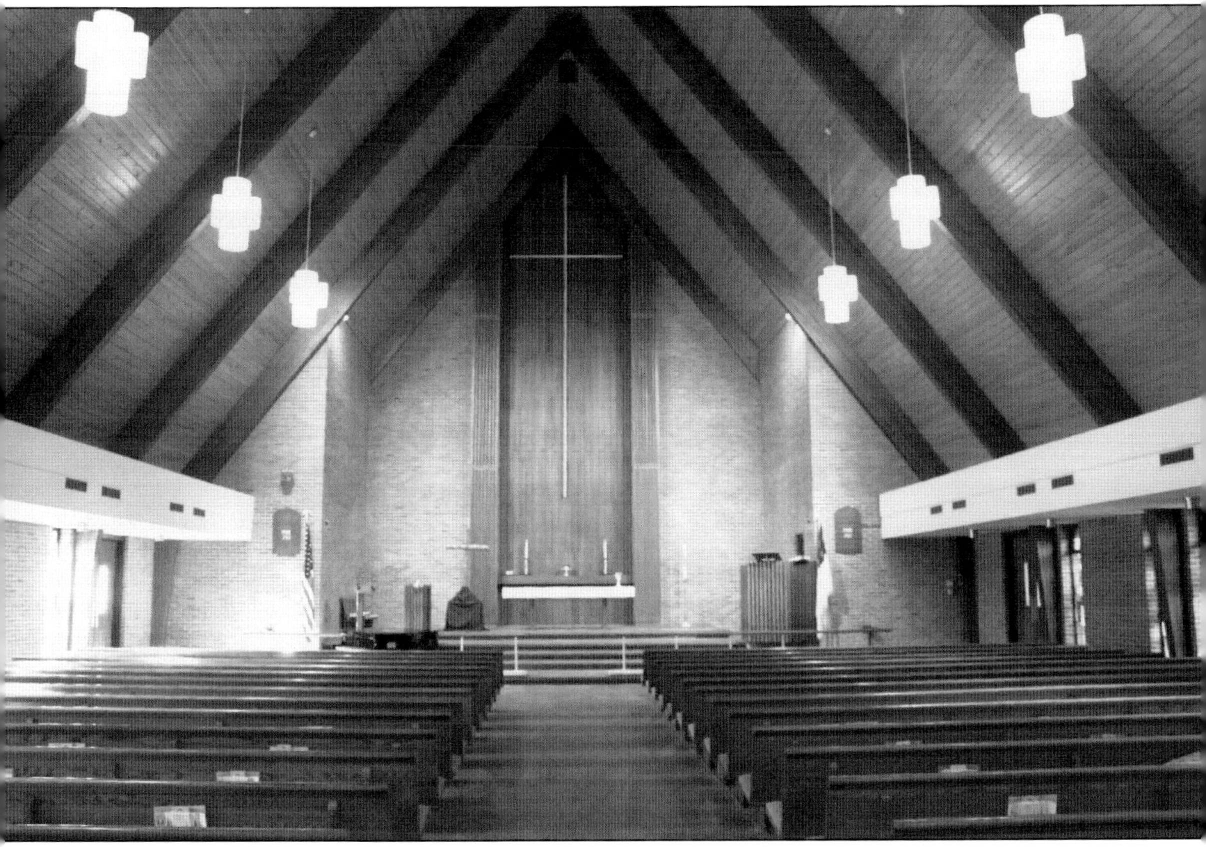

Bethel Methodist Church pioneered organized religion 100 years before Forest Acres became an incorporated city. Their first brick church was built in 1948 partially with $5,000 raised by the women of the church led by Mae Dent (1894–1988), wife of Benjamin M. Dent (1886–1941). The interior of the Bethel sanctuary is beautiful and welcoming. (Photograph by Warner M. Montgomery.)

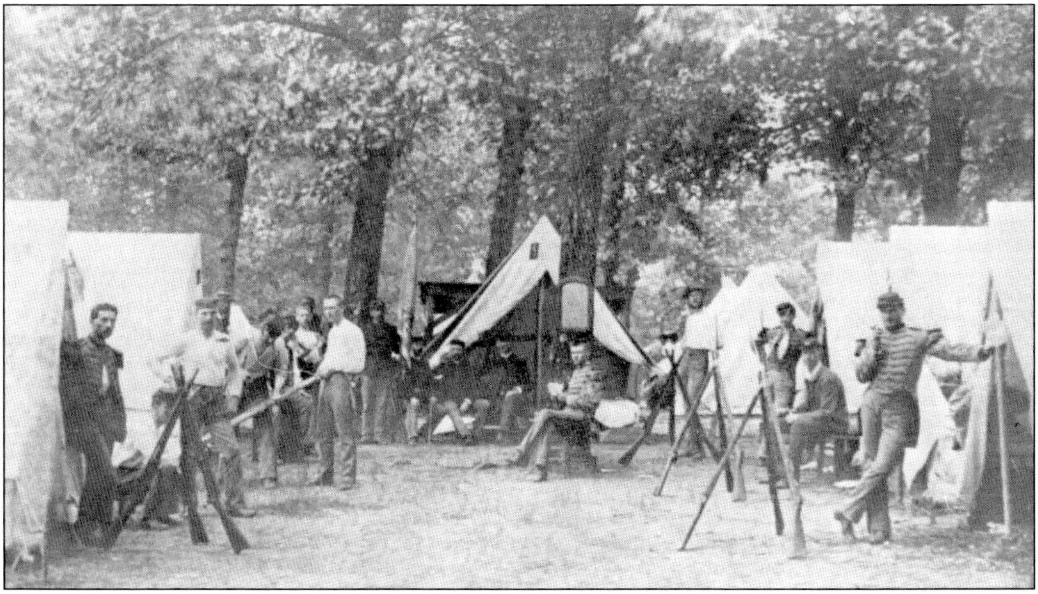

The families of Hezekiah H. Dent and Samuel Dent suffered while they were away at war. Samuel and Alice had at least 12 children. Three of their sons fought with the Confederate army. Several Dent men (seated in left of the center tent) were at this Confederate army camp at Lightwood Knot Springs on the Columbia and Charlotte Railroad in August 1861. The location is now on Farrow Road south of Blythewood. The Dents became profitable farmers once again after the war. (Courtesy of Pete Dent.)

The progeny of Samuel and Alice Dent continued to work the land, and Dent families expanded their farmland along Gills Creek, Two Notch Road, and the Old Camden Road. They were John (1814–1897) and Rebecca (1814–1892) Dent, James (1837–1897) and Hester (1843–1904) Dent, Benjamin (1841–1909) and Harriet (1844–1901) Dent, Samuel H. (1849–1933) and Lucia (1849–1919) Dent, and William (1839–1913) and Martha (1839–1896) Dent. The grave of Martha Dent is in the Bethel United Methodist Church cemetery. William Dent ran the mill at Dent's Pond. Jesse E. Dent (1810–after 1880), son of Hezekiah, served as sheriff of Richland County three times—1855 to 1858, 1863–1866, and 1873–1880. (Photograph by Warner M. Montgomery.)

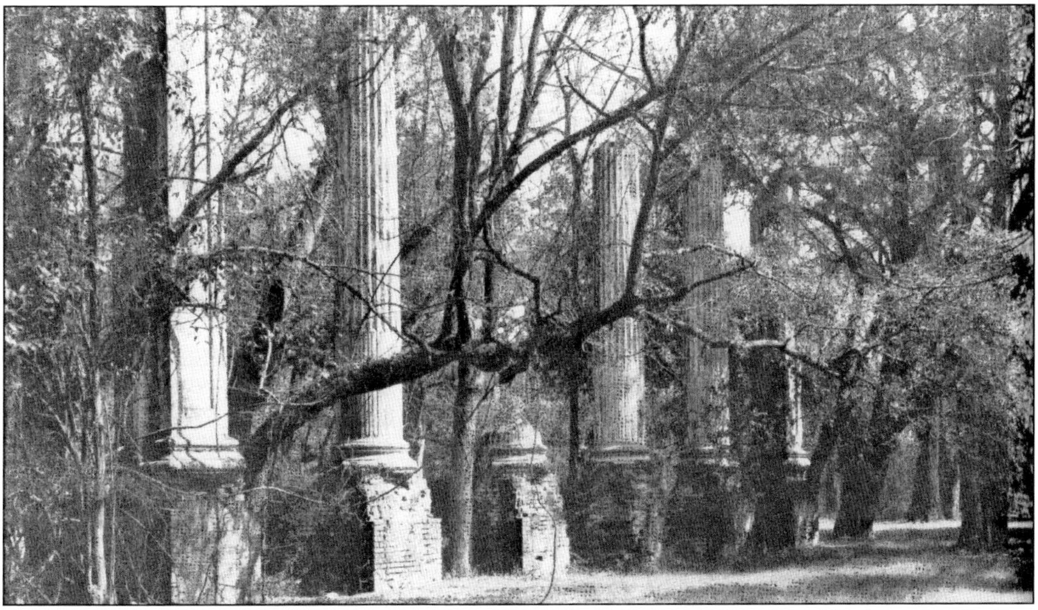

Wade Hampton III inherited the property on Gills Creek originally owned by his grandfather, Wade Hampton. It was valued at $70,000 in 1860. He organized Hampton's Legion and fought with Gen. Robert E. Lee in Virginia. The Millwood mansion was burned by Sherman's men soon after Columbia burned on February 17, 1865. The Hamptons lost their fortune during the war but retained Woodlands and Millwood Plantations, much of which remains in the family today. Wade III became governor in 1876 and served in the US Senate (1879–1891). (Photograph by Russell Maxey.)

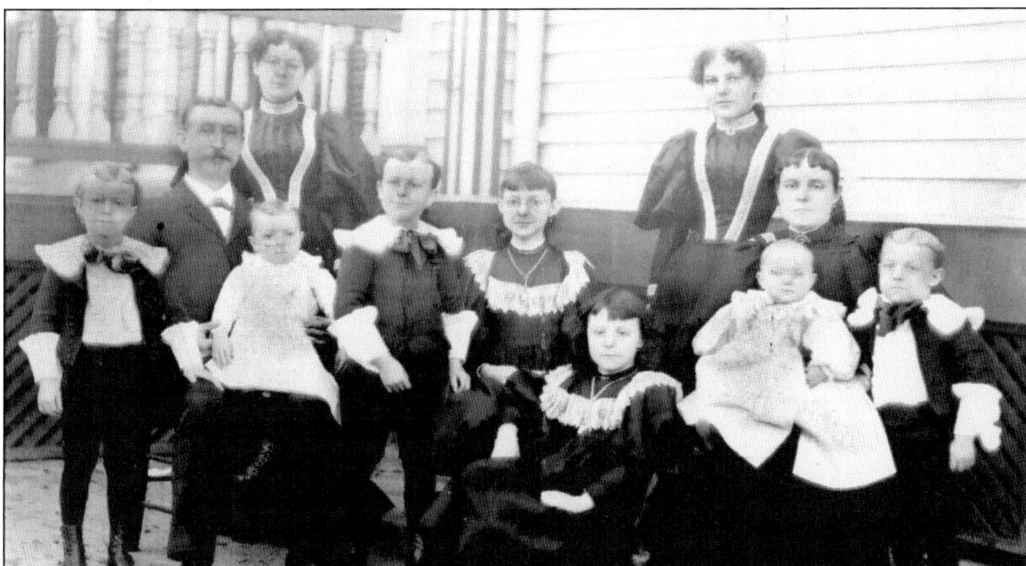

Christopher C. Habenicht, a Columbia resident who owned a farm in the area, sold ice, mineral water, fuel wood, lights oil in Columbia and also rented out night watchmen. He and his wife, Sophia, had two children in 1880. Habenicht's father-in-law and nearby neighbor, John C. Seegars, owned a brewery and saloon in Columbia. He retired to his farm north of the Old Camden Road in 1880. (Courtesy of Historic Columbia Foundation.)

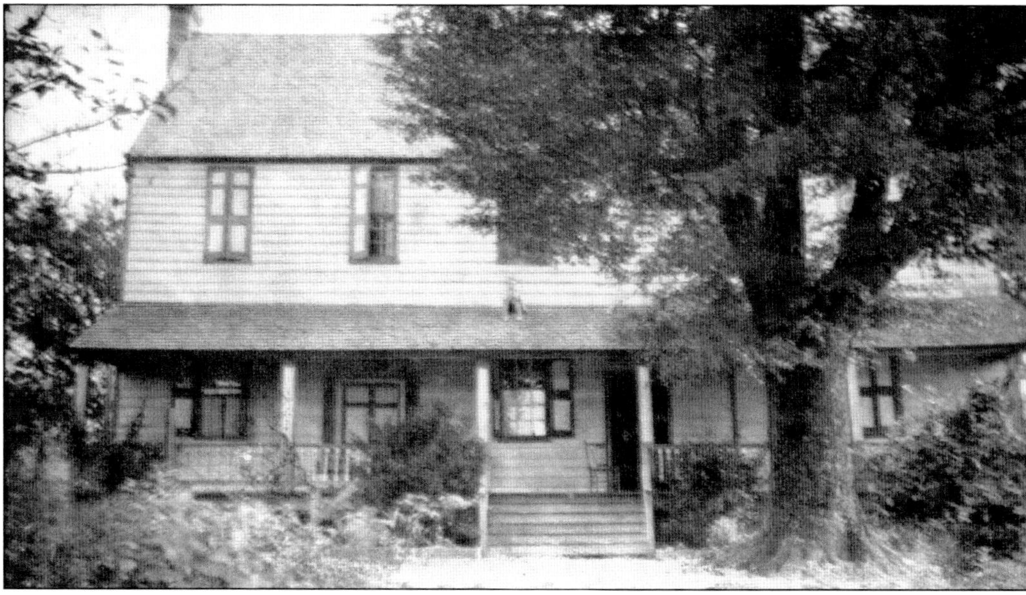

William J. Taylor (1779–1857) served in the South Carolina Legislature and in the state militia. He managed much of the Taylor property along the Old Camden Road. His son William Jr. left the South Carolina College to join Hampton's Legion during the Civil War. His teenage son, James, was killed at the Battle of Gaines' Mill. Dr. Benjamin Walter Taylor (1834–1905) was present at the battles of Fort Sumter, Manassas, and Gettysburg. He resumed his medical practice after the war and became a regent of the South Carolina Lunatic Asylum in 1876. This Taylor home on Richland Street in Columbia survived the Civil War but was demolished in 1915. (Courtesy of Dr. Edmund R. Taylor.)

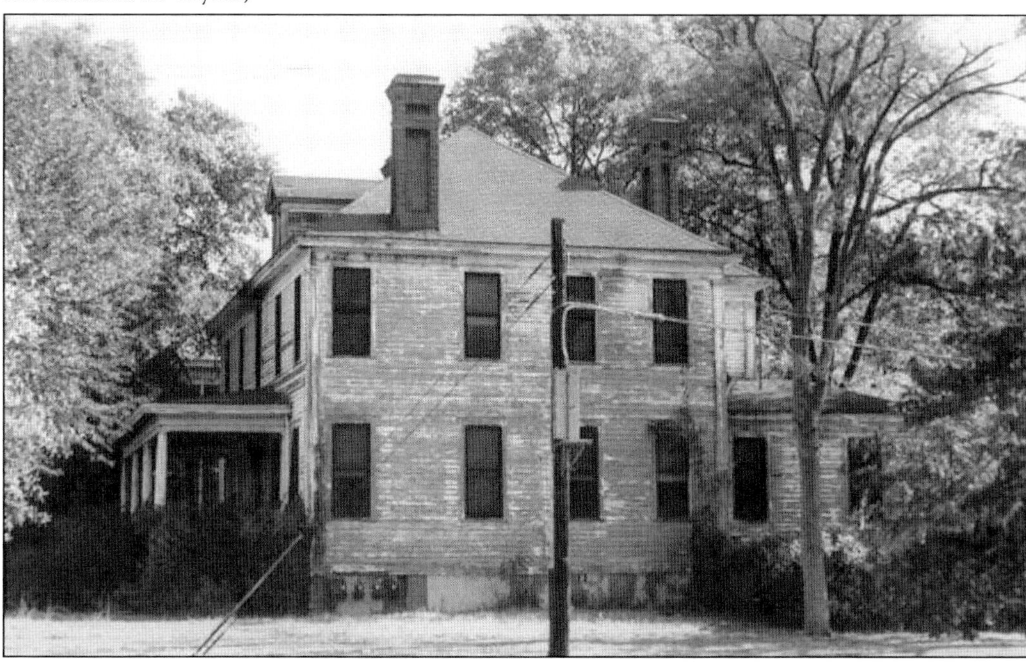

This house at 1800 Senate Street in Columbia is the last house lived in by Wade Hampton III. It was demolished in 1963. (Courtesy of Historic Columbia Foundation.)

Four

Cooper and Hammond Bring New Direction

At the dawn of the 20th century two ambitious young men left their family farms in rural South Carolina and sought better lives in the growing capital city. They graduated together from the University of South Carolina (USC) School of Law in 1910 and became influential attorneys, land speculators, and real estate developers. Within 25 years, John Hughes Cooper (1885–1945) and James Henry Hammond (1885–1970) became the founding fathers of a new city along the Old Camden Road on property once owned by Revolutionary War heroes Thomas Taylor and Wade Hampton. The city of Forest Acres is their legacy.

John Hughes Cooper fled his once prosperous but then impoverished family farm in Williamsburg County after graduating from Kingstree High School. He worked his way through the University of South Carolina and established a law practice specializing in defending the poor and downtrodden. In trial after trial Cooper amazed judges and juries alike with his rhetorical wit. Lawyer Cooper struck an almost comical pose at 5-feet-6-inches tall, 250 pounds, and a distinctive southern twang. Even after automobiles became popular, he continued to drive his small white mare and buggy around town.

James Henry Hammond left rural Blackville in Barnwell County to play football for the Citadel and then moved on to Columbia. His grandfather, for whom he was named, had been a U.S. congressman and senator, governor of South Carolina, and owner of Redcliffe Plantation in Aiken County. Upon being admitted to the bar, Hammond focused his attention on banking, politics, and public service. His lifestyle and unusual habits earned him the reputation of being an eccentric genius.

Hammond's business ventures included organizing the Security Federal Savings and Loan Association in 1923 and serving as president of savings and loan associations in Columbia, the state of South Carolina, and the Southeastern region. He chaired the board of directors of the South Carolina Ports Authority and the South Carolina Public Service Authority. He was elected to the South Carolina House of Representatives in 1915 and to the South Carolina Senate in 1927, where he served until 1934. He was known thereafter as Senator Hammond.

Cooper and Hammond were colleagues and friends, passing each other on the way to and from their nearby offices in downtown Columbia. Cooper was usually on his way to court and Hammond on the way to the state house.

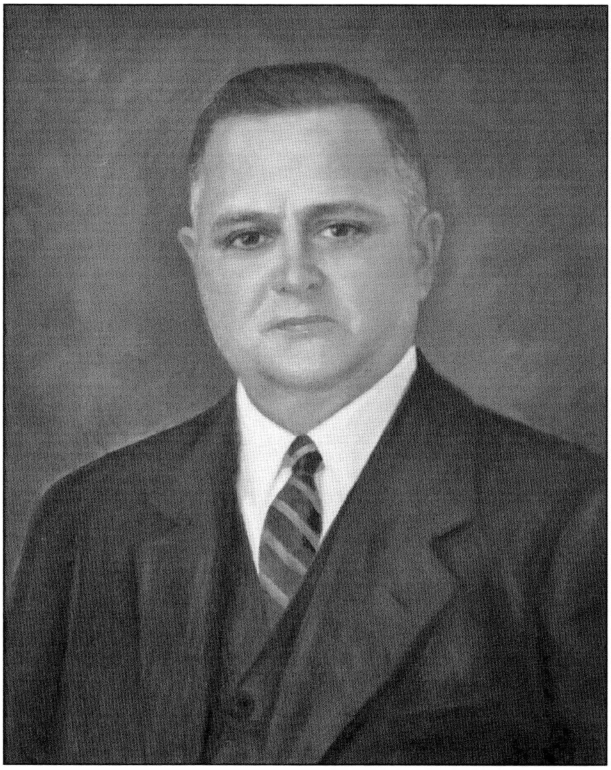

John Hughes Cooper (1885–1945) graduated from the USC School of Law in 1910. Within a few years, Cooper had earned enough money to bring his eight brothers and sisters to Columbia. He took care of them and made sure they completed their schooling. His dedication to his family and business did not allow him time to find a wife. He remained a bachelor and became known to all as "Uncle John." (Courtesy of Richland County Public Library, Cooper Branch.)

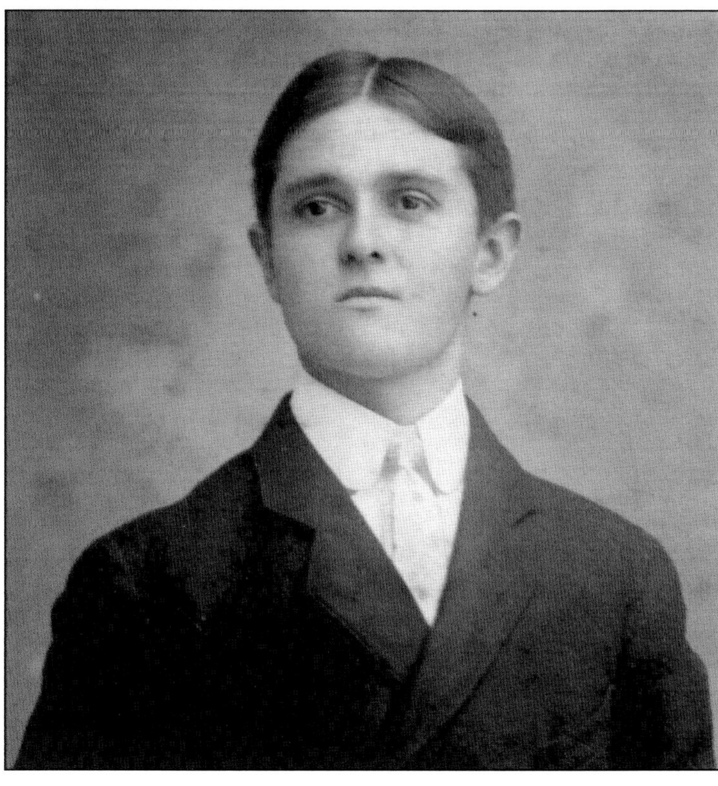

According to James Hammond, "John Hughes Cooper (pictured here while a student at USC) was a good debater, always having some curt, witty expression to emphasize his remarks. He was a good campus politician, genial and cordial conversationalist and always found in the middle of groups on the campus where rumors, protests, complaints, scandals, suspicions and misinformation were received and broadcasted." (Courtesy of Richland County Public Library.)

John Hughes Cooper purchased Lake View from Benjamin Abney and Lee Lorick and established Forest Land Company in 1920. Cooper (upper left) is shown here with Capers Power (upper right) Eldridge Barnes (lower left), and Calhoun Boineau (lower right) at Lake View (now Forest Lake) in June 1918. (Courtesy of Richland County Public Library.)

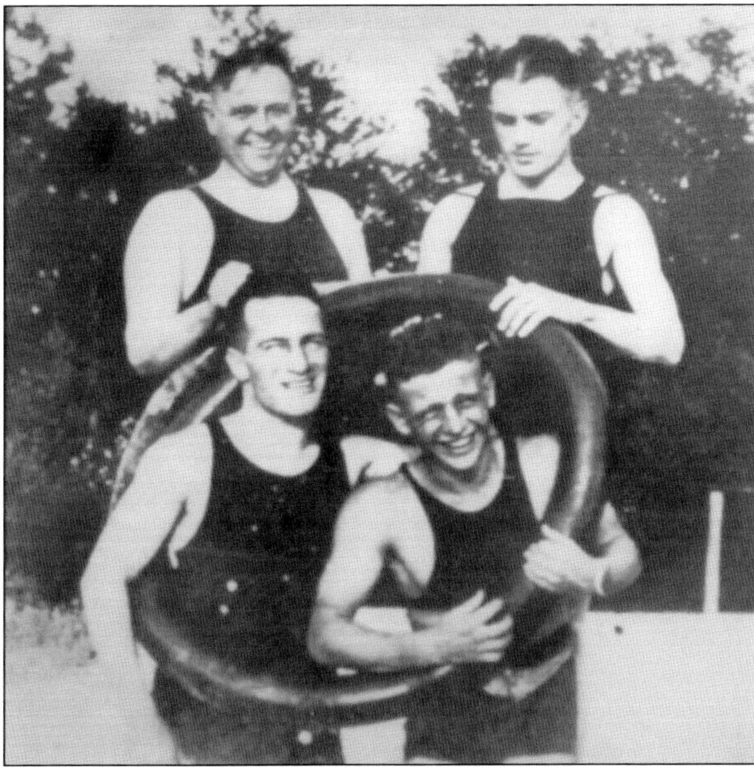

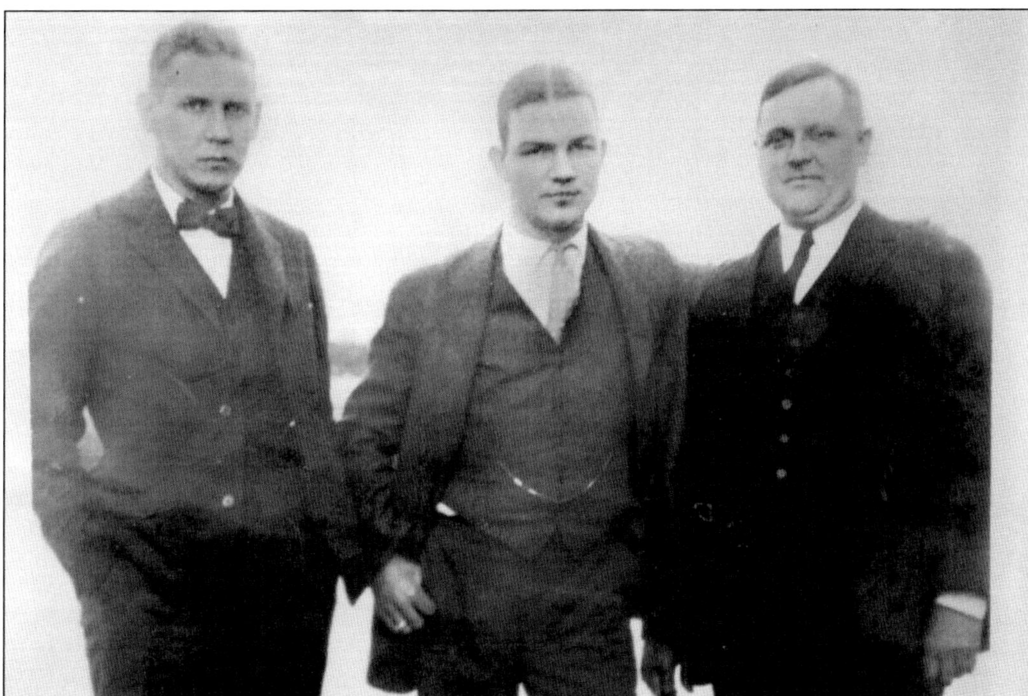

In more formal attire are Eldridge Barnes (left), Capers Power (center), and John Hughes Cooper in 1918. (Courtesy of Richland County Public Library.)

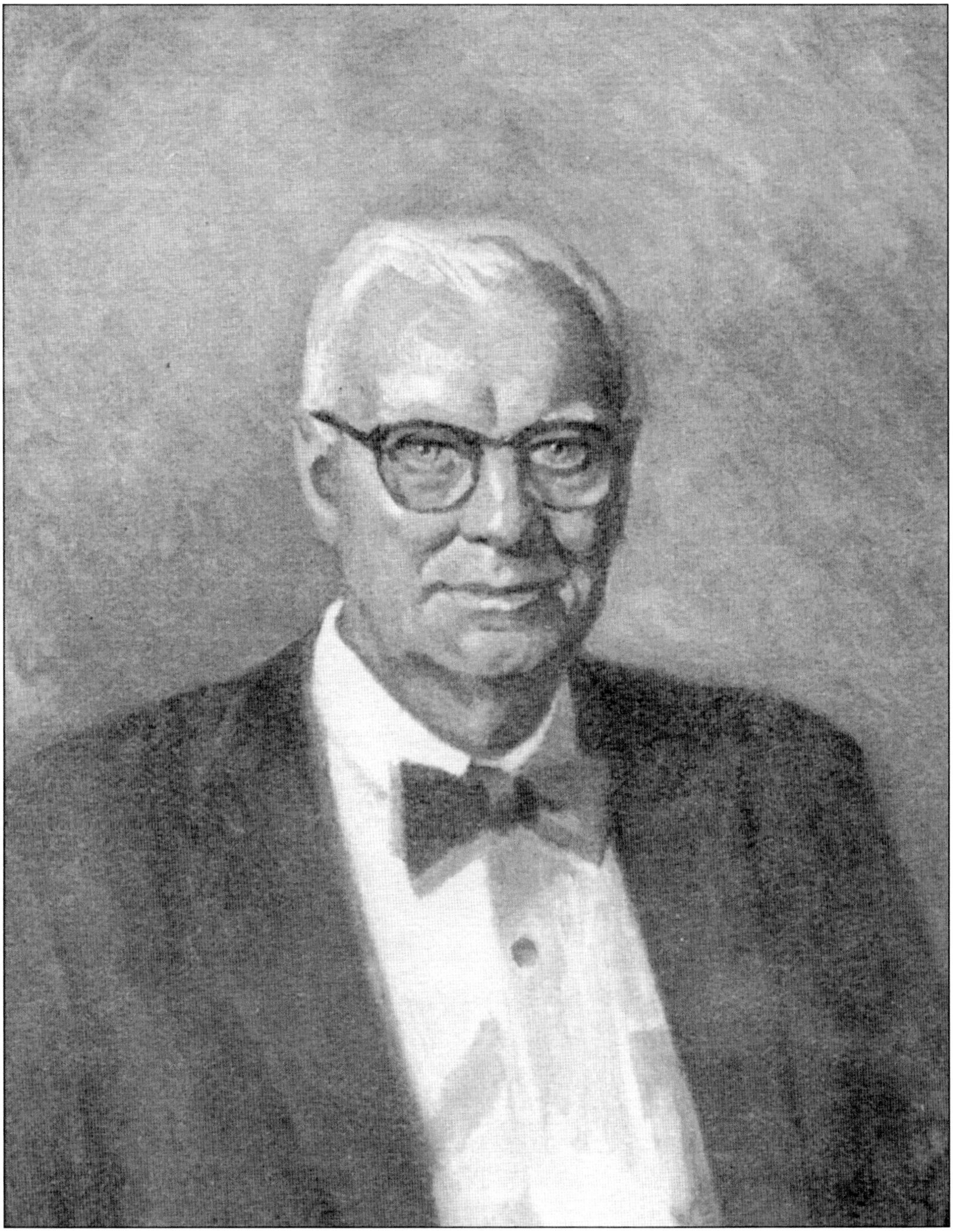

James H. Hammond (1885–1970) graduated from the USC School of Law in 1910 and became successful by representing banks and public service agencies. He served in the South Carolina Legislature as a representative and senator. In 1914, Hammond married into the influential DeBruhl-Marshall family, who lived in an 1820 home in downtown Columbia designed by Robert Mills. He and Janie Marshall had four children—Spann, James Jr. (who died in infancy), Quitman (who was known for his eccentricities), and Laura (a beautiful woman who married Cotesworth Jeffords). (Courtesy of Adele Jeffords Pope.)

Five

Dent's Pond Becomes Forest Lake

An event in 1911 drew the attention of Cooper and Hammond. The Lake View Investment Company purchased Dent's Pond and the surrounding 1,700 acres for about $8,000 from Samuel III (1853–1933) and William (1868–1932) Dent, sons of Samuel W. Dent II (1839–1913), who was seriously ill.

Chief officials in the Lake View Investment Company were Benjamin Abney (attorney for the Columbia Electric Street Railway, Light, and Power Company and for most of the local railway companies) and Lee A. Lorick (owner of Lorick and Lowrance Hardware). Other principals were W. Boyd Evans (a railroad attorney), G. A. Guignard, and T. C. Williams (partners in the Columbia Railway and Navigation Company and advocates of what became the Santee Cooper Public Service Authority in 1934), A. G. LaMotte (architect and engineer with Niernsee and LaMotte), Dr. F. D. Kendall, and Columbia mayor W. S. Reamer.

When soldiers departed after World War I, Abney and Lorick gave up on Lake View and mortgaged it to John Hughes Cooper, who had his eye on investment property along the Old Camden Road. Cooper established the Forest Land Company in 1920 to manage his new property.

Cooper created a new Lake View Club. Above the dam he built a large bathhouse, a two-story dance pavilion, and boat docks, and then invited families to join for $20 a year and individuals for $10. His nephews camped out in the old Dent log cabin and served as cashiers and lifeguards. During the summer months the bumpy, dusty Old Camden Road from Columbia was crowded with "Tin Lizzies" heading for the Lake View Club.

The idea of selling farmland at city prices came to Cooper during a 1925 trip to Miami, where he witnessed the Florida land boom. He imagined nice homes surrounding a beautiful lake in a country setting with boating, fishing, golf, and tennis not so far from offices in the city. With this in mind, John Hughes and his brother, Paul, organized the Forest Lake Club in 1923 on 141 acres of land surrounding the newly named Forest Lake. The club was chartered in 1924 by R.J. Blalock and R. Beverley Herbert with $20,000 in capital stock.

Cooper moved into the old Dent home overlooking Forest Lake and named it Forest Lake Gardens (104 Country Club Drive), then began to buy up more of the Dent property between Satchel Ford Road and Gills Creek. He attempted to entice his friend James Hammond to move to his new development by offering him a 2-acre lot on the lake and free lifetime membership in the Forest Lake Club. Hammond turned him down, saying it was too far from town, but he did buy 67.3 acres on Quinine Hill from Cooper.

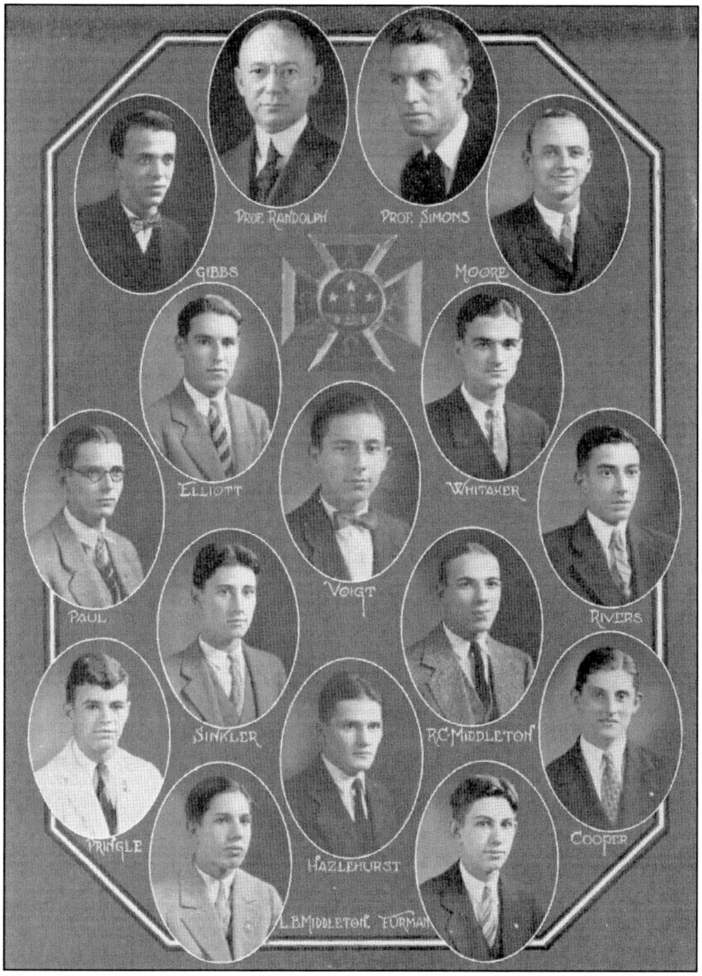

William Hazlehurst (second row from the bottom, center) and Edwin Cooper (second row from the bottom, right) were members of the ATO fraternity at USC in 1926. Hazlehurst settled in Quinine Hill and was the second mayor of Forest Acres. Cooper succeeded his uncle John Hughes Cooper as president of Forest Land Company. (Courtesy of Elizabeth Hazlehurst Cantey.)

This plat of Lake View Development Company property prepared by B. L. Abney in 1916 shows Gills Creek, Dent's Pond dam, Lake View swimming pool, bathhouses, Old Taylor Mill, and a Dent residence that later burned. The Dent Pond Road is now Old Mill Court. (Courtesy of Edwin Cooper Jr.)

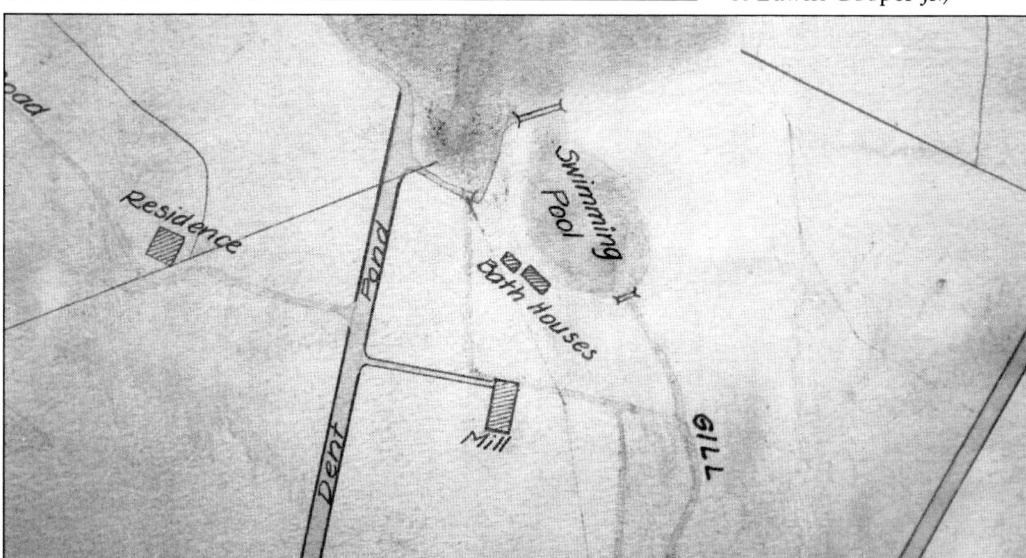

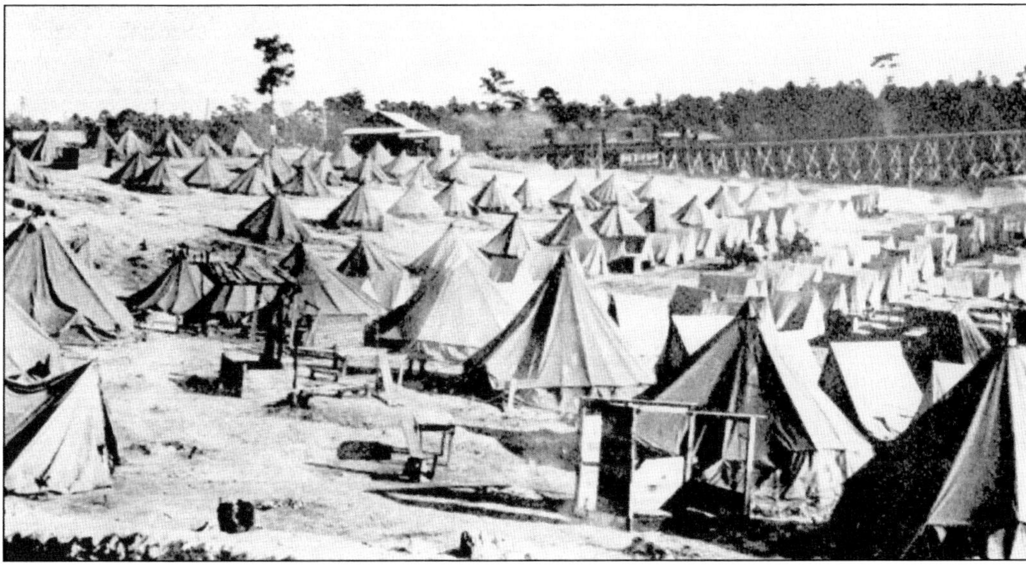

While World War I was raging in Europe, Maj. Charles E. Kilbourne reported to Gen. Leonard Wood that the vast Wade Hampton estate east of Gills Creek would make an excellent U.S. Army training camp. It was approved by Maj. Douglas MacArthur, and the government began acquiring rights of way and property. The Columbia Chamber of Commerce raised $50,000, purchased the Hampton estate, and turned it over to the federal government. Columbia residents donated 1,192 acres and another 19,742 acres were purchased by the government. The trolley line ran from Columbia down Devine Street to Kilbourne Road and into Camp Jackson. (Courtesy of Fort Jackson.)

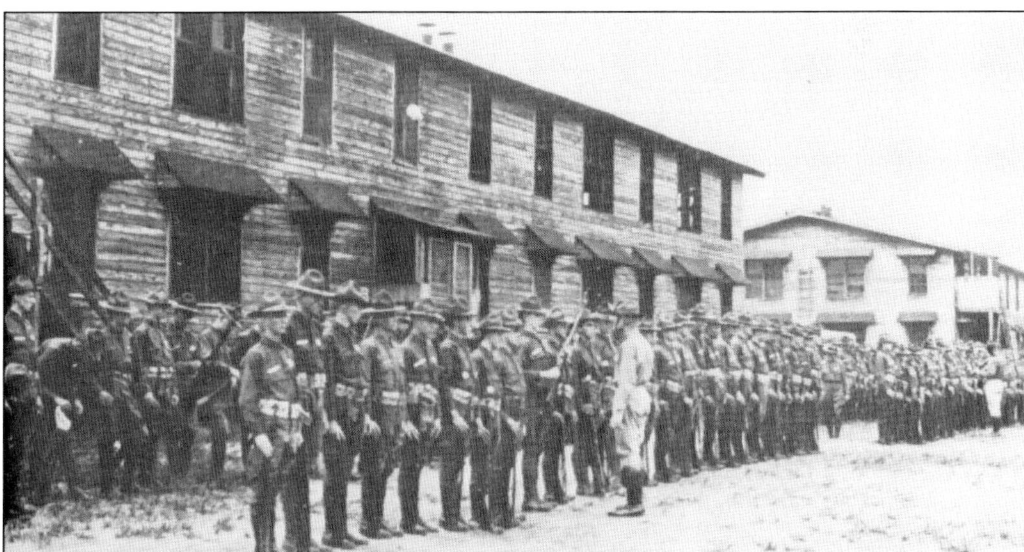

Camp Jackson was training soldiers by 1917 for America's entrance into World War I. These soldiers stand at attention outside their newly constructed barracks. (Courtesy of Fort Jackson.)

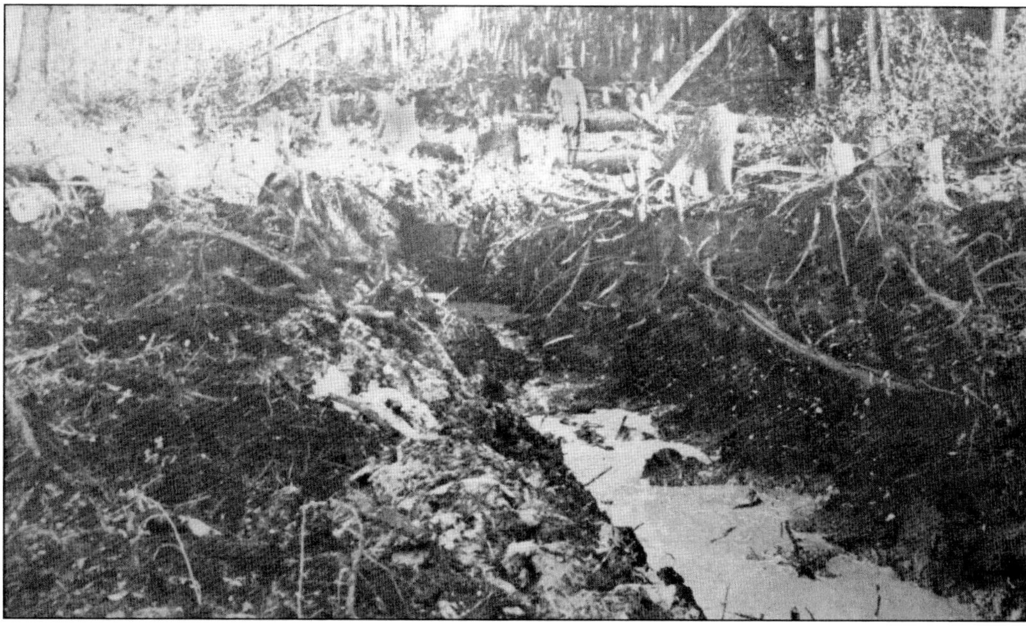

The Gills Creek swamp was drained and the creek straightened with mule-drawn dredges and wagons for Camp, Jackson where over 1,500 buildings were constructed. Harwell descendants—Bowers, Daniels, Devereauxs, Kellys, Marshes, and Drehers—capitalized on the situation by taking labor jobs, selling produce and cooked meals to workers, and providing housing to military families and workers. (Courtesy of Fort Jackson.)

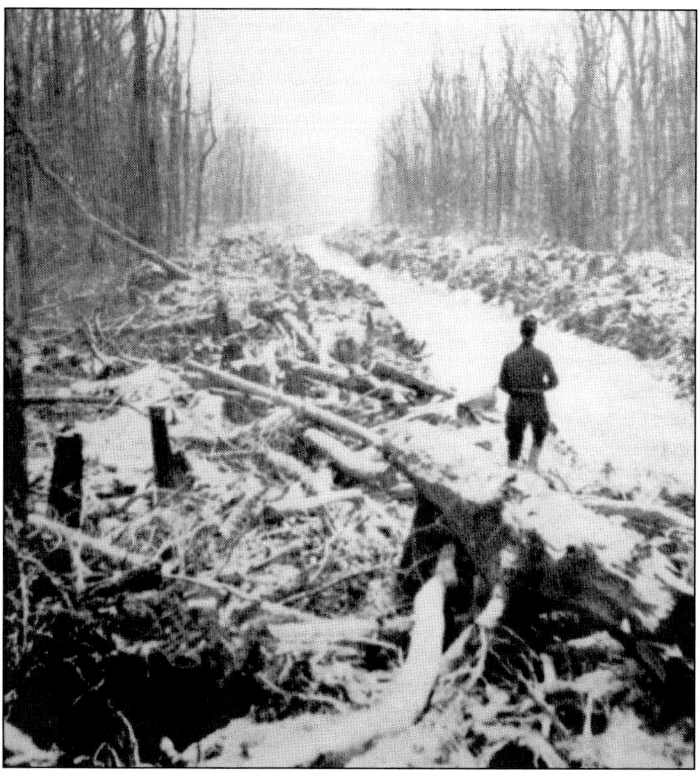

This photograph looks south from Trenholm Road in 1917. The meandering Gills Creek that flowed slowly from Dent's Pond was changed to a straight, swift, deeper stream into order to drain the land for construction of Camp Jackson. (Courtesy of Fort Jackson.)

Benjamin Abney was one of the original investors in the Lake View Development Company. He was attorney for the Columbia Electric Street Railway, Light and Power Company, and for most of the local railway companies. (Courtesy of Historic Columbia Foundation.)

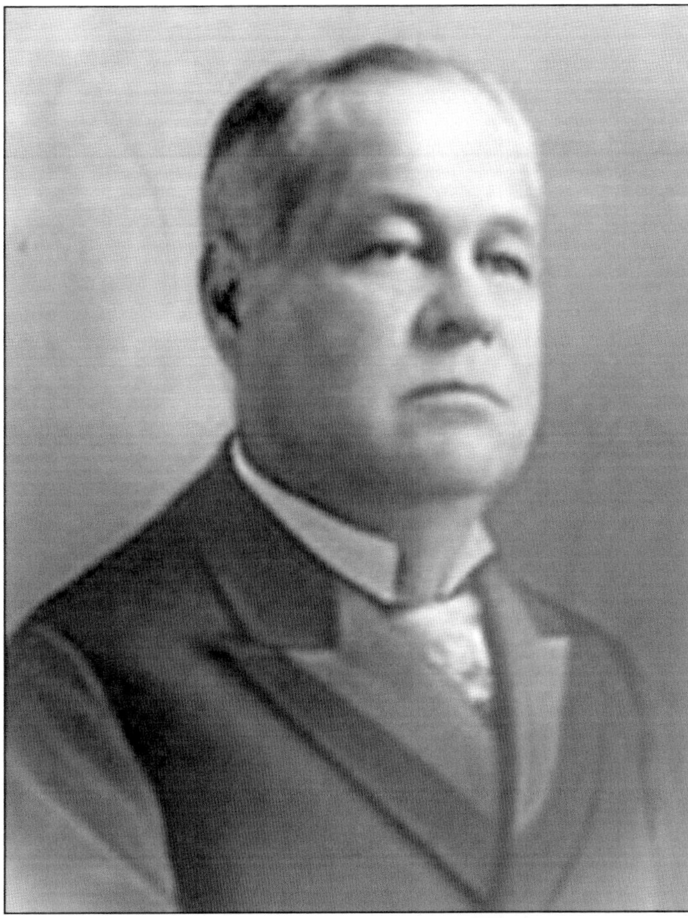

The Lake View Club closed at the peak of its popularity when Forest Lake Club opened in 1926. Cooper sold the land to the Forest Lake Club ($100 per acre) with the stipulation that he would receive 50¢ per member since he would be losing revenue from closing Lake View. This was the first club house in 1925. Capt. Jack Blalock was the first president of Forest Lake Club. (Courtesy of Forest Lake Club.)

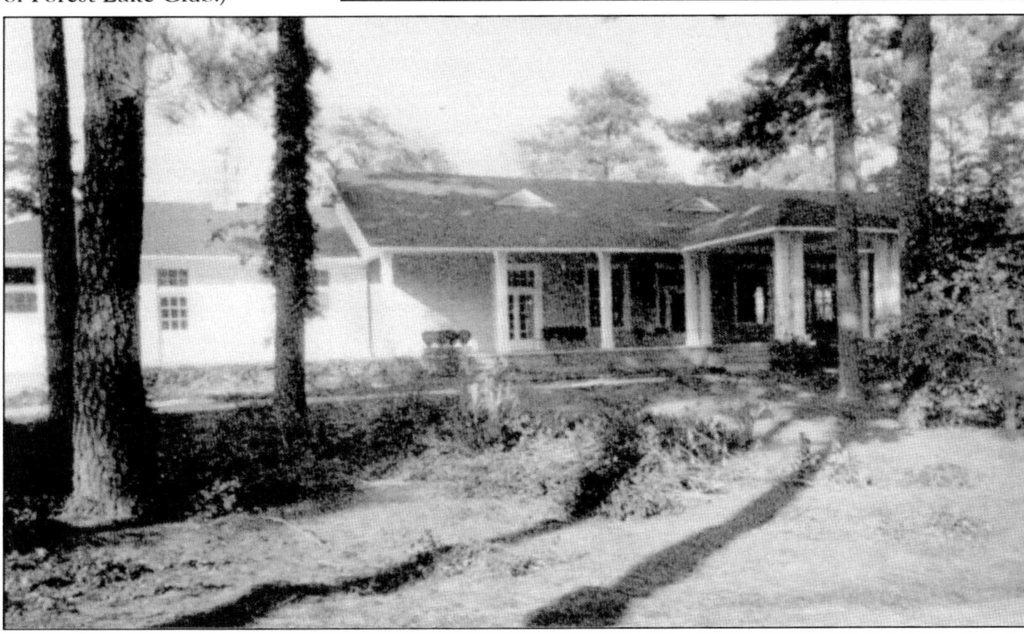

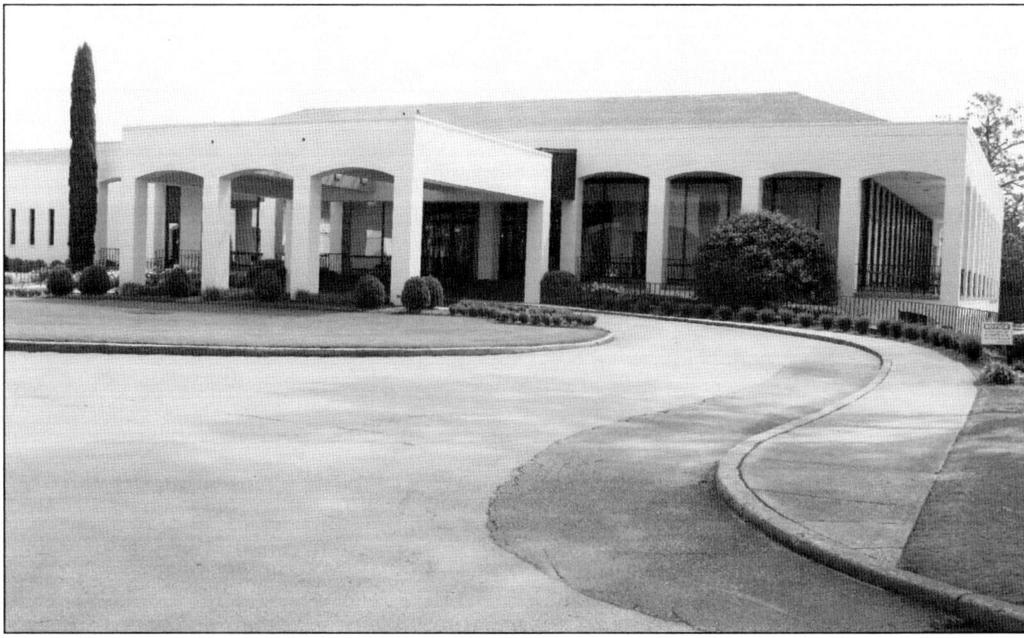

The Forest Lake Club in 2010 is a private country club. (Photograph by Warner M. Montgomery.)

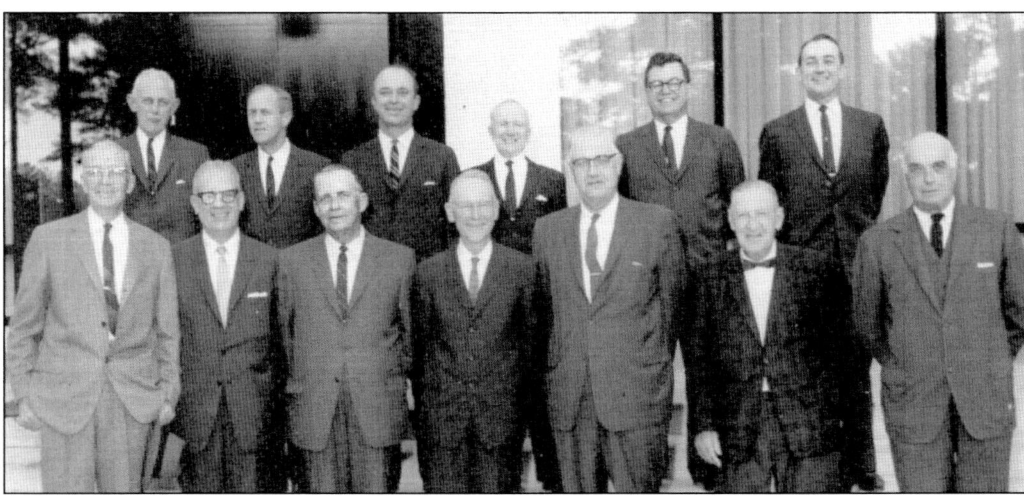

The presidents of Forest Lake Club posed for this picture in 1965. Pictured from left to right are (first row) R. Beverley Herbert (1927–1928), G. Richard Shafto (1944–1945), Ernest M. Spong (1947–1948), Frank J. Dana (1949–1950), Rufus R. Clarke (1951), W. Dixon Foster (1952), William L. Boyd (1953–1954), (second row) Dr. Frank C. Owens (1955–1956), A. Mason Gibbes (1957–1958), John W. Thomas (1959–1960), William B. Love Jr. (1961–1962), T. Howard Timberlake (1963–1964), and Alex D. Graham (1965). (Courtesy of Forest Lake Club.)

On March 20, 1937, golfers Patty Berg and Olympic champion Babe Didrikson (soon to be Zaharias) gave an exhibition match at Forest Lake Club. Pictured here from left to right are Jane Cothran of Greenville; Patty Berg; J. B. Urquhart, president of Forest Lake Club; Babe Didrikson; and Kathryn Hemphill of Columbia, known as the "Number One Girl Golfer in the U.S." (Courtesy of Forest Lake Club.)

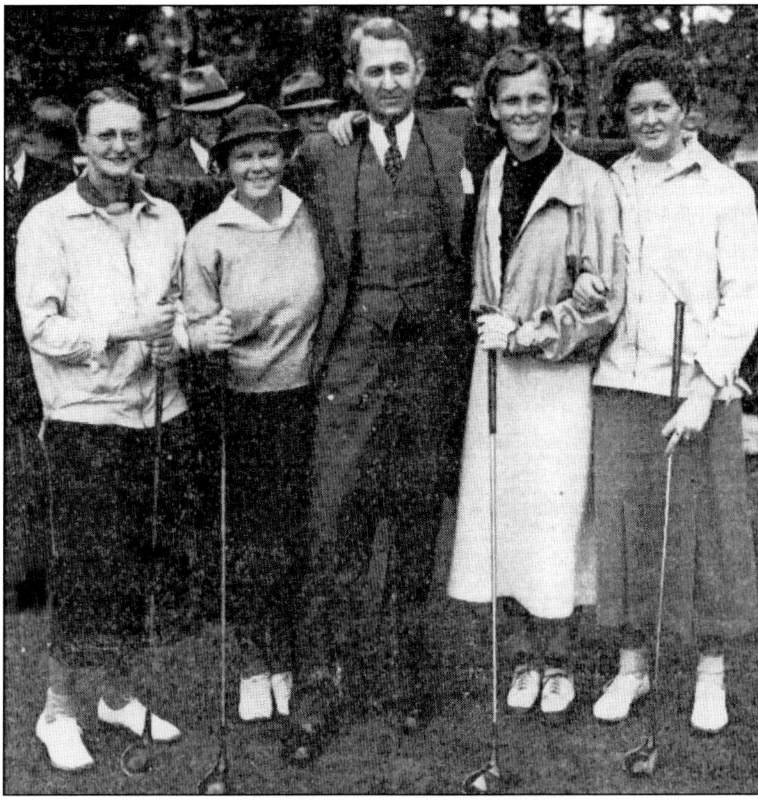

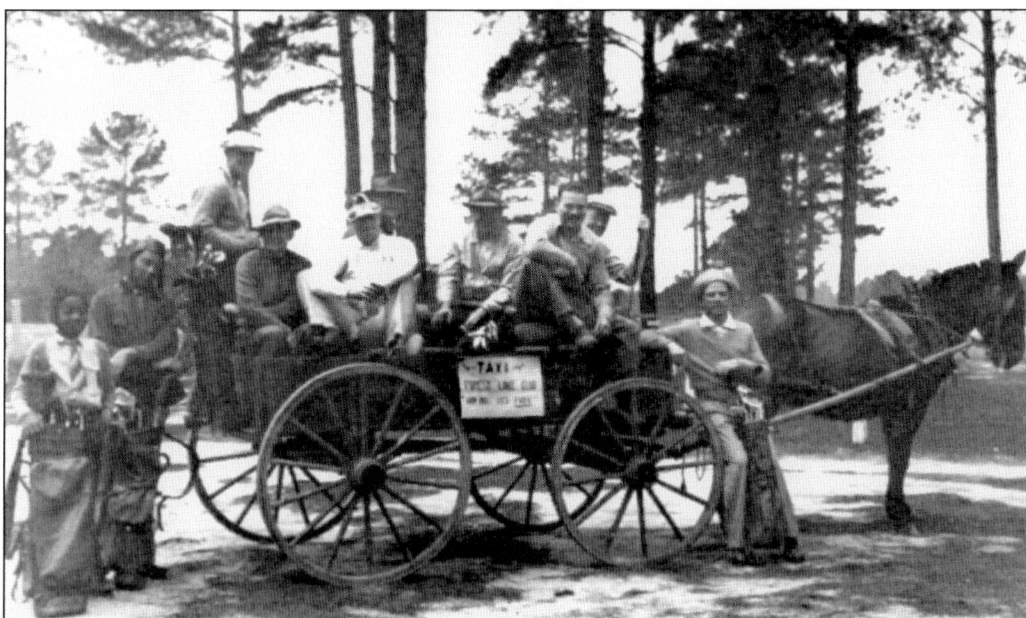

During World War II, Forest Lake Club members Melvin Hemphill and Charlie Barron hitched a mule to a wagon and provided transportation from the near bus stop to the club a mile away. The wagon was nicknamed "The Hayburner Express." (Courtesy of Forest Lake Club.)

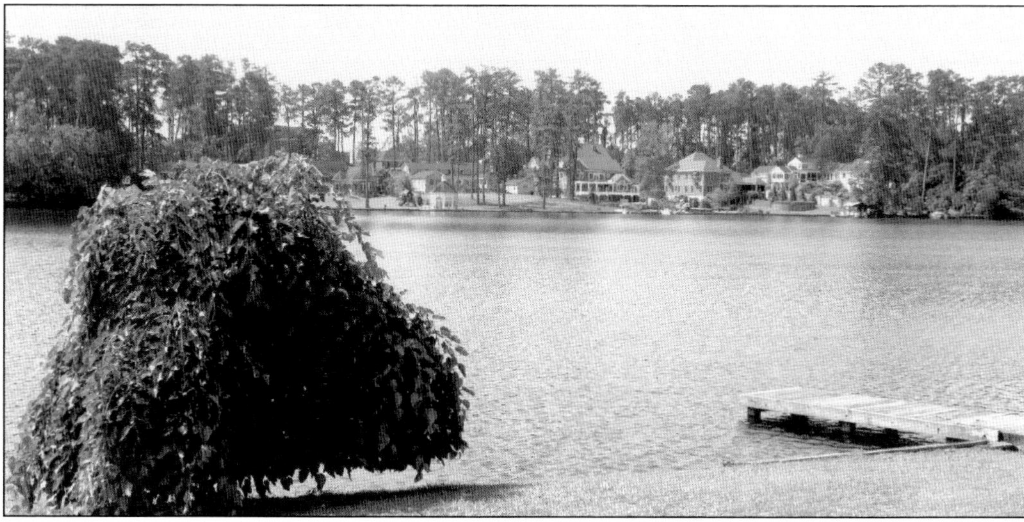

Fort Jackson grew by leaps and bounds during World War II. Forest Drive became a major road from Columbia to the fort. New families working at the fort or serving in the army sought homes in Forest Acres. The town's population exploded from 323 in 1940 to 3,240 in 1950 and to 6,808 in 1970. Edwin, Charles, James, and Frank Cooper took over their uncle John's Forest Land Company. With Edwin at the helm, they initiated subdivisions at Forest Lake and along Satchel Ford Road. In 1950, they turned over their small water system to Forest Acres. Today Forest Lake is a beautiful residential development shared with the Forest Lake Club. (Photograph by Warner M. Montgomery.)

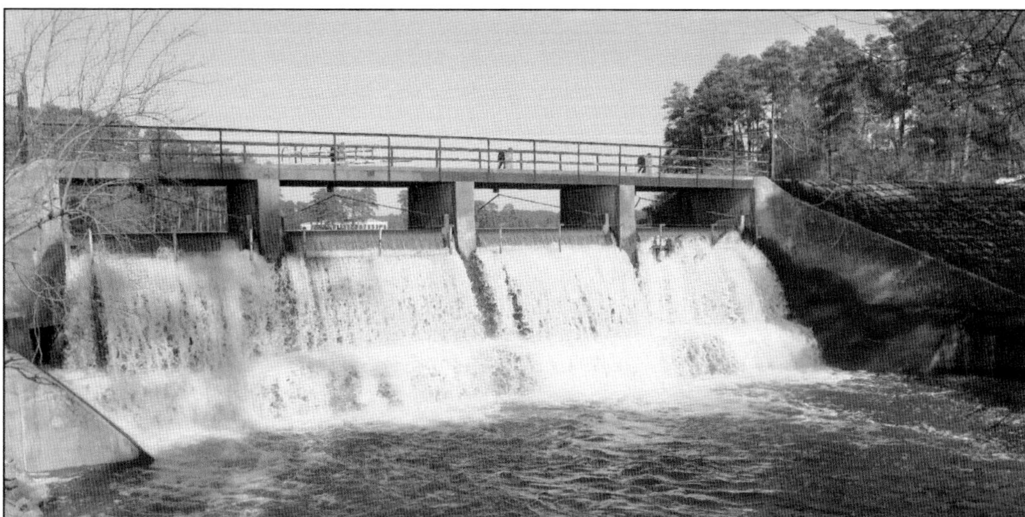

The Forest Lake dam, built before the Civil War by Samuel Dent, was improved in 1912 by the Lake View Development Company. Weston and Brooker Contractors built an 80-foot reinforced concrete dam at Dent's Pond. The swimming pool below the dam was improved, the water level raised two feet, and a walkway paved around the pool. A dozen bathhouses were constructed on the beach. Lake View became Columbia's first swimming resort, a welcome retreat from the summer heat for Columbians and soldiers from Camp Jackson. The Columbia streetcar line was extended to Lake View, which made it easily accessible from Columbia. (Photograph by Warner M. Montgomery.)

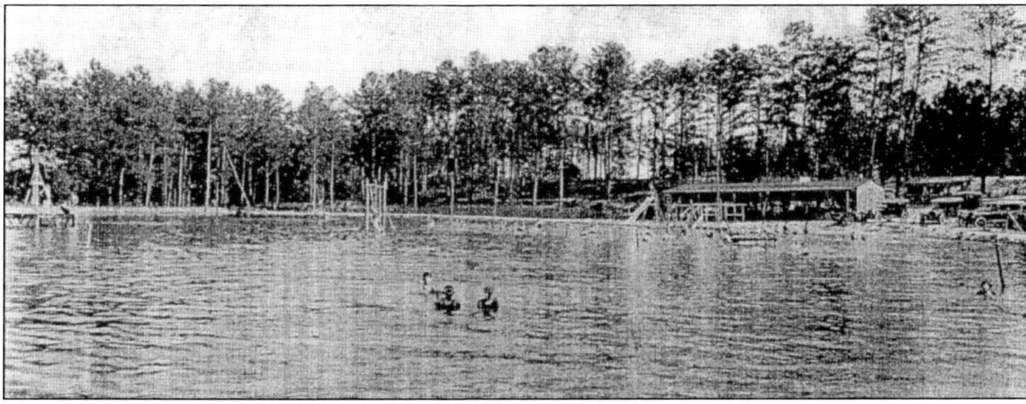

After World War I, brothers William (1865–1940) and Thomas Bowers (1863–1926) built a lake known as Bowers' Beach on Gills Creek, where Hampton had a pond in the late 1800s. It was on Kilbourne Road on the trolley route to Camp Jackson. They built a bathhouse, dancing hall, concession stands, and outhouse toilets. Their brothers John (1868–1939) and Charlton (1871–1936) ran the operation. Bowers' Beach was very successful until trolley service ended in 1923. The Bowers sold the property in 1936 to a real estate developer. The much larger Lake Katherine was built at the site in the 1940s. This photograph was taken in 1921. (Courtesy of the Bowers family.)

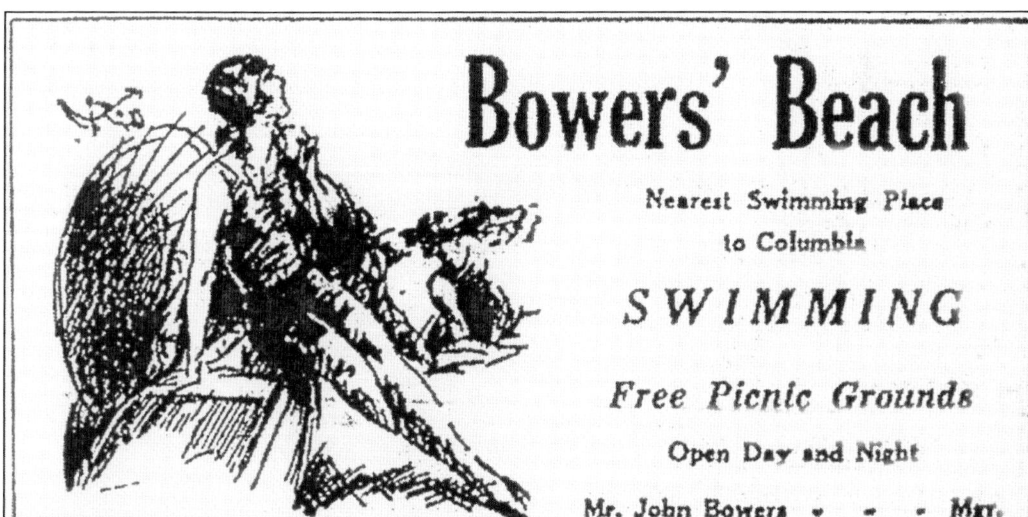

Columbia claimed to be "the Largest Inland Bathing Resort in the Country" during the 1920s and 1930s. Bowers' Beach, along with Twin Lakes, Lake View, Moore's Pond, Adams' Pond, and Barron's Pond, were among Columbia's beautiful and charming swimming places. John Bowers operated his resort on Kilbourne Road until his death in 1940. (Courtesy of the Bowers family.)

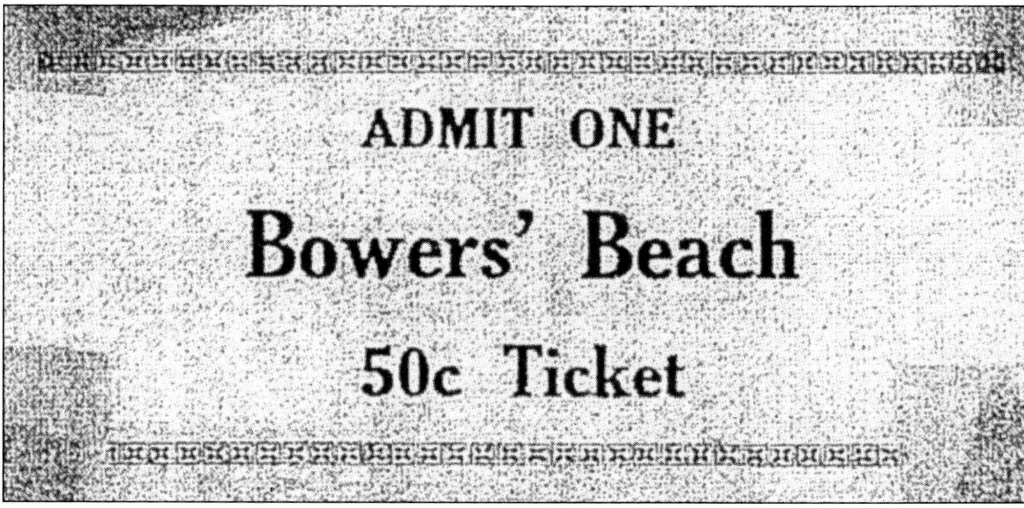

Admission to swim at Bowers' Beach in 1923 cost 50¢ including rental of a swimming suit or only 25¢ for visitors who brought their own suits. Concessions sold Coca-Cola, Orange Crush, and grape soda drinks and Shacks, Baby Ruths, Bit-O-Honey, and Big Sticks for 5¢ each. Children from Epworth and Carolina Children's Homes were admitted free. (Courtesy of the Bowers family.)

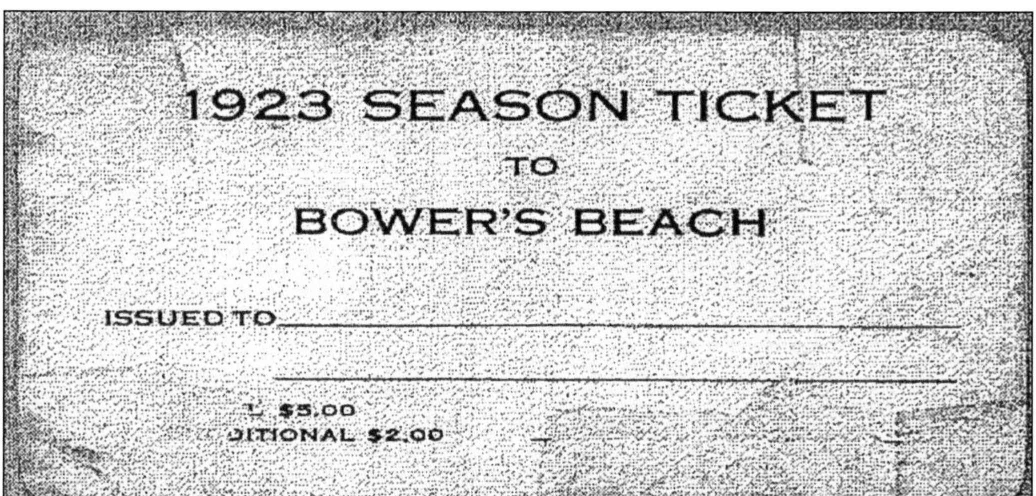

A season pass to Bowers' Beach was only $5 in 1923. Kilbourne Park (Springdale) Baptist Church conducted baptisms in the lake on Sunday mornings in warm weather. Square dances were held on Saturday nights in the late 1920s. (Courtesy of the Bowers family.)

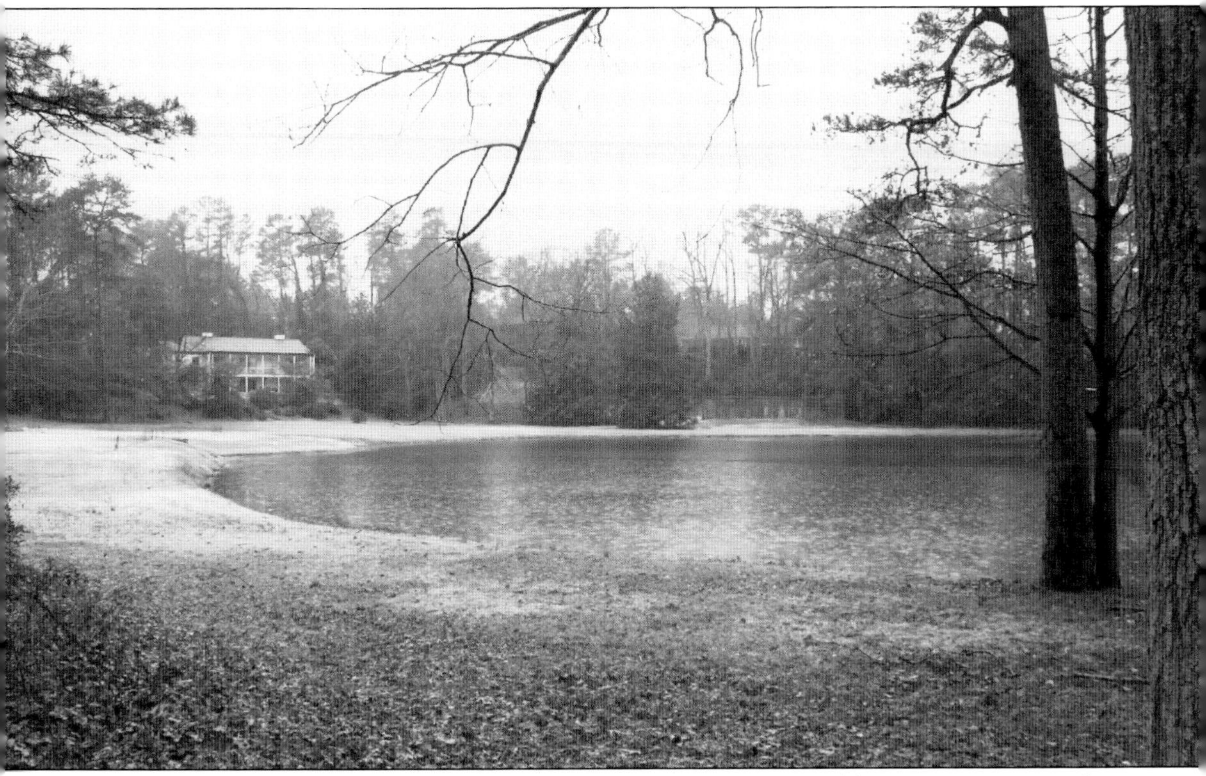

When Bowers' Beach closed, the name was changed to Lake Lelia, and houses soon appeared around the lake. This is the lake in 2010. (Photograph by Warner M. Montgomery.)

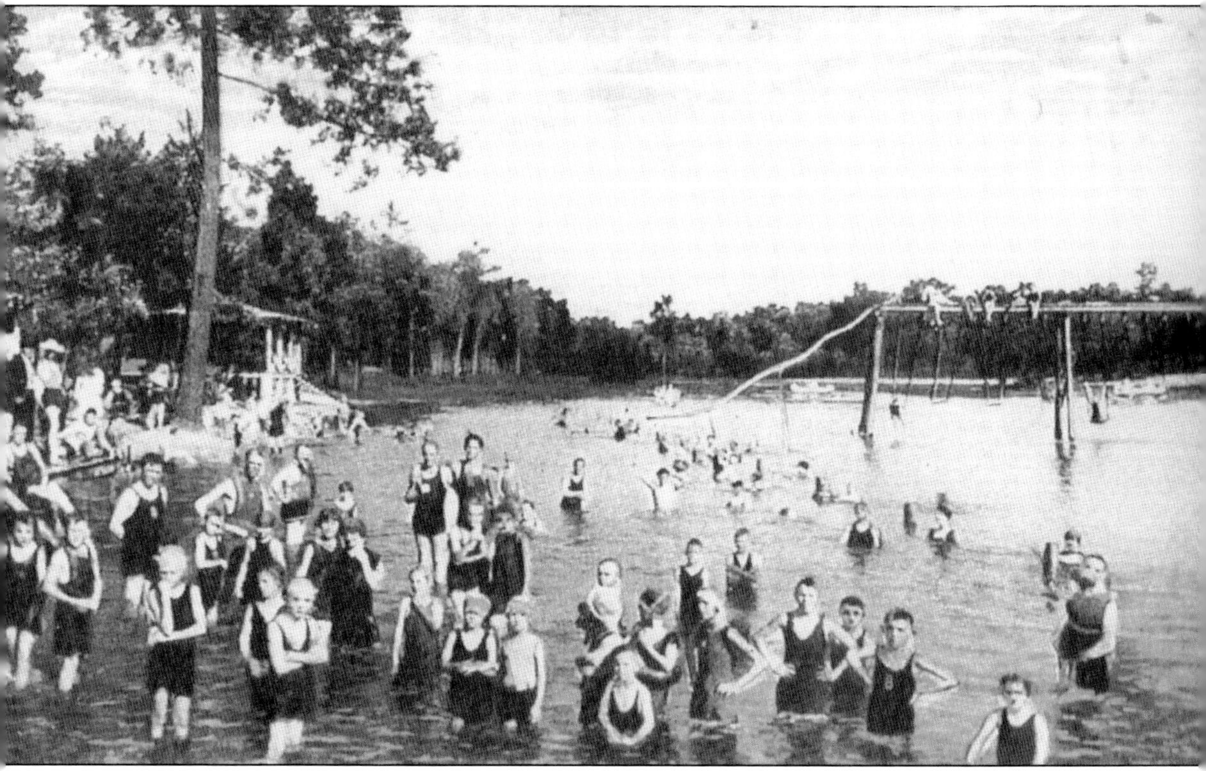

Boyden Arbor was constructed on Gills Creek north of Forest Lake during World War I as a recreation area and tourist camp for the soldiers and their families. After the war ended, it became popular with families from Columbia and Northeast Richland County. (Courtesy of David Sennema.)

Six

Hammond Recreates Quinine Hill

After the city of Columbia was founded on the Taylor plantations, Quinine Hill became a refuge from the summer heat and pesky mosquitoes. Several Taylor families, John Francis Dalloz, Dr. James Davis, and others built summer retreats on the hill.

By the time Hammond purchased it from Cooper in the mid-1920s, all that remained were shanties and crisscrossing dirt trails. A huge farm bell with a hand-painted sign at the end of Troy Road announced this Hammond "plantation" as Belle E Acres. The house at the entrance became Hammond's office and the place he spent most of his time. A brick-and-stone wall was constructed around the nearby spring at the corner of Hammond and J. B. McLauchlin property on Forest Drive. The "curative" water was offered free to all.

Quinine Hill became a great suburban project for the urbane lawyer. Hammond wanted his friends to move into his neighborhood and enjoy the trees, animals, and fresh air. He got William Y. "Bill" Hazlehurst, a civil engineer working on government projects, to survey his property in 1929 and lay out the streets.

The early property owners were Mrs. E. W. Heyward, Moak, Woodson, Evans, Bultman, W. H. Rose, Foster Marshall, E. H. Talbert, E. A. Mucklow, C. M. Munson, Quattlebaum, W. J. Taylor, Dr. P. V. Mikell, E. J. Plumer, R. E. Plumer, G. D. Huiet, M. S. Culler, T. J. Hendrix, J. D. McRae, H. L. Bynum, Kibler Dent, Arthur Holler, and Frank Tompkins. William and Ellen Taylor bought 4 acres on the northwest corner of Verner and Dalloz (3823 Verner Street). One of their four sons, James, had a law office next to Sen. James Hammond.

In 1934, Bill and Valeria Hazlehurst bought a small house and 1.17 acres on Vallie (Valley) Road from Hammond for $985, becoming the first modern residents of Quinine Hill. The Hazlehursts were soon joined by Foster and Walton Marshall (brother of Janie Hammond), Henry and Evelyn Richardson (Walton Marshall's mother), William Richardson (Henry's brother), William and Callie Rose, Edward H. Talbert, and Harry Taylor (descendant of Thomas Taylor as was his brother, William).

The residents of Quinine Hill got together on Christmas Day 1934 and elected officials of their small community. William Taylor became mayor, Foster Marshall and Edward Talbert became councilmen, and Harry Taylor became game warden. Sen. Hammond "sanctioned" the event and promised that bigger things were yet to come.

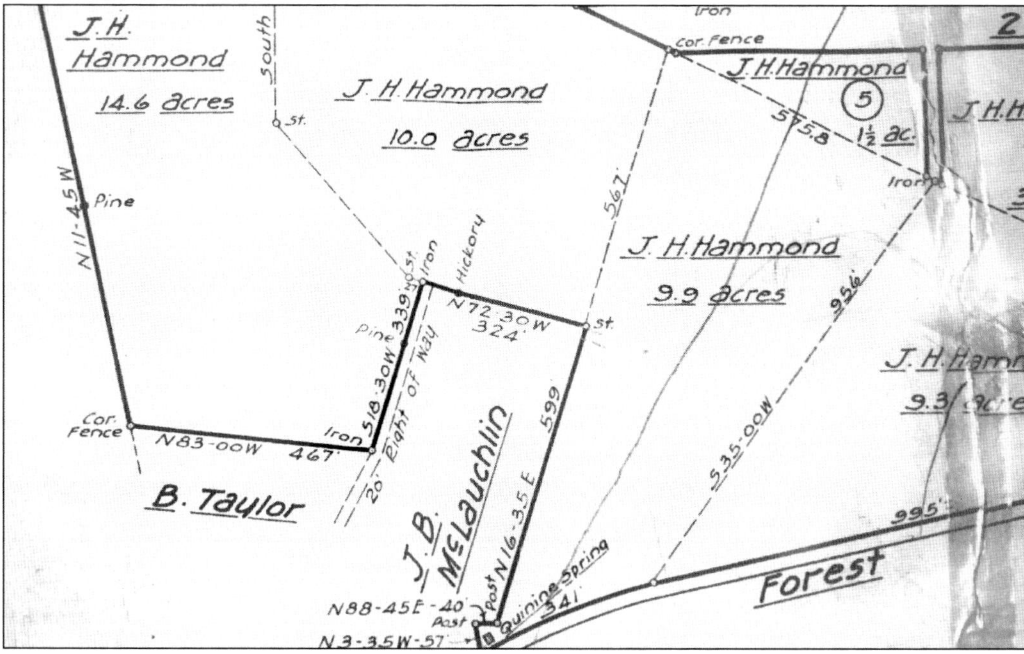

This 1929 map shows the Hammond property on Forest Drive. At the junction of Hammond and McLauchlin property on Forest Drive is the famous Quinine Spring. The spring was piped when Beltline Boulevard was constructed in 1938 and now runs beneath Richland Mall. (Courtesy of Elizabeth Hazlehurst Cantey.)

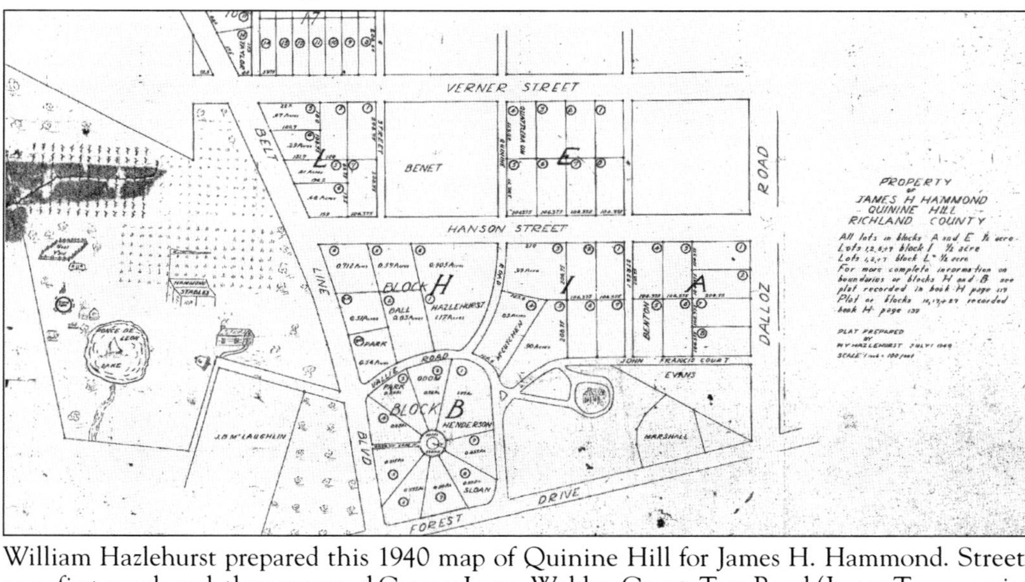

William Hazlehurst prepared this 1940 map of Quinine Hill for James H. Hammond. Streets were first numbered, then renamed Groggy Lane, Walden Court, Troy Road (James Troy married Kate Dalloz), Vallie Road (Bill Hazlehurst's wife's name was Vallie, which was later corrupted to Valley), John Francis Court, Hanson Road (Senator Hammond's mother was Laura Hanson), Verner Street (James Verner was a lawyer friend of Hammond), Beverly Drive (Beverly was the mother of John DuBose who built DuBose pond on northern side of Quinine Hill), Quitman Street (Quitman was Senator Hammond's son), Quinine Road, Spencer Street, and Dalloz Road. These names remain today. (Courtesy of Elizabeth Hazlehurst Cantey.)

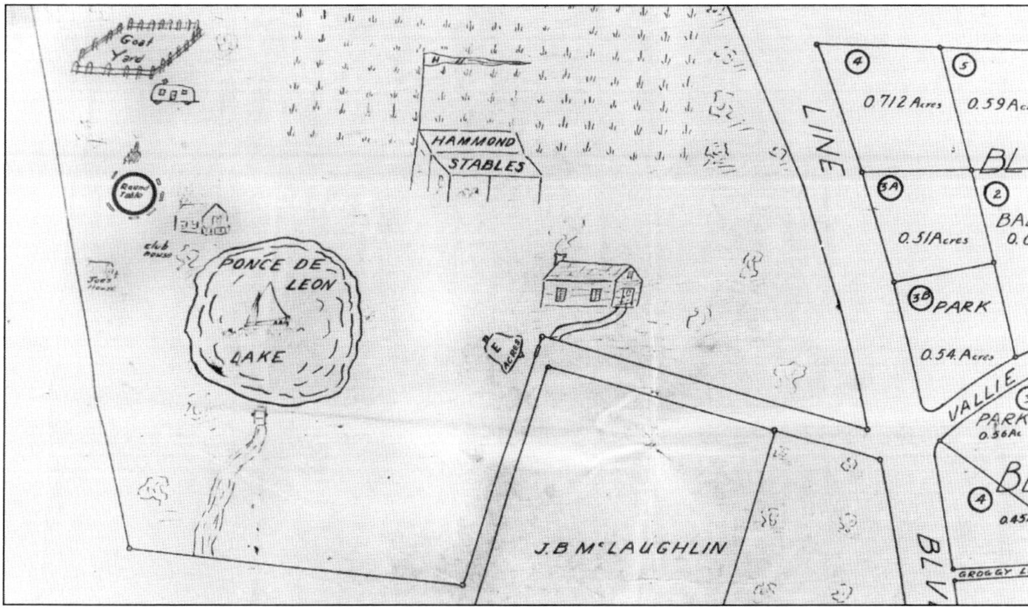

At the bottom of Quinine Hill, Hammond built a fish pond and a swimming pond, which he named Ponce de Leon Lake. He raided Fisher's Mill at Lake View of scores of millstones and scattered them around the pond. Stables and other outbuildings were constructed for cows, donkeys, horses, and goats. A ramshackle building that became known as the "Pond House" was reserved for weekend parties. Beside it were a "Round Table" and a barbecue pit. The caretaker, Joe, had his own house by the pond. Hammond planted dogwood, holly, cedar, and pecan trees. (Courtesy of Elizabeth Hazlehurst Cantey.)

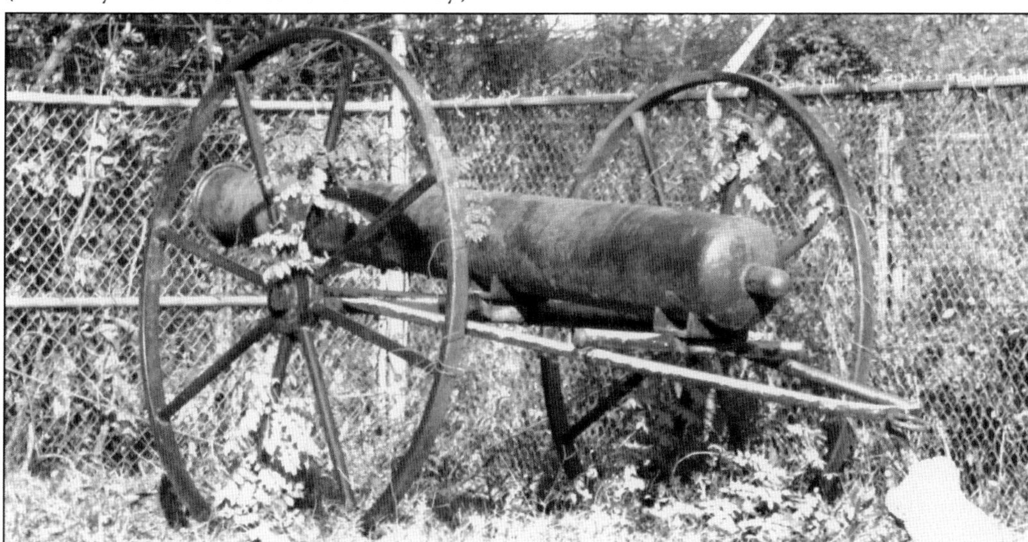

Hammond built an archway entrance to Belle E Acres inscribed with "Queenie" for his daughter's favorite donkey. The aging senator continued his pack rat ways, collecting pinball machines, buggies and carriages, plantation bells, millstones, an 1853 Spanish cannon, and an old train caboose in which his son, Quitman, lived. One of his prized possessions was a boot spur he claimed once belonged to Ponce de Leon. Sen. James Hammond had this 1853 cannon in his collection at Belle E Acres. (Photograph by Warner M. Montgomery.)

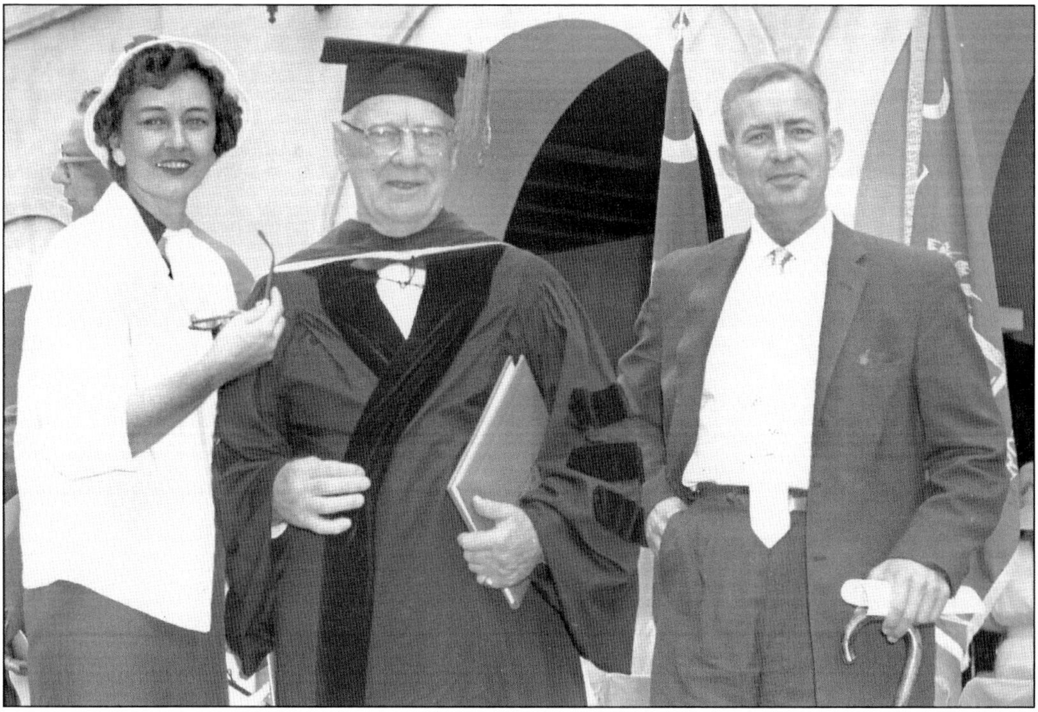

Sen. James Hammond received an honorary doctorate from the Citadel in 1969. He is shown here with his daughter, Laura, and son, Spann, after the ceremony. (Courtesy of Adele Jeffords Pope.)

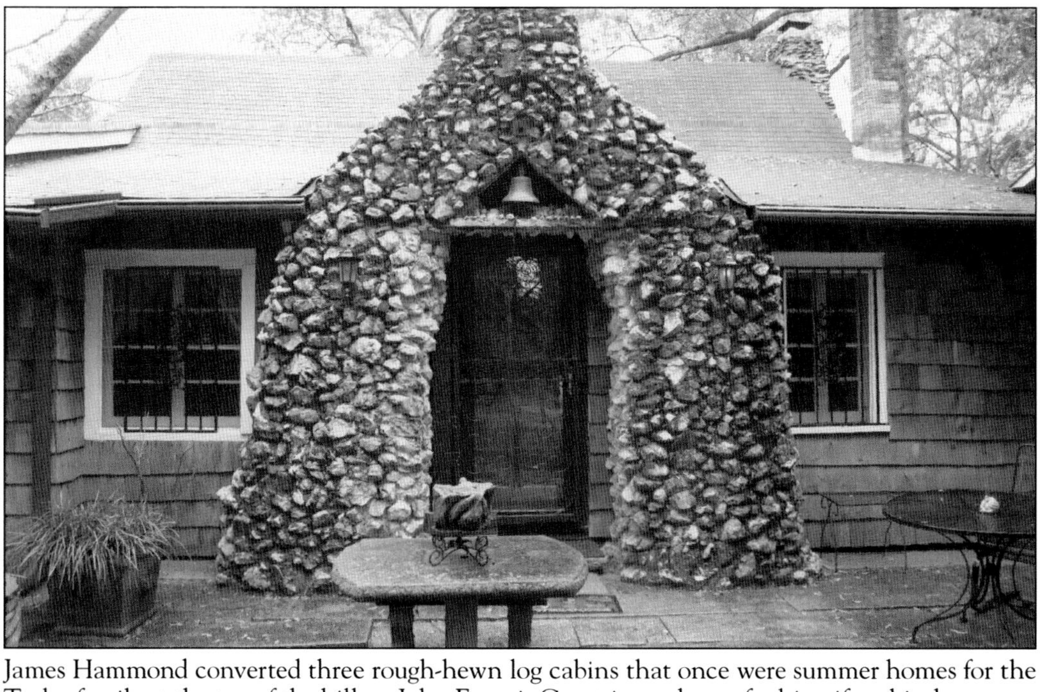

James Hammond converted three rough-hewn log cabins that once were summer homes for the Taylor family at the top of the hill on John Francis Court into a home for his wife, a kindergarten, and a storehouse. Over the years, the three cabins were connected. Since 1992 the home has been owned by Jean Berry. (Photograph by Warner M. Montgomery.)

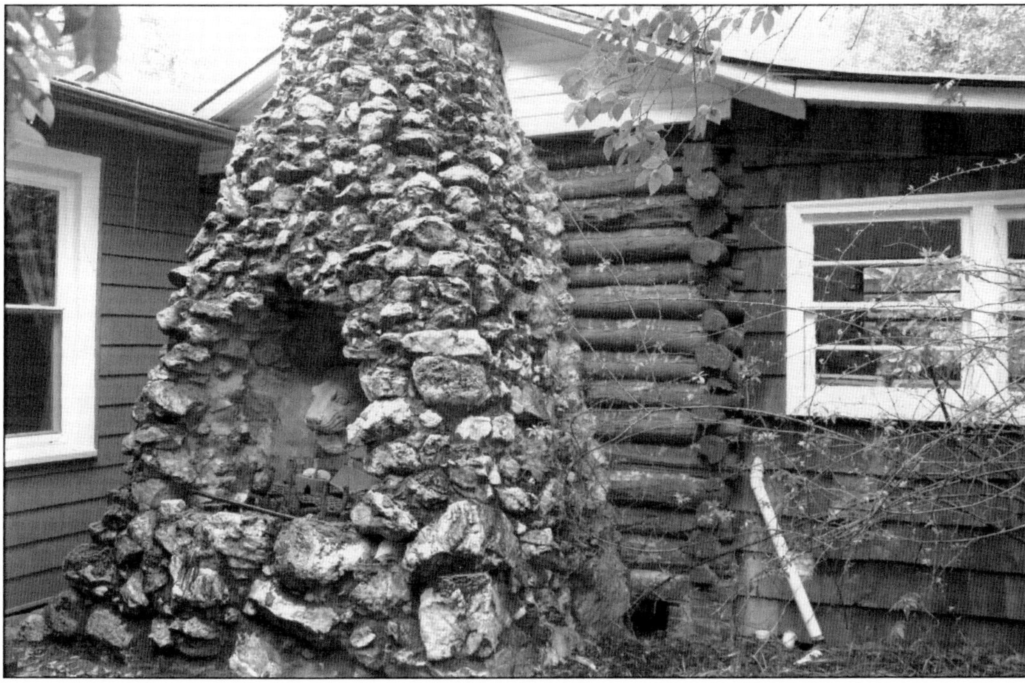

This stone chimney on the Hammond home features a lion motif. (Photograph by Warner M. Montgomery.)

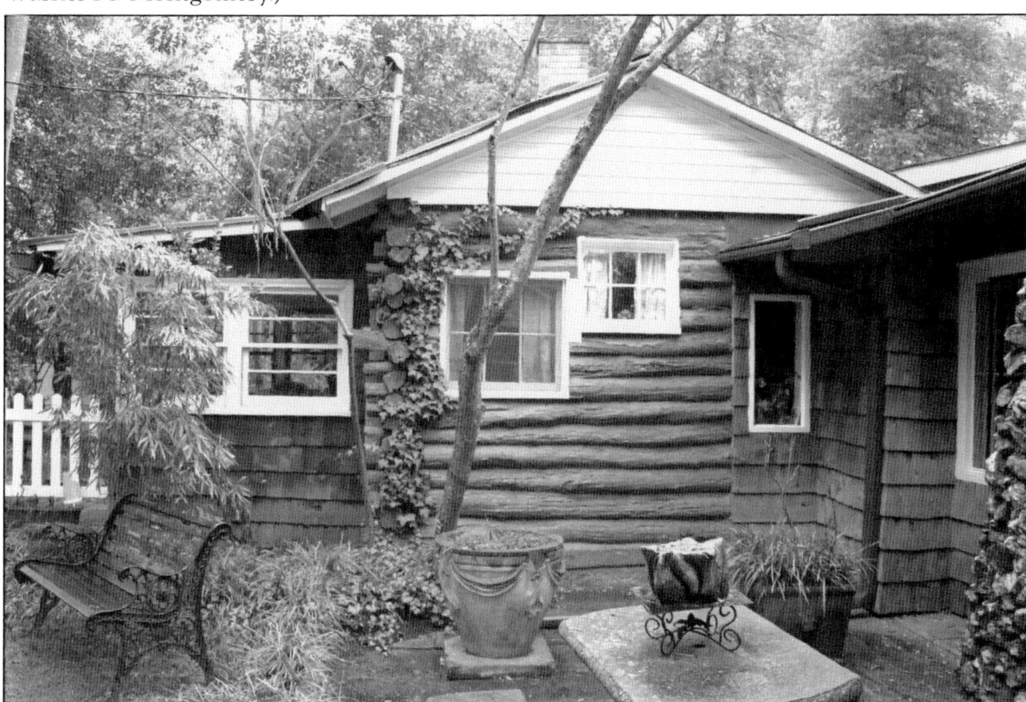

This view of the Hammond home shows where the cabin that served as Mrs. West's Kindergarten (on the left) was joined to the cabin that served as a warehouse. The enclosed porch is a recent addition. (Photograph by Warner M. Montgomery.)

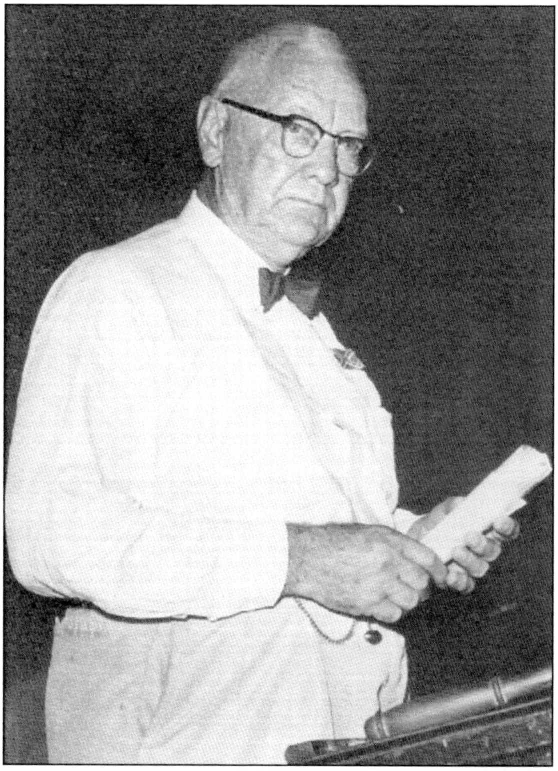

In 1953, some 15 friends and relatives of Senator Hammond gathered at Belle-E Acres and organized the Acres Club. They elected Cotesworth Jeffords, Hammond's son-in-law, the first president. Membership was limited to 36, an initiation fee was set at $1 per person and dues at $1 per month. Charter members were James H. Hammond, Clark and Hazel Brockman, Jane and Herbert Jervey, Cotesworth and Laura Jeffords, Bell and Pack Childress, Christine Willis, Kathleen Holliday, Hattie Johns, Julia Kennerly, and Mozelle and Guy Malone. The club was still meeting in 2010. In this 1969 photograph, Senator Hammond speaks to the Acres Club. (Courtesy of Adele Jeffords Pope.)

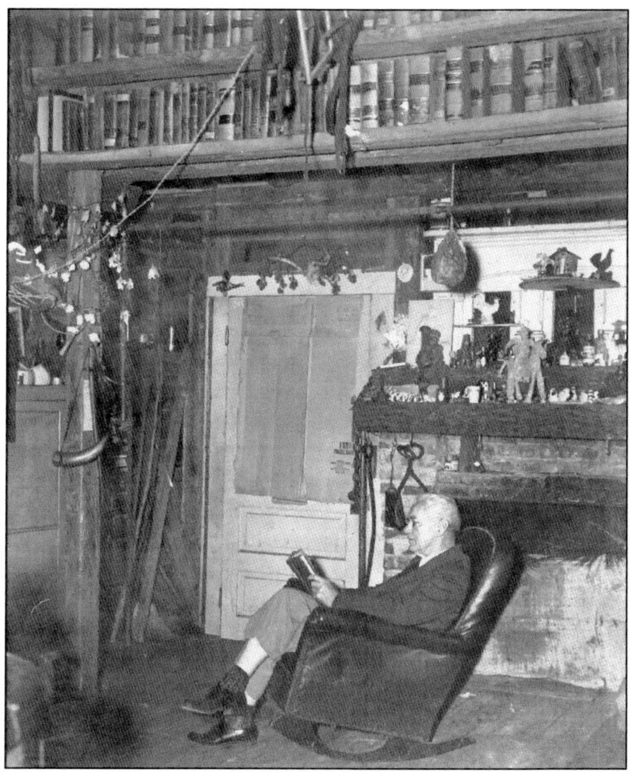

Senator Hammond's Quinine Hill property was cut in half by Beltline Boulevard. On the northwest corner of Beltline and Forest Drive, he built a commercial strip. His first tenant, Jim Scoggins, set up a drug store with a popular soda fountain. Hoover's Gulf Station and Embers Drive-In soon followed. Through it all, he spent most of his time in his office at The Pond where he kept his law books and his other collections. Senator Hammond died in 1970 without a will. Attorney Hal Green handled his estate and sold the Quinine Hill property in 1978 to Zan Heyward and Bloomwood Development Company who developed it as residential subdivision called Mill Pond. (Courtesy of Adele Jeffords Pope.)

Janie Hammond (center) and her daughter, Laura (right), had their picture snapped in 1948 on Main Street in Columbia. (Courtesy of Adele Jeffords Pope.)

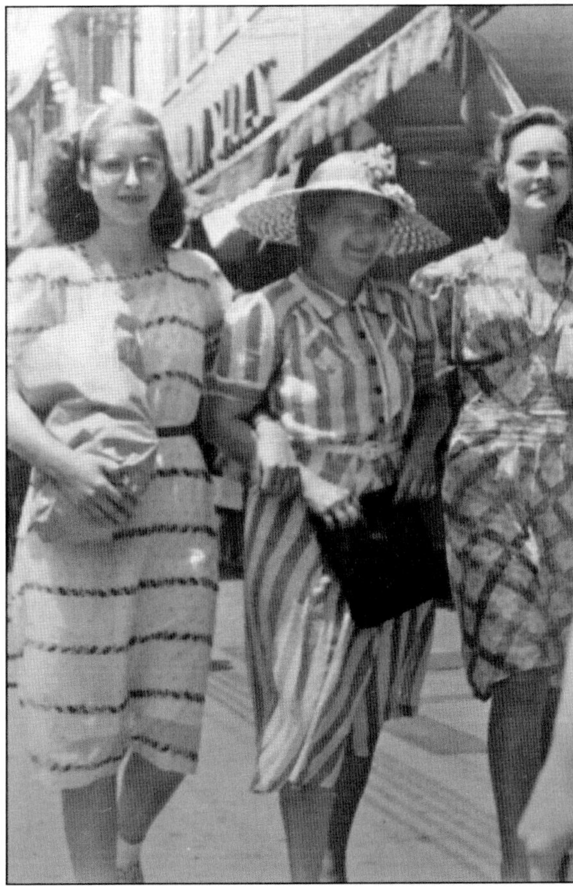

Hammond renovated his pond house with old doors, windows, and planks from his razed office building in Columbia, floorboards from the old Seibels house in Columbia, and timbers from a stable at Redcliffe, his grandfather's plantation in Aiken County. He purchased a washbasin and marble stand for $10 from the home of Episcopal bishop Peter Shand, which was being demolished. The pond house chandelier was made from antique guns, Indian axes, and old swords. A pine trunk Hammond's grandmother brought from Europe filled with silverware sat in the corner next to a modern jukebox. Senator Hammond collected old millstones from the Taylor Mill on Gills Creek. They now line the streets of the Millpond development at the end of Troy Road. (Photograph by Warner M. Montgomery.)

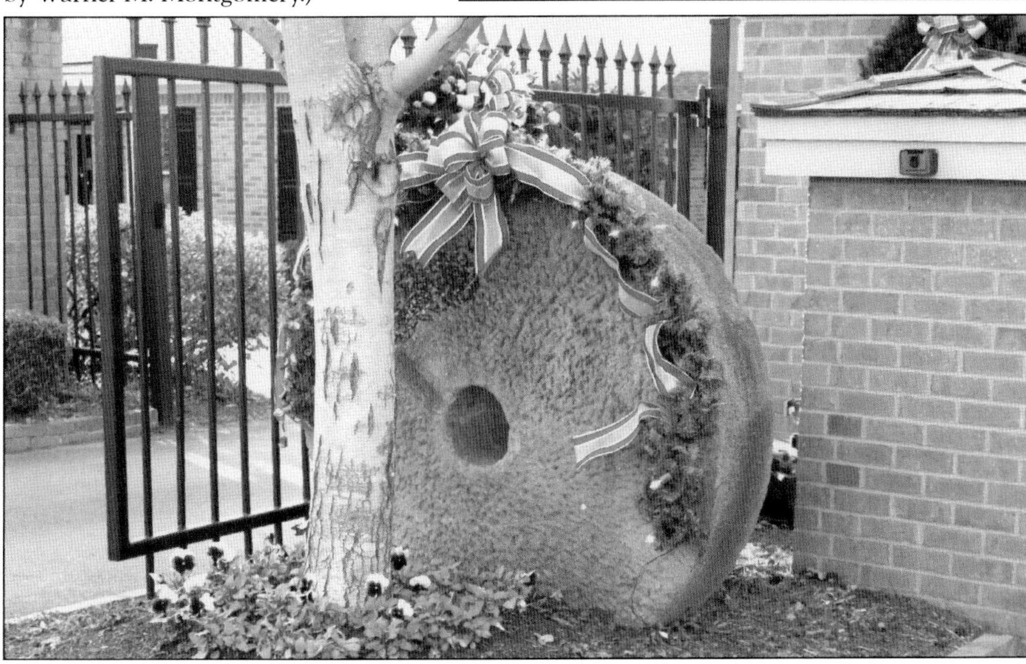

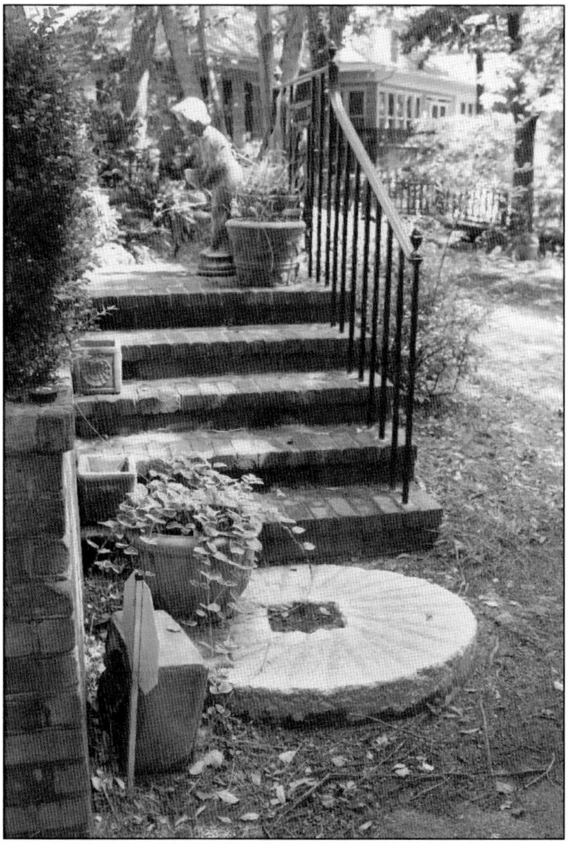

Hammond's millstones are still used on personal walkways in the Millpond development. (Photograph by Warner M. Montgomery.)

The mill pond was once Hammond's Ponce de Leon Lake. (Photograph by Warner M. Montgomery.)

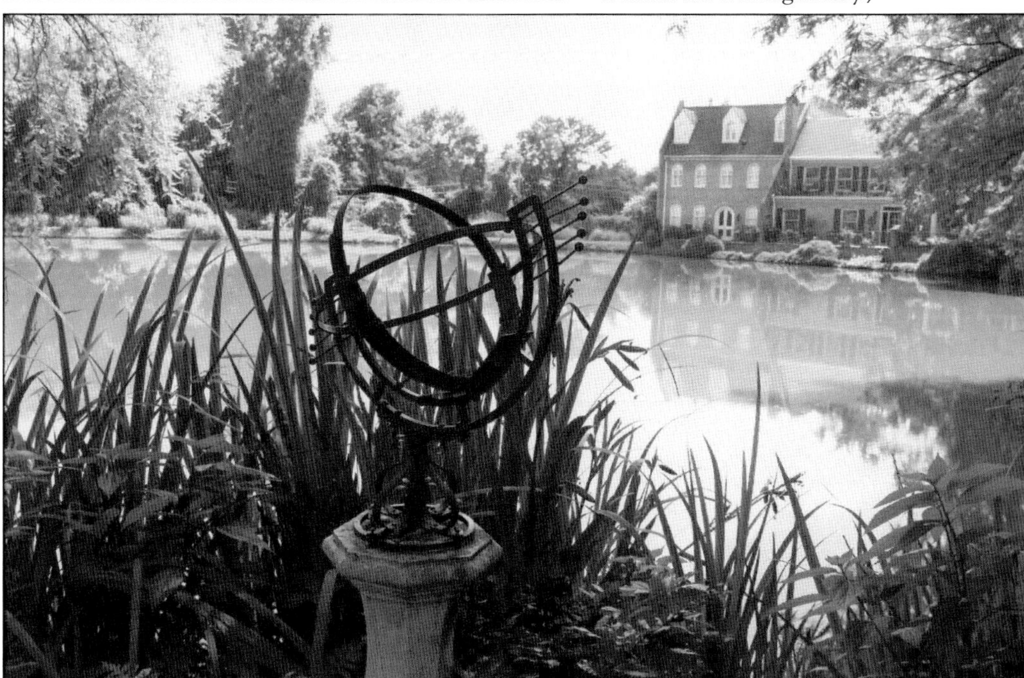

Seven

City of Forest Acres Is Born

Funds from the Works Project Administration (WPA) put millions to work during the Depression building highways, roads, streets, public buildings, and public utilities. Hammond and Cooper became aware of plans by the South Carolina Highway Department to build roads connecting the Old Camden Road to Two Notch Road using WPA funds. The road between the two was Satchel Ford Road, which forded Eightmile Branch just beyond Bethel Church and wound through the farms ending where the railroad tracks crossed Two Notch Road.

Seeing an opportunity for improvement of Quinine Hill and Forest Lake, Hammond and Cooper gathered citizens at the Huiet's 15-acre dairy farm on the Old Camden Road. Those attending included William and Callie Rose, who had established a paint factory on Quinine Hill in 1920; many Dent families; Boykin and Fannie Davis, who had operated the B. T. Davis Grocery since 1909; the Evans, who owned property along the Old Camden Road; and banker-developer Emmette Groover, who would become the new town's third mayor in 1949. Groover developed Idalia Road (his wife was Ida) and built the first house on the street in 1936.

Hammond pointed out that municipal incorporation would be necessary in order to qualify for WPA funds. The town had to have a name, corporate limits, registered inhabitants, and a government, but first a petition had to be signed by a majority of the citizens. Cooper recommended the name Forest Acres. Hammond suggested Quinine Hill. They put it up for a vote in the petition.

The southern and northern boundaries would be one-half mile on either side of the Old Camden Road. The eastern boundary would be 1,000 feet east of Gills Creek and the western boundary two miles to the west just beyond Hammond's property. The petition included a ballot with Cooper as mayor and William Rose, A. G. Dent, and G. D. Huiet as councilmen. The election committee of Hammond, A. G. Dent, Fannie Davis, and William Rose filed the petition on August 28, 1935, with the South Carolina secretary of state, which gave them the right to hold an election on September 24, 1935. Hammond, Dent, and Davis were appointed election commissioners.

On September 24, 1935, approximately 100 voters went to the polls at the Davis Store. They chose the name Forest Acres and approved the ballot for mayor and council. The election was rushed to the secretary of state's office and the town of Forest Acres was born with a population of 375.

Cooper died March 24, 1945, and was officially succeeded as mayor by Bill Hazlehurst (1905–1998), who was still serving in the Pacific theater with the U.S. Navy. Councilmen were T. K. Knight, E. M. Henderson, and J. B. Taylor.

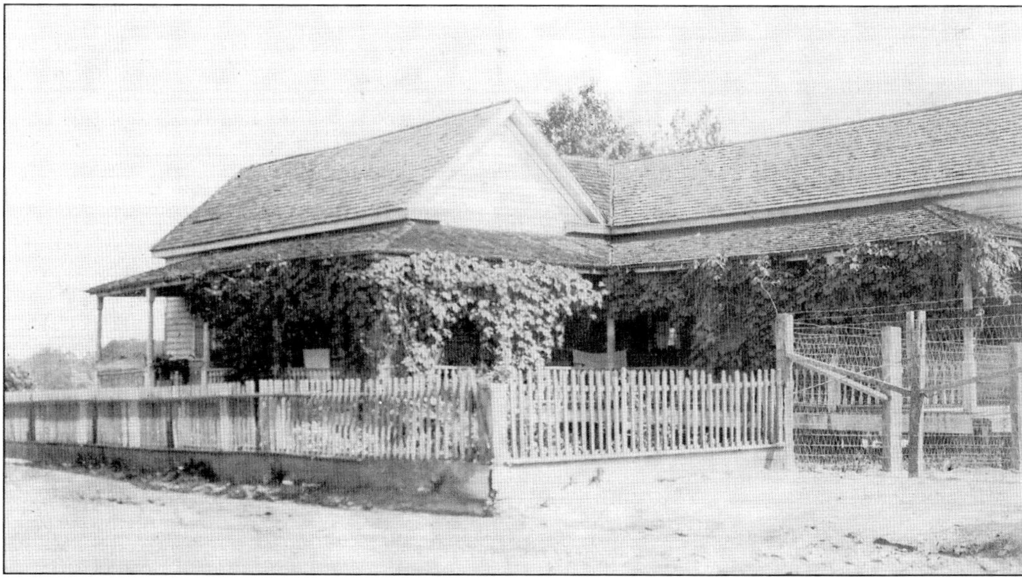

Boykin and Fannie Davis lived in this home on Forest Drive at the beginning of the 20th century. They had two children, Louise and Hugh. (Courtesy of Hammond Edwards III.)

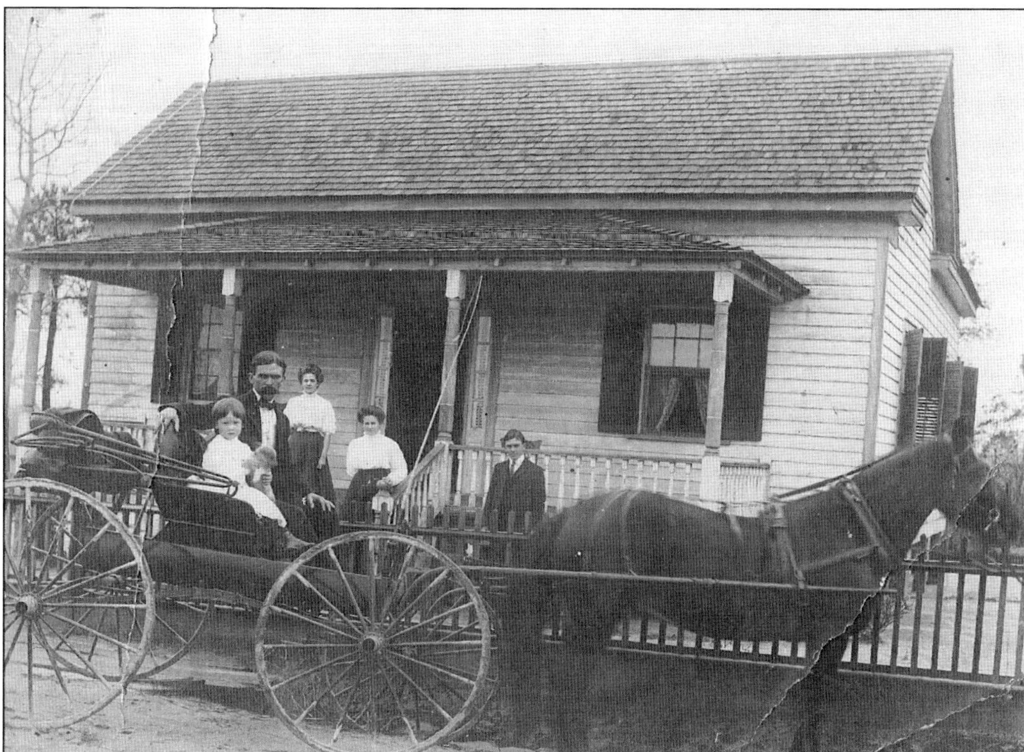

This 1909 photograph was taken in front of the Davis home. Boykin and Louise are in the carriage. Fannie Davis, Alice Cline, and Hackerd Davis are behind the carriage. (Courtesy of Hammond Edwards III.)

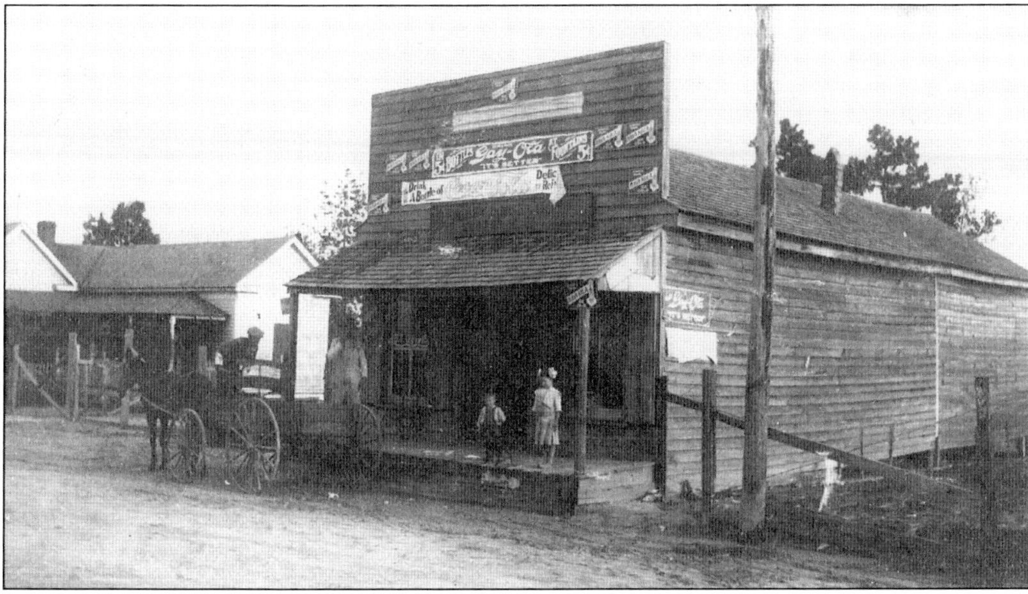

Samuel W. Dent opened this store on the Old Camden Road (4600 Forest Drive) soon after the Civil War. In 1909 Boykin Davis bought the store. It served as the voting polls for Forest Acres from 1935 until 1955. (Courtesy of Hammond Edwards III.)

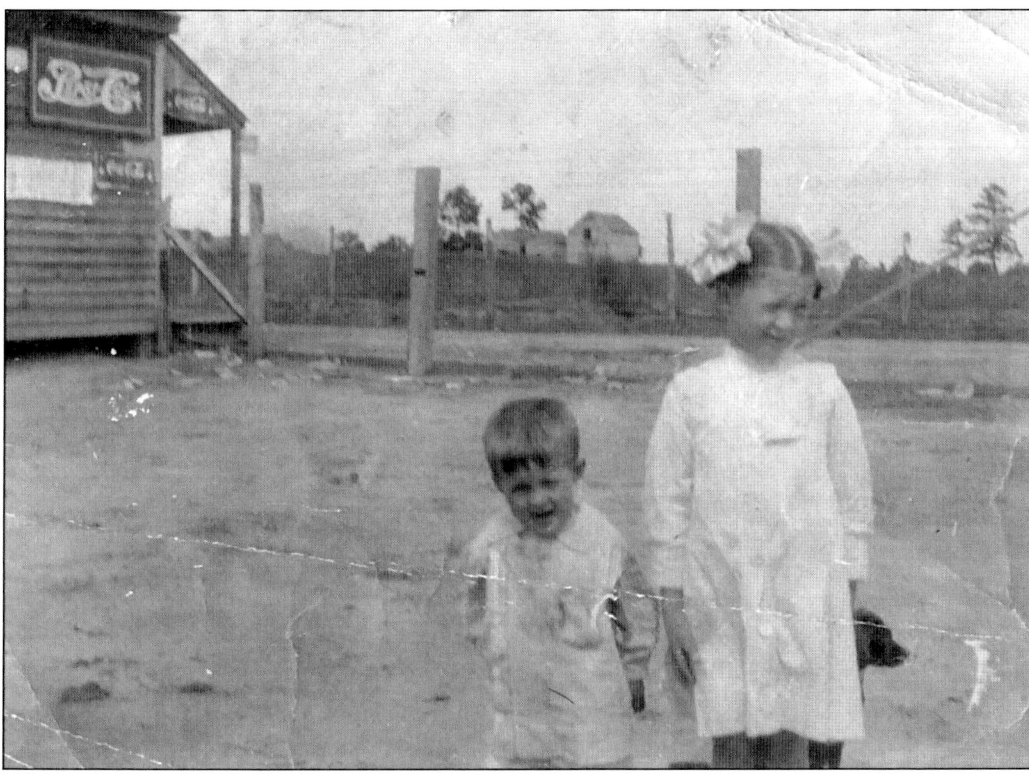

Hugh and Louise Davis play behind the Davis Store. (Courtesy of Hammond Edwards III.)

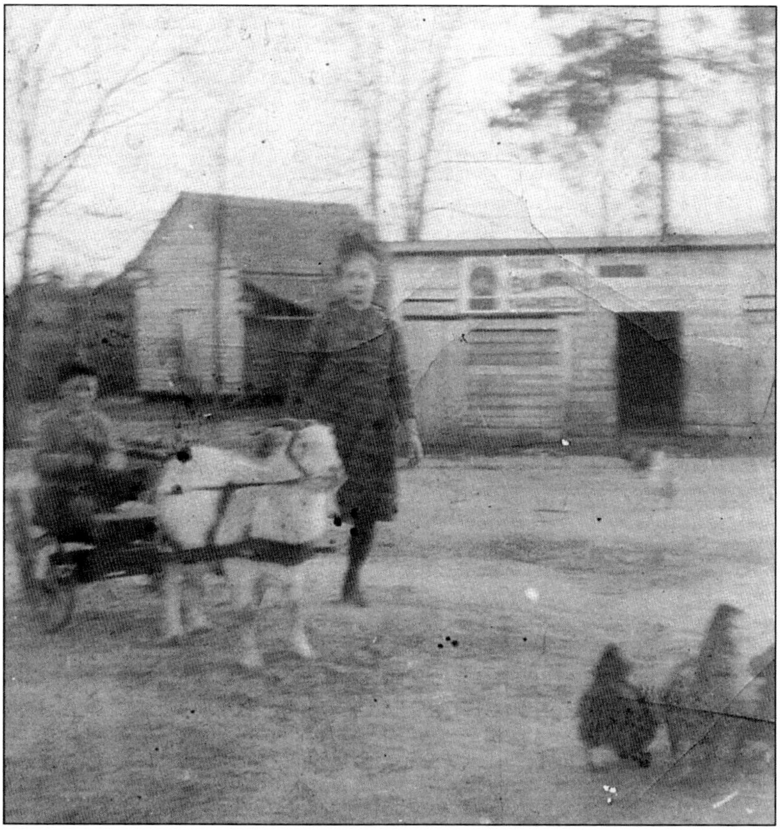

Hugh Davis rides in his goat cart while his sister, Louise, chases chickens at their home on Forest Drive. (Courtesy of Hammond Edwards III.)

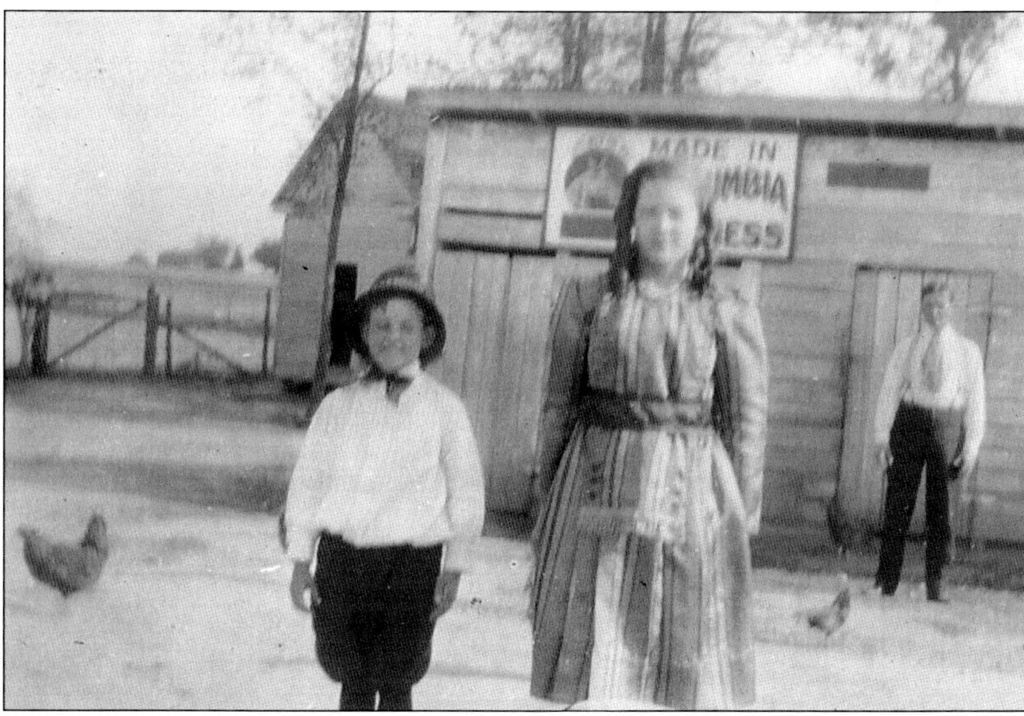

Hugh, Louise, and their father, B. T. Davis, stand behind their home on Forest Drive. (Courtesy of Hammond Edwards III.)

The Dent family continued as a major influence in the area. Benjamin T. Dent (1841–1909) had owned much of the land south of Eightmile Branch along Satchel Ford Road. Consuela "Sue" Dent (1896–1969) attended and later taught at Bethel School. Sue Dent was a beautiful baby in this 1898 photograph. Benjamin's grandson, A. G. (1879–1946, known as Archie), lived on Forest Drive and ran a meat market on Assembly Street in Columbia. Archie and Ethel (1884–1967) Dent's son, Bubba (1923–1992), opened a meat market on Forest Drive. (Courtesy of Pete Dent.)

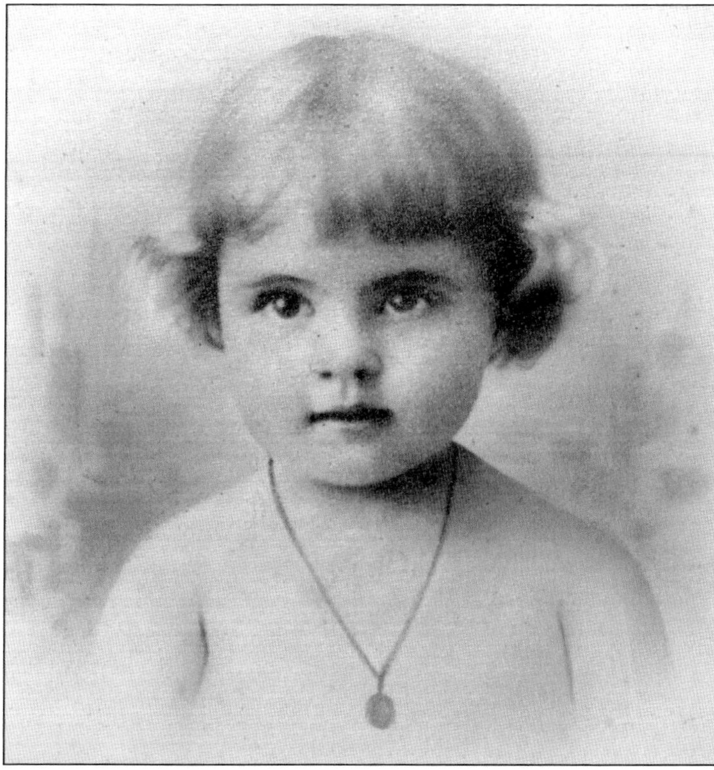

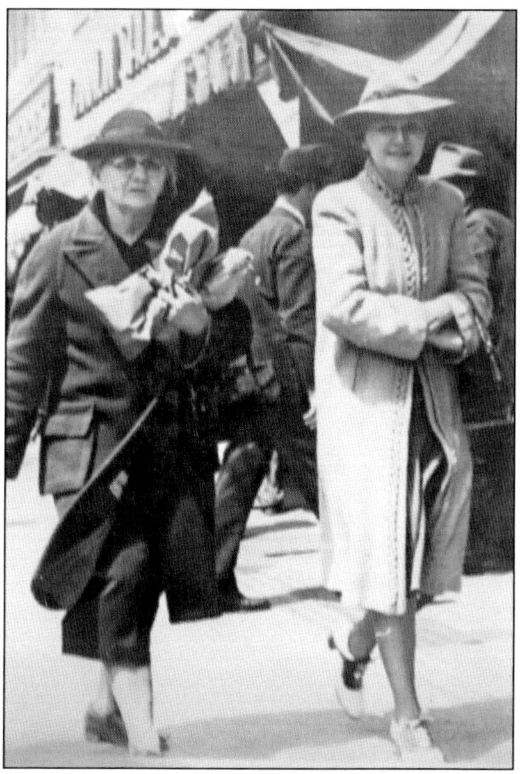

Roberta "Birdie" and Sue Dent had their picture snapped in 1948 on Main Street in Columbia. (Courtesy of Pete Dent.)

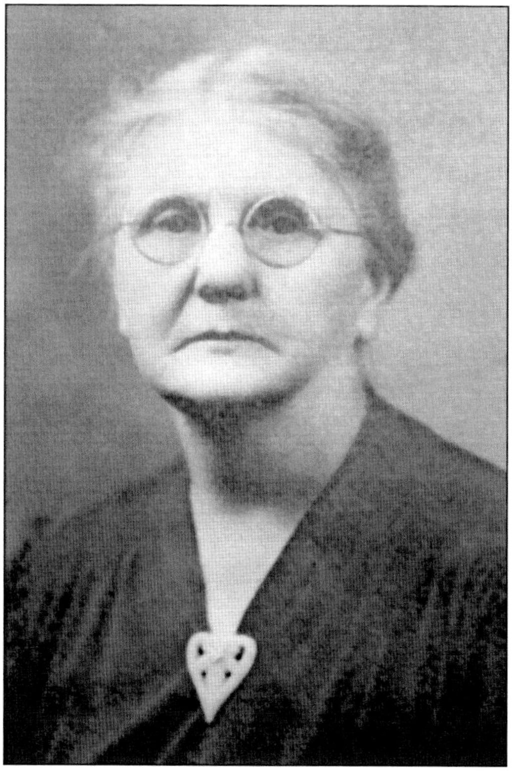

Roberta "Birdie" Dent (1872–1957) had this portrait taken a few days before her death. (Courtesy of Pete Dent.)

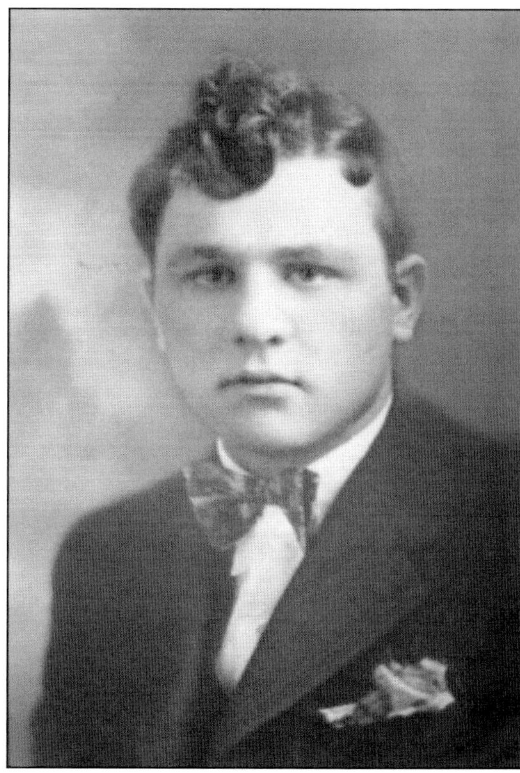

Neil Dent (1907–1986), Sue's brother, poses for a formal photograph in 1929. A. G. "Bubba" Dent Jr. (Neil and Sue's great-nephew) and his wife, Margie, inherited property along Forest Drive and operated Dent's Open Air Market for decades. Bubba served on the city council from 1935 to 1949. Bell's 19¢ Hamburger Drive-In and Pop's A&W Root Beer were among the early fast food joints on Forest Drive. W. J. Stubbs Jr. was elected mayor in 1957. The council was made up of incumbents Lonnie Garrick and W. H. Tillotson and newcomers C. D. Hill and A. S. Thomas Jr. G. S. McKibben, Alex A. Dickson, and R. C. Johnson were elected to the public works commission were. (Courtesy of Pete Dent.)

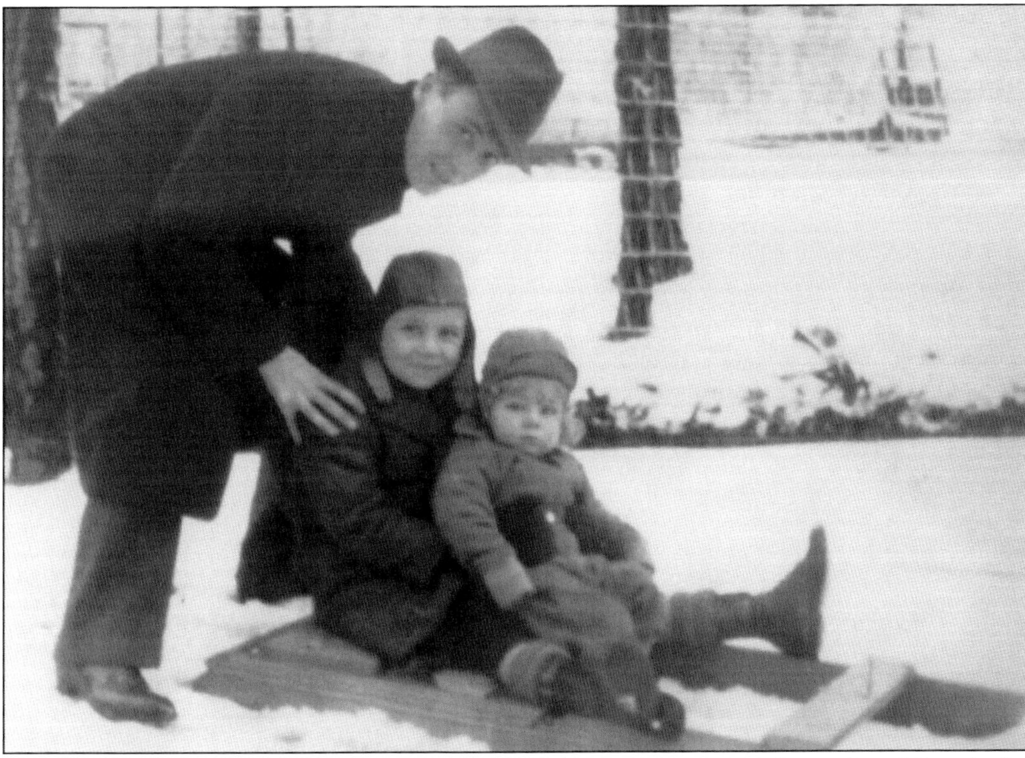

During a snowstorm in 1936, Kibler Dent (left) pushes his sons Sonny (center) and Pete (right) on a homemade sled. (Courtesy of Pete Dent.)

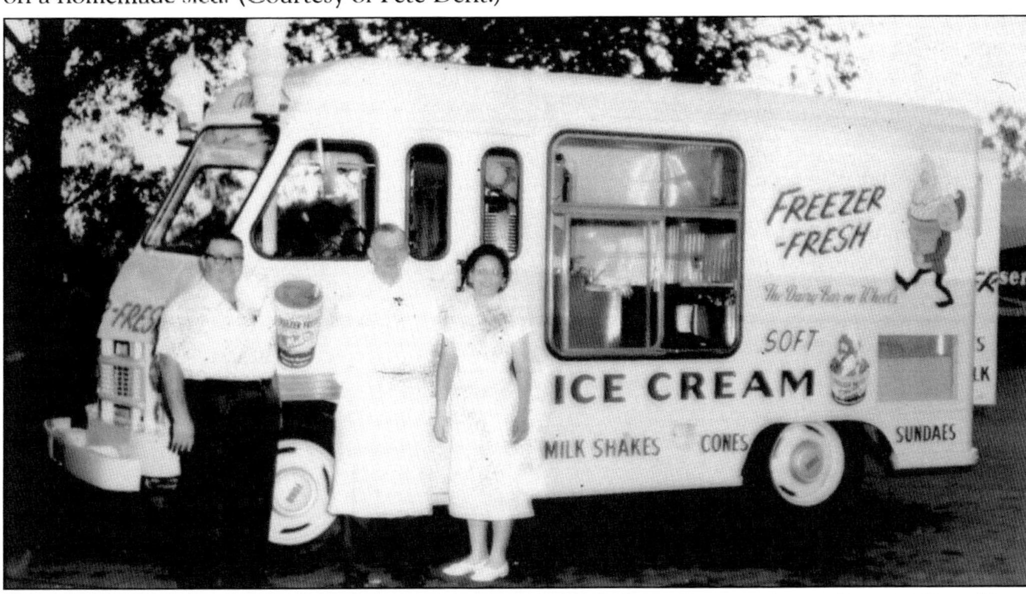

Businesses in the new city of Forest Acres included B. T. Davis Grocery Store, Rose-Talbert Paint Company, Jack Small's Grocery Store (later Mr. Grainger's Store, then Kelly's Open Air Market), and Monckton's Golf Course. The most popular mobile business was the "Ice Cream Man," who rang his bell as he cruised the streets of Forest Acres. Children rushed to get their freezer-fresh treats. (Courtesy of Frankie Garrick.)

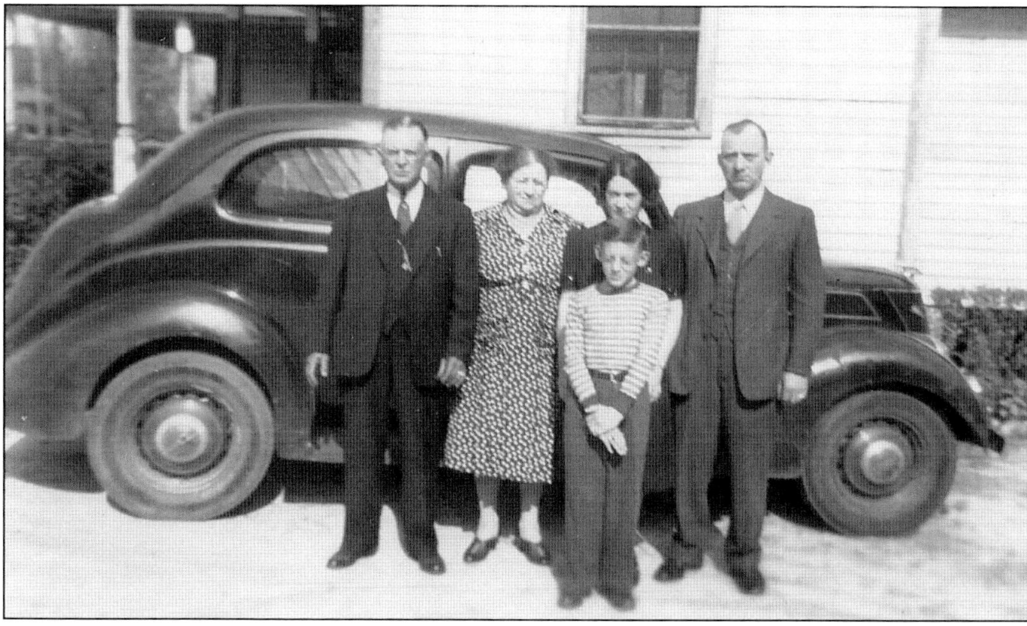

The Davis family poses proudly in front of their new 1937 Ford V8 sedan. From left to right they are Boykin and Fannie Davis, their daughter Louise (b. 1905) and her husband, Hammond Edwards (b. 1903), and Hammond Edwards Jr. (1932–2009) in front. (Courtesy of Hammond Edwards III.)

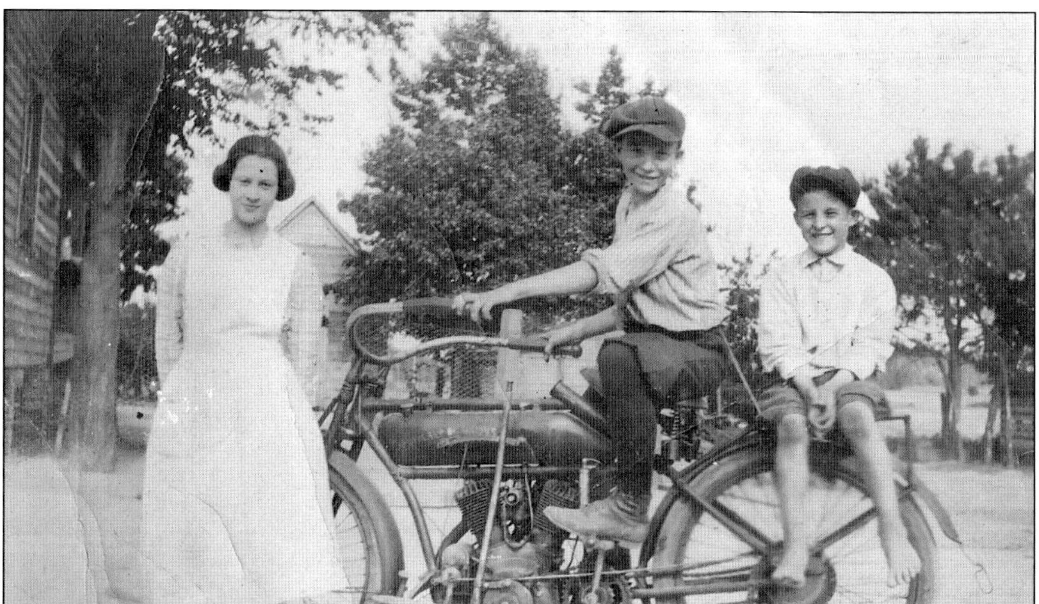

Louise Davis admires Andrew Allen (driving) and her brother, Hugh, on their Flying Merkel motorcycle. (Courtesy of Hammond Edwards III.)

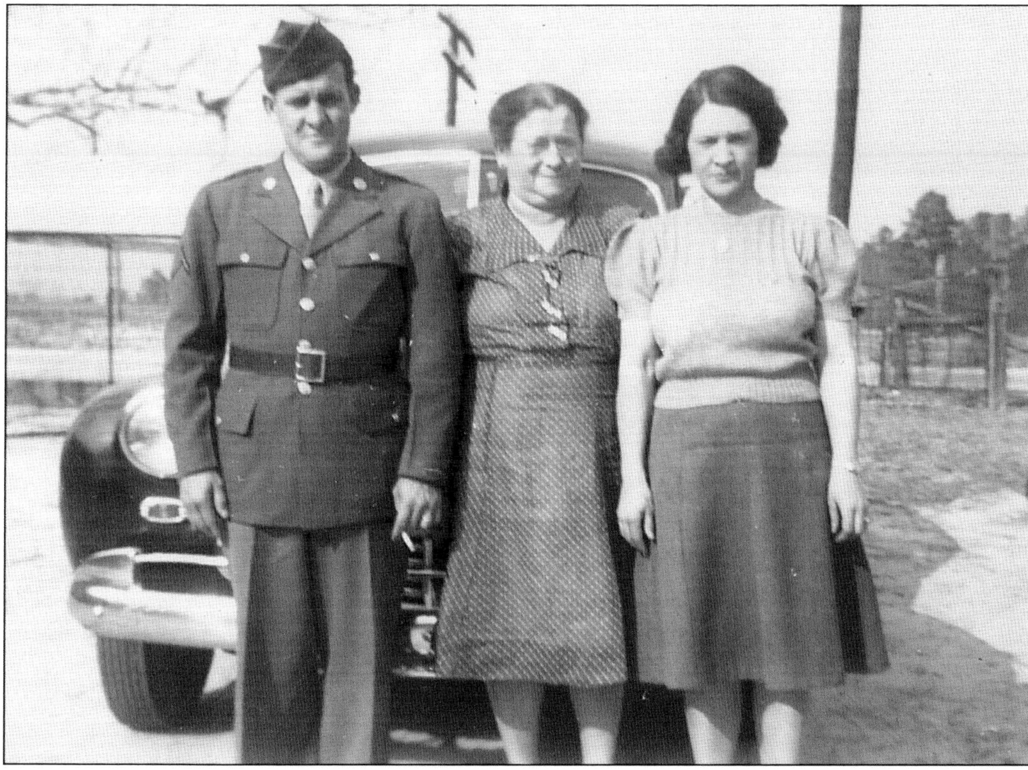

Hugh Davis returns from the war in 1947 and is greeted by his mother, Fannie, and his sister, Louise. (Courtesy of Hammond Edwards III.)

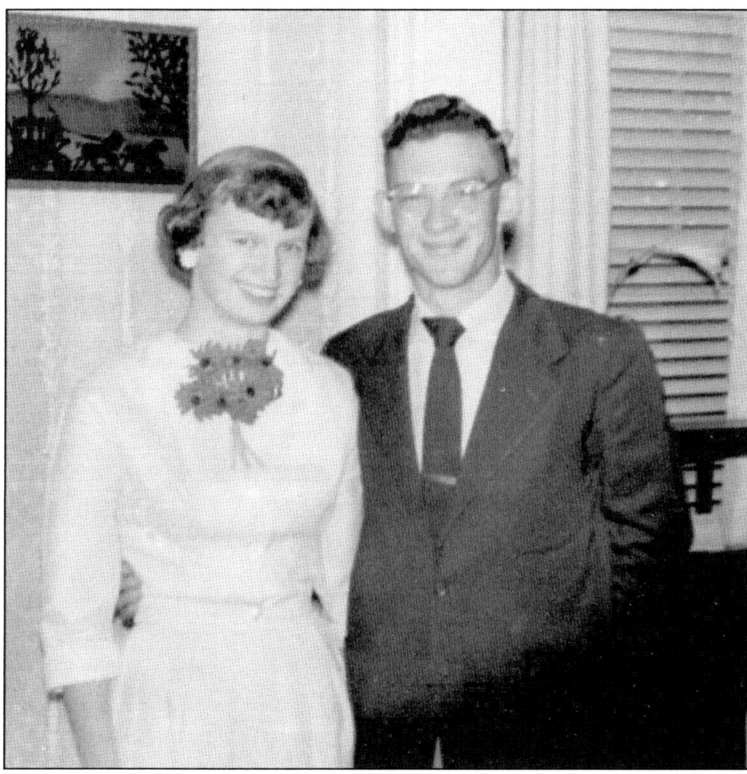

Wilhelmina (b. 1935) and Gene (1932–2009) Edwards are pictured in their 1956 wedding photograph. (Courtesy of Hammond Edwards III.)

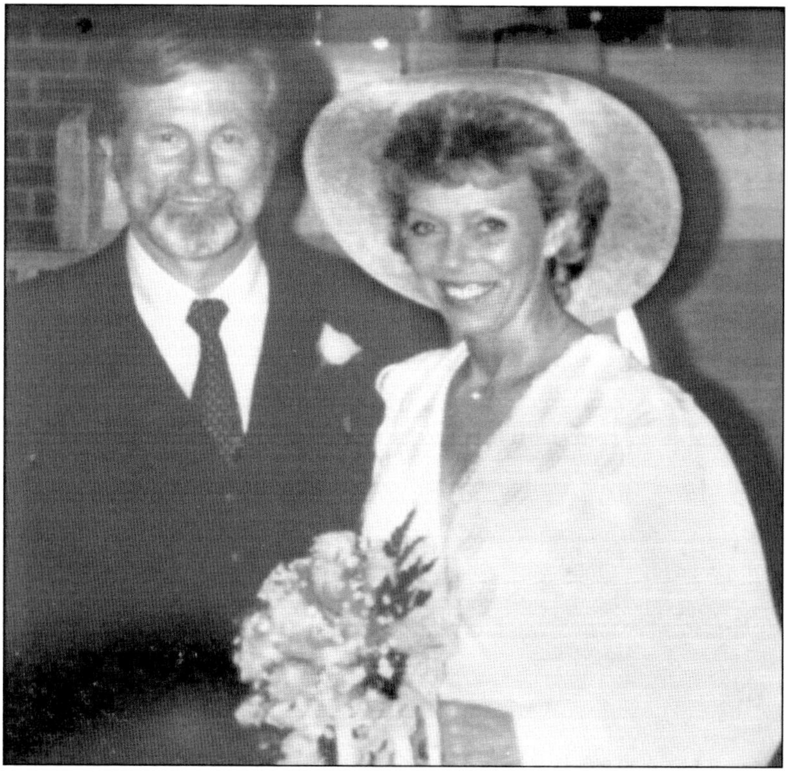

Pete Dent, son of Kibler Dent who owned a jewelery store on Main Street in Columbia, grew up on Forest Drive across from the Hi-Hatt Club and rode the bus to Taylor School. When he got off the bus in the afternoon, he would buy candy from Goldie, the proprietress of the Hi-Hatt Club. She often bragged to him about having three husbands. Pete is shown his new bride, Mary, in their 1984 wedding photograph. (Courtesy of Pete Dent.)

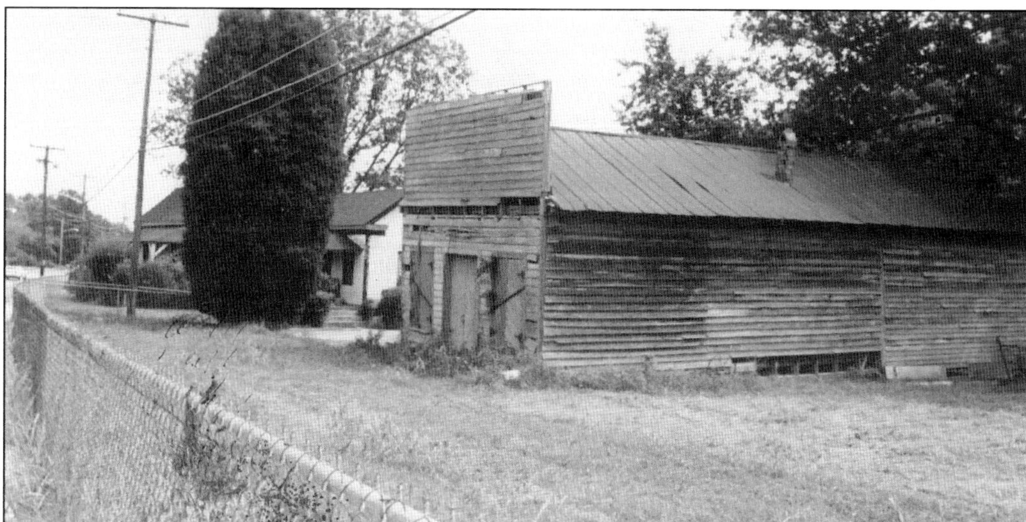

In 1949, Forest Acres mayor Emmette Groover and councilmen Lonnie Garrick, W. H. Tillotson, W. J. Stubbs, and S. R. Spann held their monthly meetings in Groover's home. Public hearings and elections were held at the Davis Store until 1955, when they were moved to Crayton School. The newly created public works commission was led by M. S. Culler, G. D. Huiet, and A. H. Gibert. W. E. Tighe became city recorder. Spann Hammond (owner of a motorcycle shop on Forest Drive) was appointed the city's first chief of police, an honorary position since the Richland County sheriff was responsible for law enforcement. The Davis Store is pictured here in 1985 just before it was demolished. (Courtesy of Hammond Edwards III.)

Dr. George McCutchen of Quinine Hill shows his award-winning dog, Pete, in 1950. (Courtesy of George McCutchen Jr.)

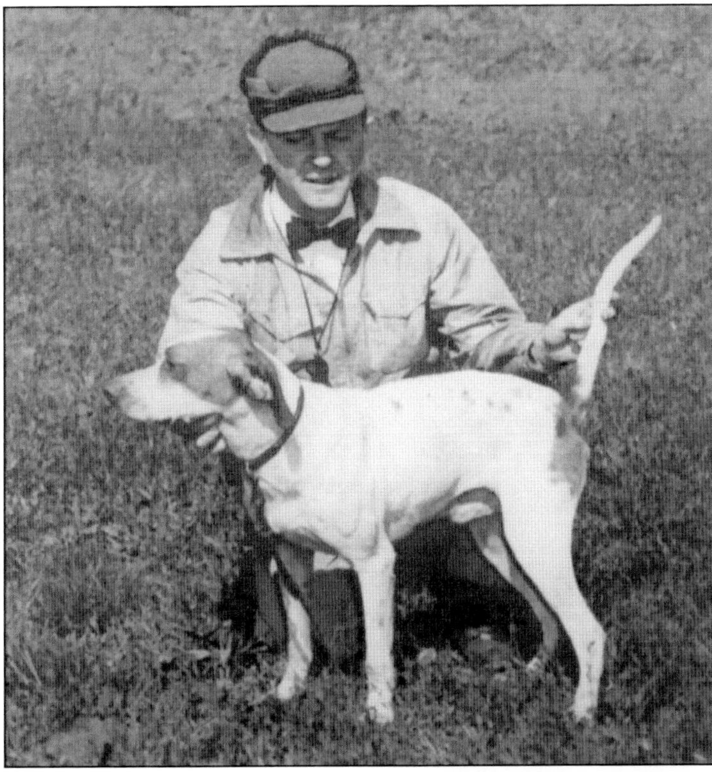

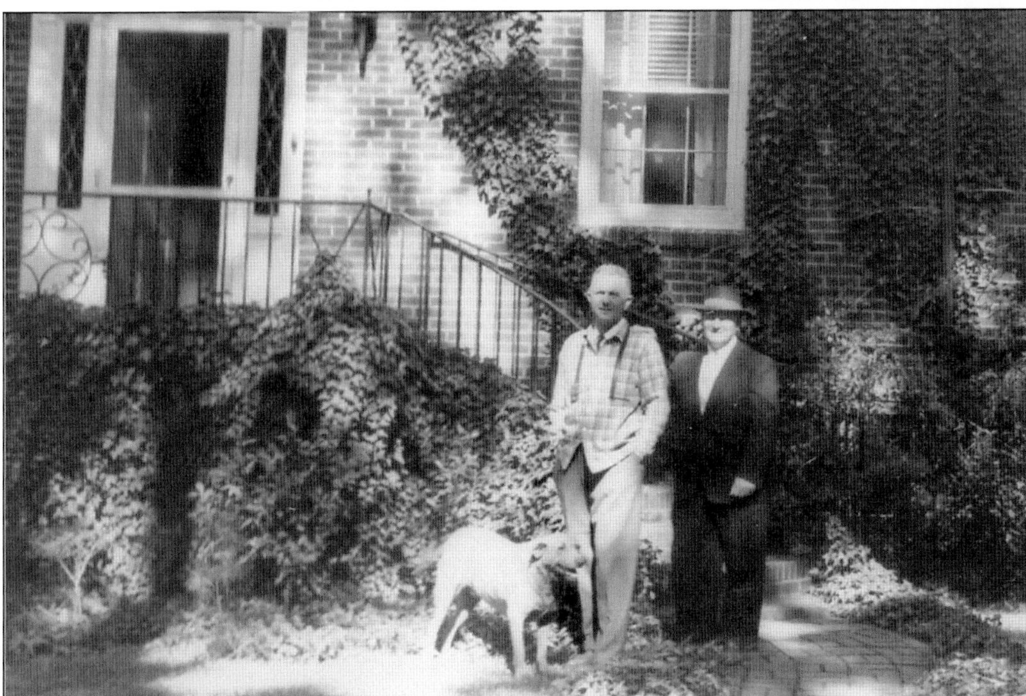

Dr. George McCutchen (left) and Bill Hazlehurst stand in front of the Hazlehurst home on Valley Road in 1957. (Courtesy of Elizabeth Hazlehurst Cantey.)

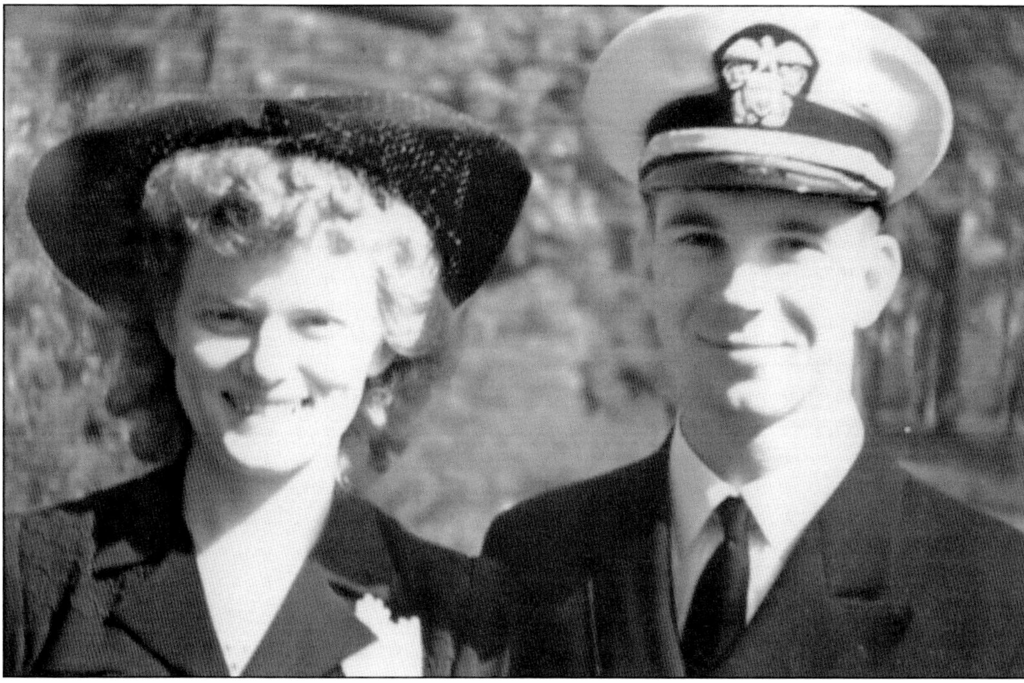

James and Nell Seay returned from California after serving in World War II and developed a section of Forest Acres. They named their streets after favorite places in the west: Atascadero Drive, Juarez Court, Monterey Place, Vallejo Circle, Ponte Vedra Drive, and Havana Court. Frankie and Lonnie Garrick (pictured above) were married while Lonnie was in the navy. They bought a home in 1946 on Verner Street next to a cow pasture. Lonnie began a long tenure on city council in 1949. (Courtesy of Frankie Garrick.)

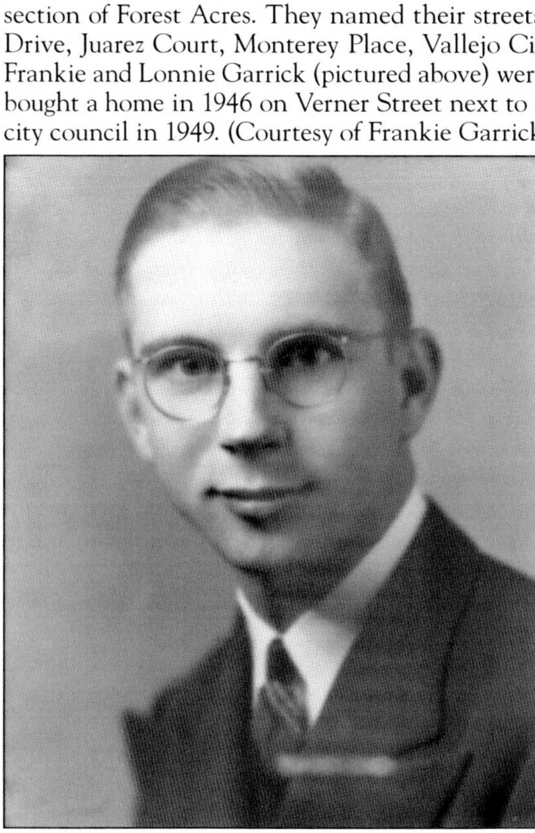

Forest Acres was connected to the Columbia water system by 1939 with the help of WPA funds and a $10,000 bond issue. The bond debt was paid off by 1947. The city did not levy property taxes but collected a modest license fee from businesses and hired a garbage service (90¢ per family per month) to be paid for by each homeowner and business. Fire services were provided by the Columbia Fire Department on a $300 per call basis. Law enforcement was provided by the Richland County Sheriff's Department. Instrumental in this development was Lonnie Garrick, pictured here, who served on the Forest Acres City Council from 1949 to 1965. (Courtesy of Frankie Garrick.)

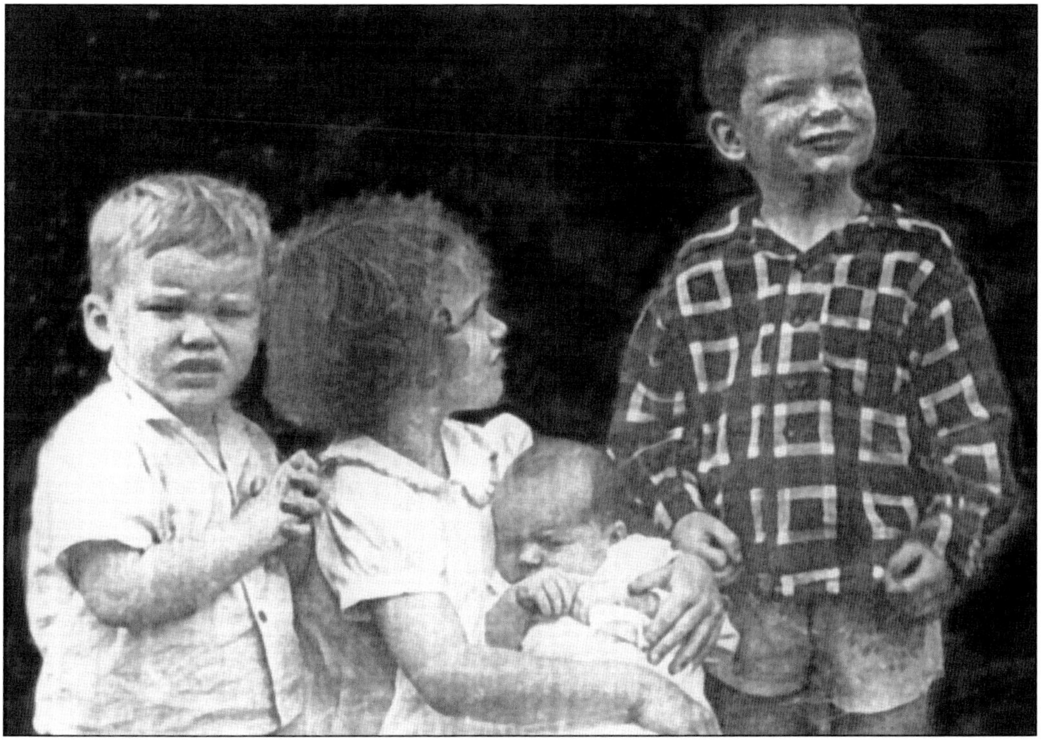

The Hi-Hatt Club served food in order to keep its liquor license, and this fact was known to the surrounding housewives. Late one afternoon, Frankie Garrick, who lived two blocks from the Hi-Hatt Club, realized she needed some groceries. She sneaked down to the club and asked Goldie for some eggs and milk. She never told her husband, who was a city councilman, what she had done. Pictured in 1951, from left to right are Frank, Jane, Fred, and Tom Garrick. (Courtesy of Frankie Garrick.)

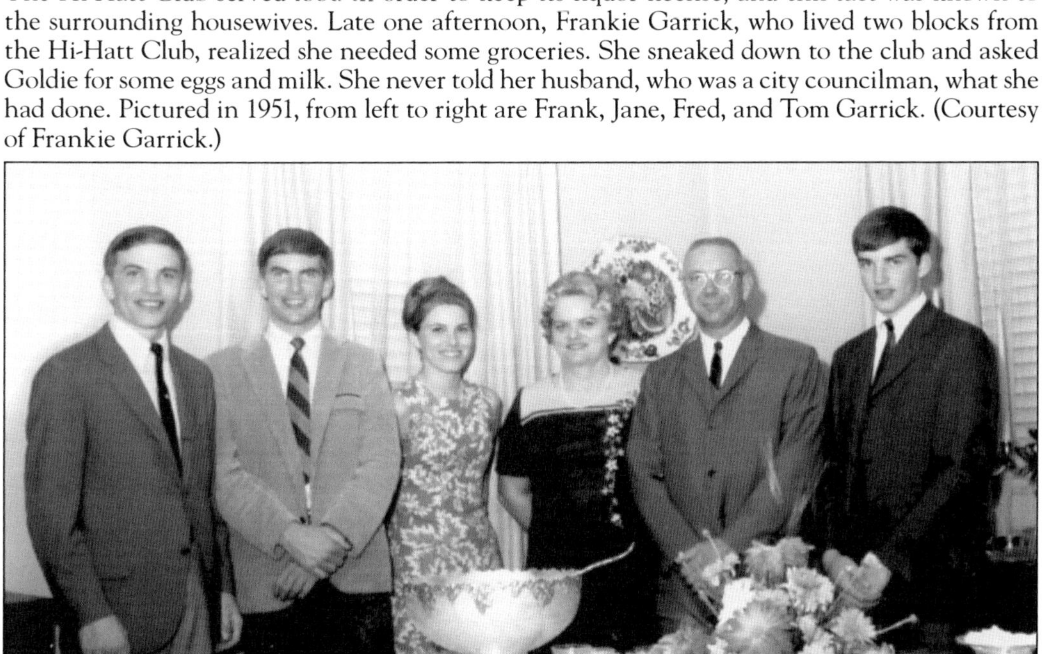

Members of the Garrick family celebrate Frankie and Lonnie's 25th wedding anniversary in 1967. Pictured from left to right behind the silver punch bowl are Frank, Tom, Jane, Frankie, Lonnie, and Fred.

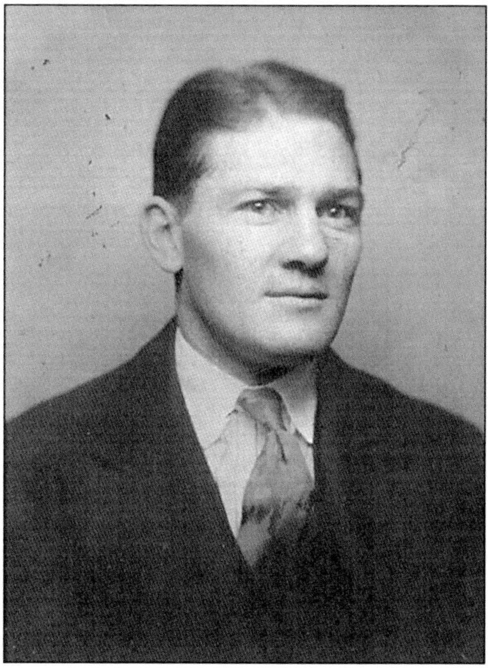

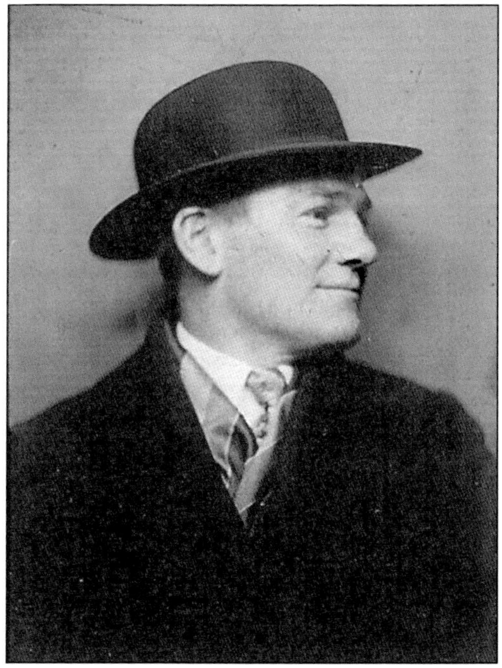

Forest Acres applied for the WPA funds in 1935, and within a few years Beltline Boulevard and North Trenholm Road were under construction. Bill Hazlehurst, shown in this photograph as an engineering student at USC, was a civil engineer on the Beltline project. Since there was no money to purchase rights-of-way and no legal authority to condemn land, Hazlehurst and his fellow engineers spent much time persuading property owners to grant permission for the road to cross their land. All of the work was done by hand labor to provide employment. (Courtesy of Elizabeth Hazlehurst Cantey.)

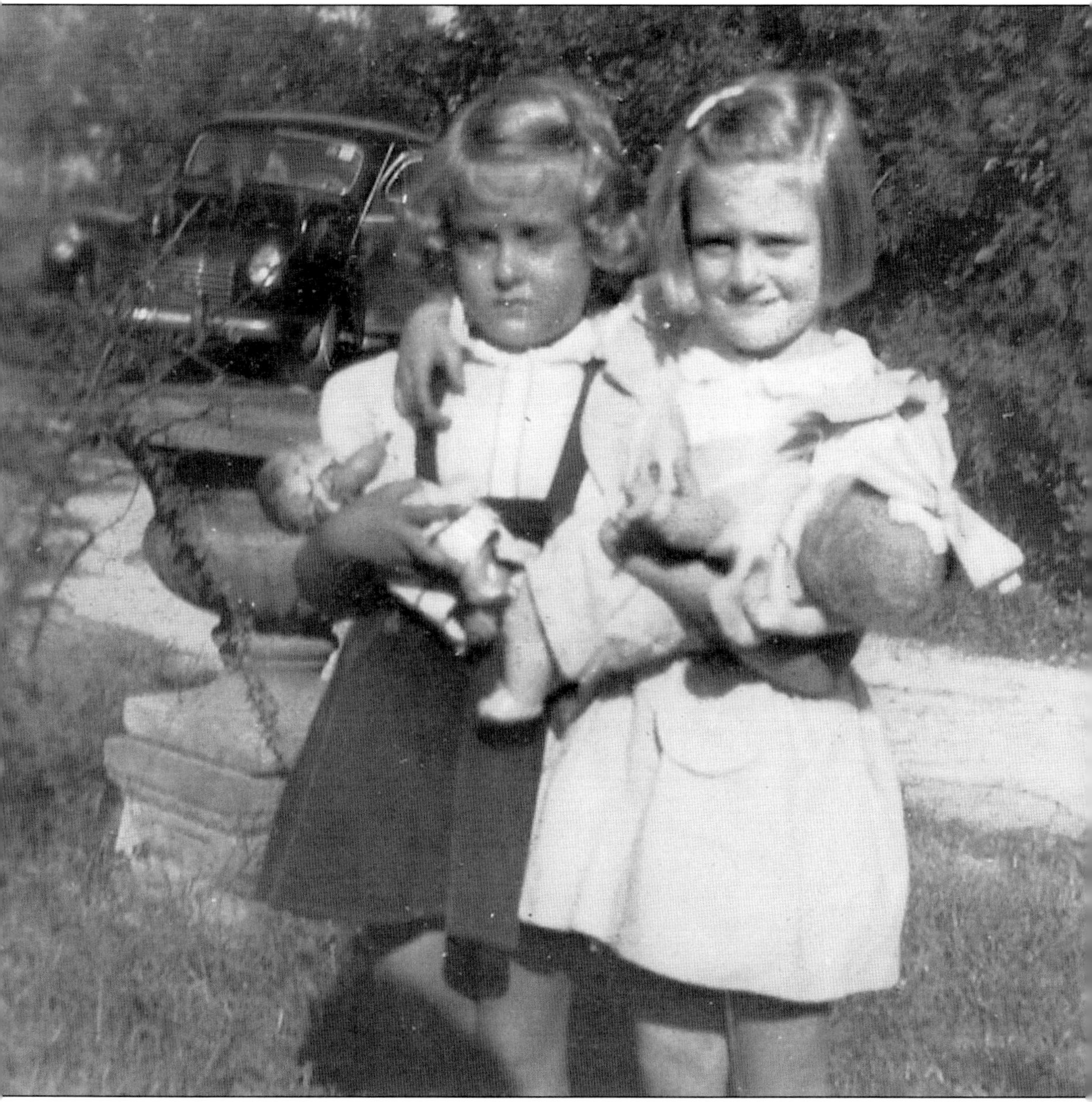

Liz Hazlehurst (right) and her neighbor Legare Benton play with their dolls in the early 1940s. (Courtesy of Elizabeth Hazlehurst Cantey.)

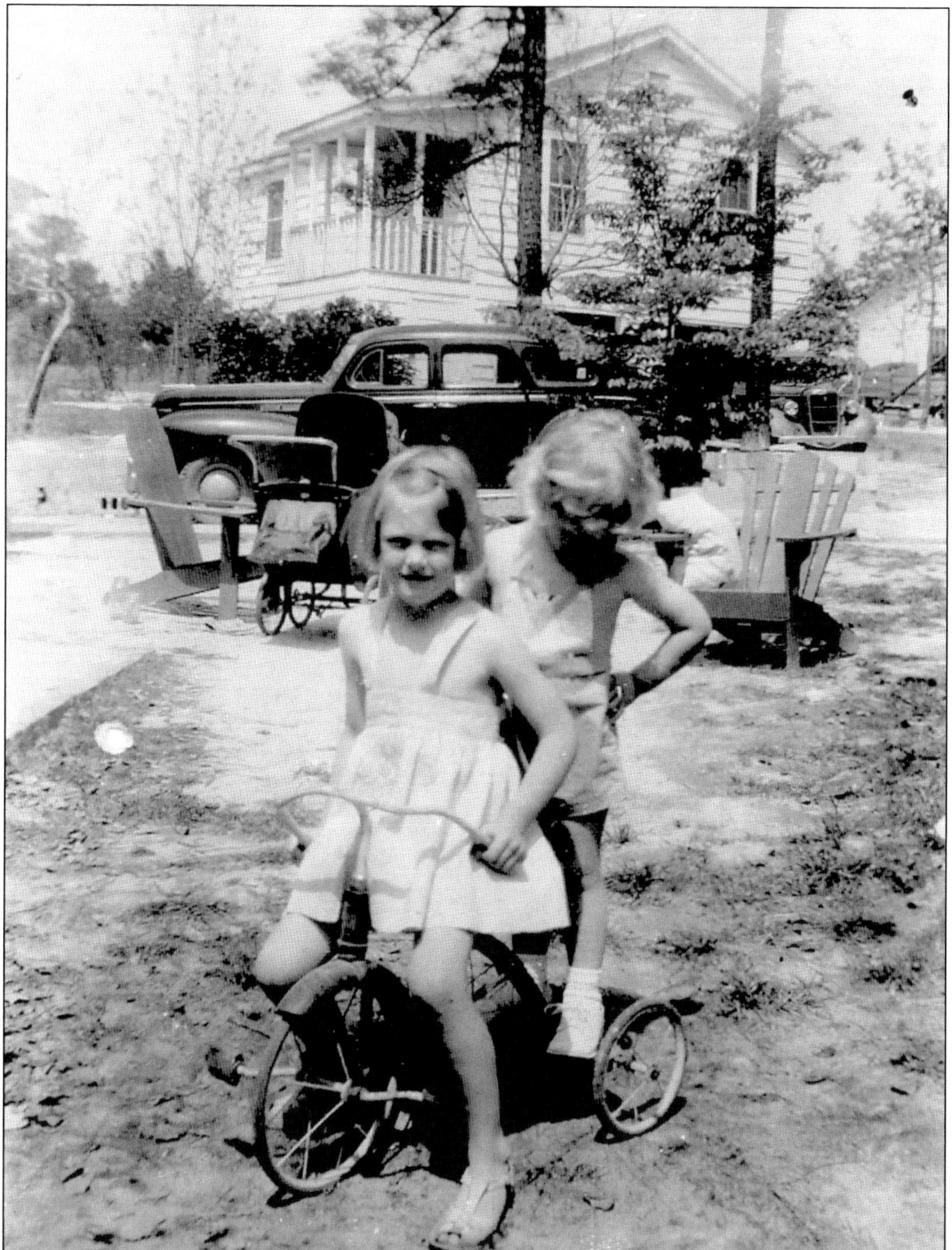

Liz Hazlehurst (left) and Legare Benton ride double on Liz's tricycle. (Courtesy of Elizabeth Hazlehurst Cantey.)

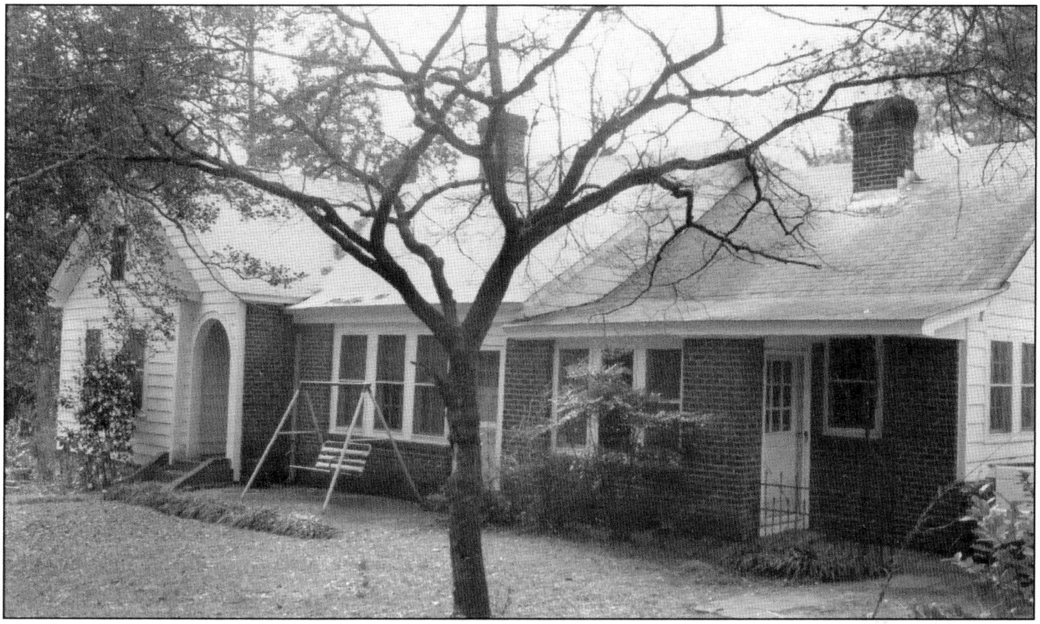

The Hazlehursts converted the garage apartment on Valley Road into this home. (Courtesy of Elizabeth Hazlehurst Cantey.)

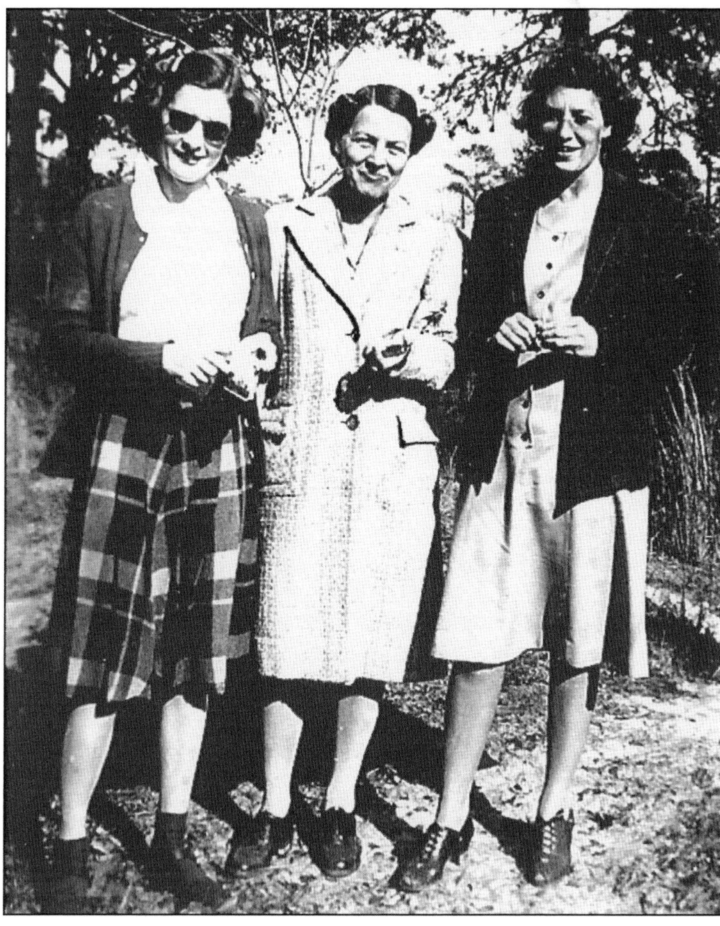

Pictured from left to right, neighbors Mary Sloan, Vallie Hazlehurst, and Amy Henderson enjoy the day on Quinine Hill. (Courtesy of Elizabeth Hazlehurst Cantey.)

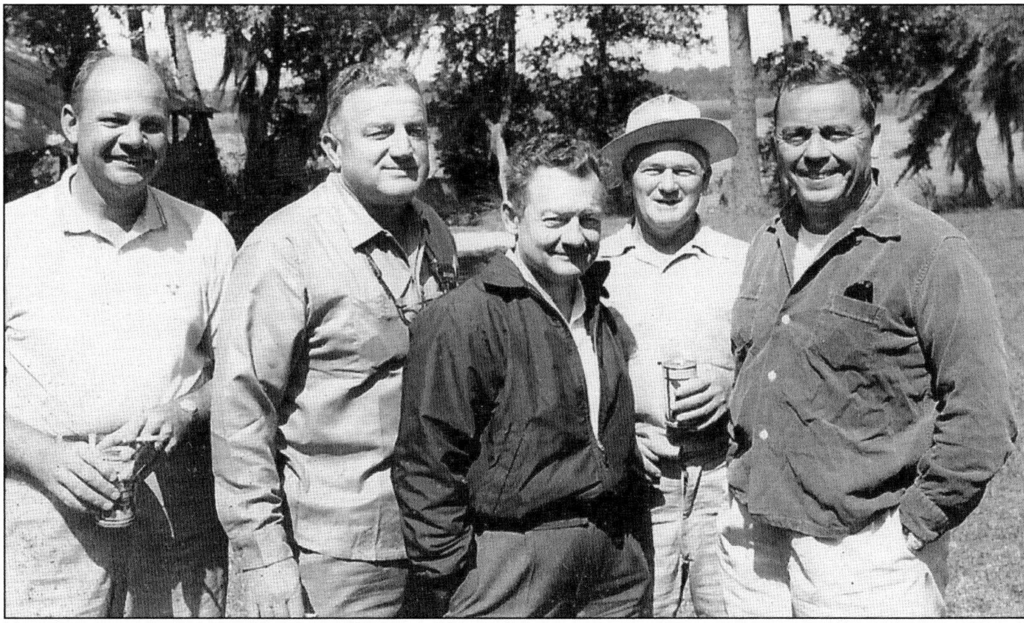

The men of Quinine Hill enjoy a day at the Hazlehurst pond in the country. (Courtesy of Elizabeth Hazlehurst Cantey.)

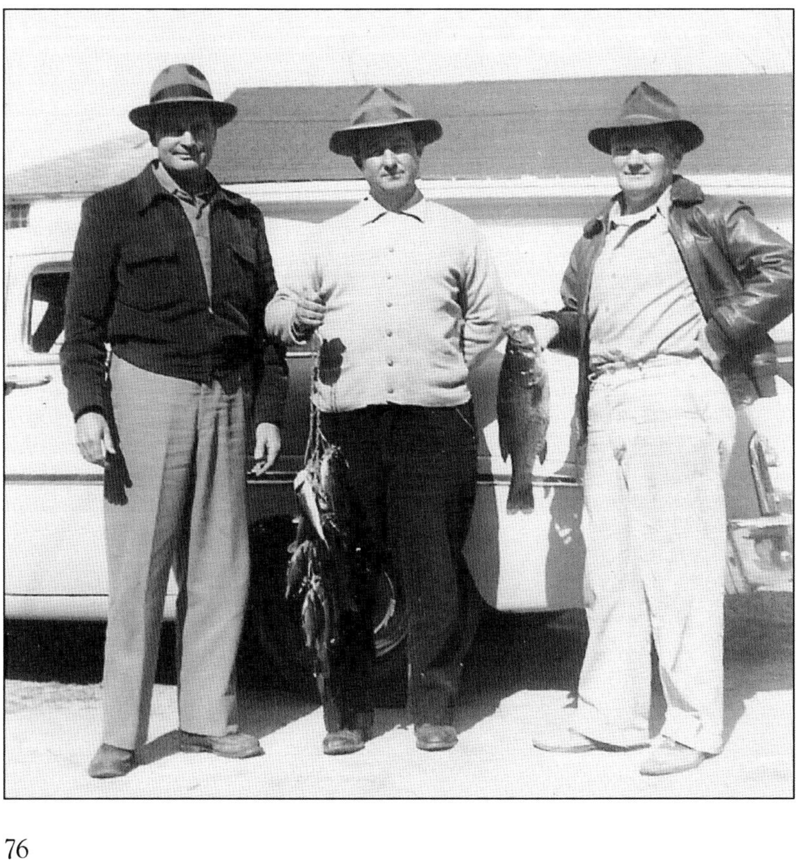

Bill Hazlehurst (right) and two of his friends bring home a mess of fish after a day on Forest Lake. (Courtesy of Elizabeth Hazlehurst Cantey.)

Bill Hazlehurst poses with his faithful dog, Joe, in 1977. (Courtesy of Elizabeth Hazlehurst Cantey.)

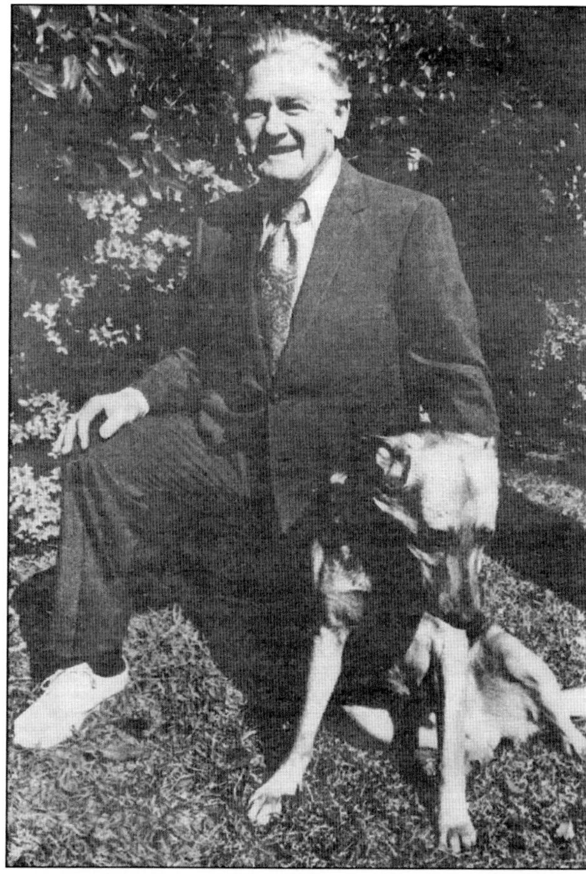

Edwin and Kathryn Powell bought a lot on John Francis Court from Janie Hammond in 1948 for $850. They built this home between the Bentons and the Spanns and raised three sons, Robert, William, and Chris. (Photograph by Warner M. Montgomery.)

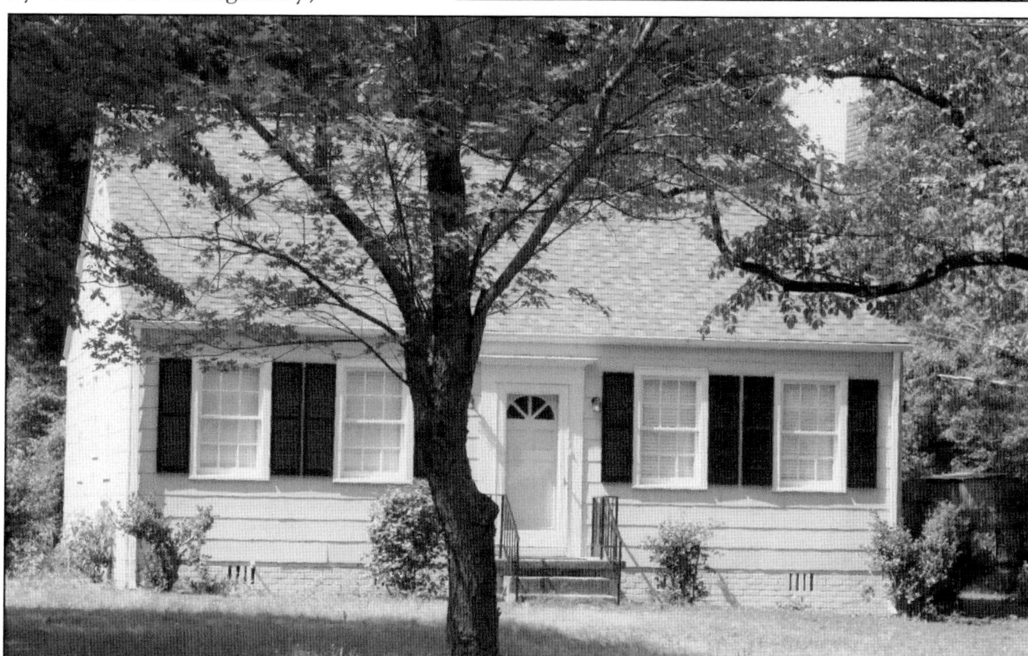

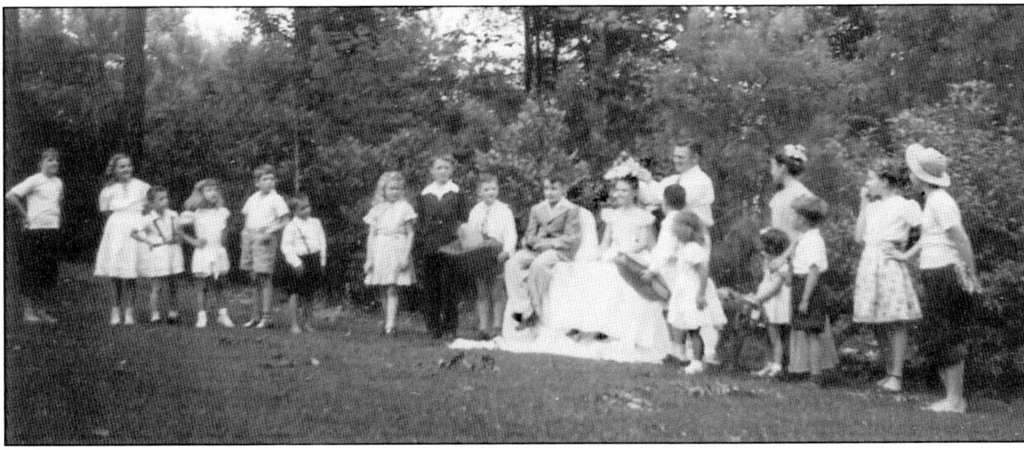

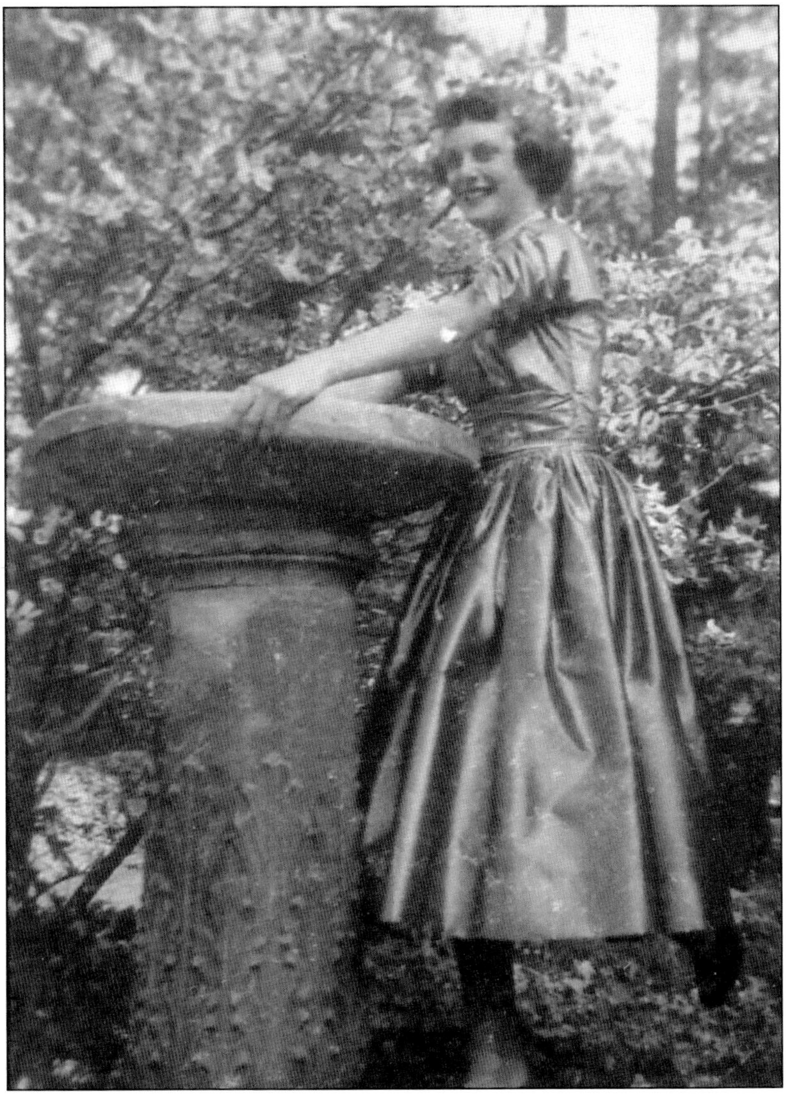

Bill Hazlehurst crowns his daughter, Liz, queen of May Day on Quinine Hill. (Courtesy of Elizabeth Hazlehurst Cantey.)

Liz Hazlehurst went to Columbia High School, as did most of the Forest Acres students until A. C. Flora High was built in 1959. In this photograph she is on the way to the junior-senior prom. (Courtesy of Elizabeth Hazlehurst Cantey.)

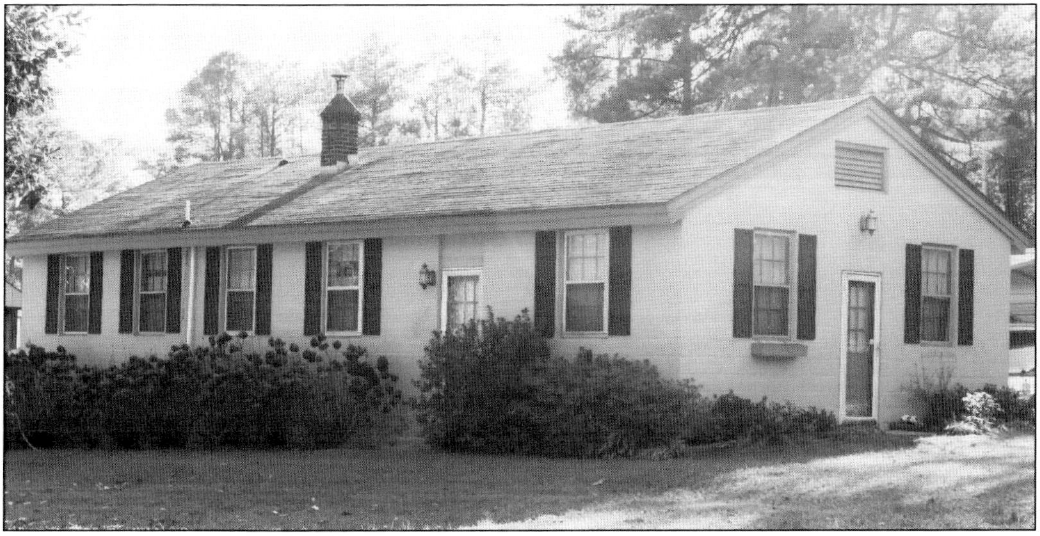

During World War II, Fort Jackson was one of 150 military bases in the United States used as internment camps for German prisoners of war. Concrete block buildings to house prisoners were constructed near the fort in what is now Forest Acres. The prisoners were hired out as laborers to local farmers and businesses. This is one of the remaining buildings and has been converted into a residence. (Photograph by Warner M. Montgomery.)

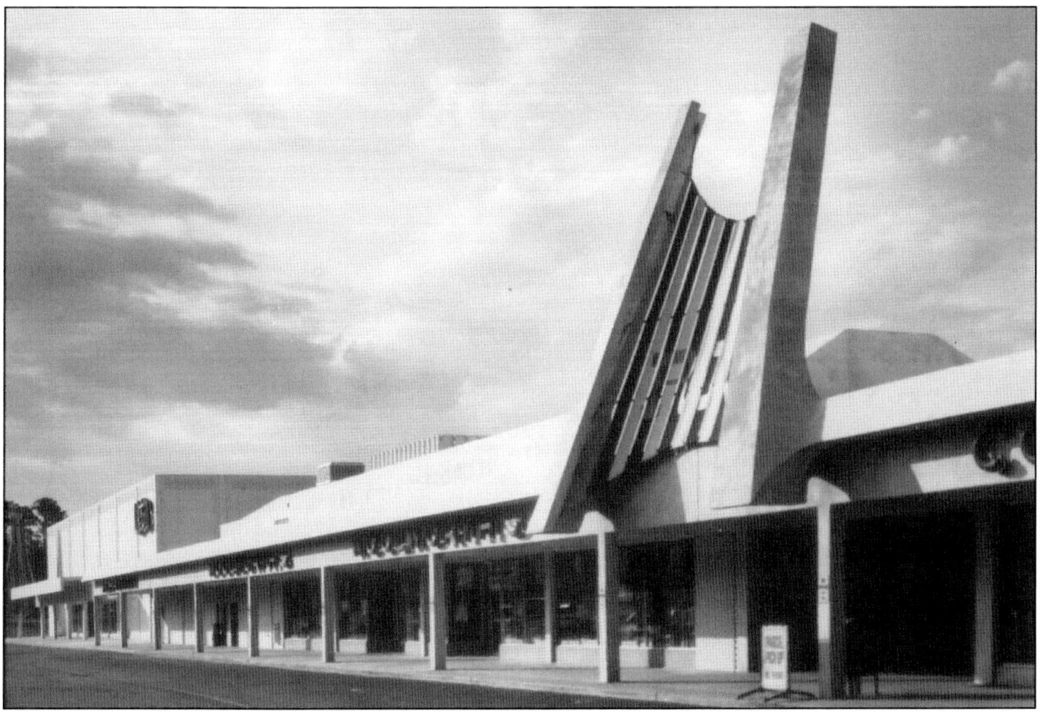

A multimillion dollar mall, the first in South Carolina, was built at the southwest corner of Beltline and Forest Drive. Manning "Pop" Evans, owner of the land, sold the property and the plans to build a mall to Liberty Life Insurance Company in 1960. The architect was Toombs, Amisanto, and Wells of Atlanta. Evans kept the corner for his gas station. The mall was constructed in 1961 by McCrory Construction Company. (Courtesy of Margaret McCrory Hicks.)

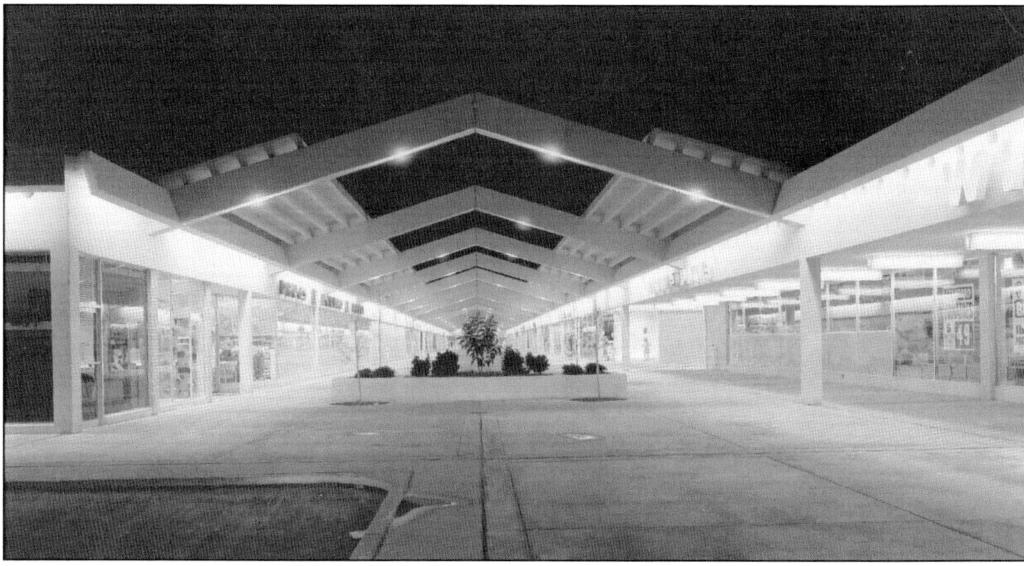

McCrory Construction Company started work on Richland Mall in January 1961. The land had to be excavated and landscaped to change it from a farm with chickens, cows, and barns. McCrory designed and built a modern structure with folded plate concrete over the main buildings and concrete beams over the outdoor central walk of the mall. Richland Mall was completed on schedule and won many design awards. This 1962 interior view of Richland Mall shows the results of the moveable shoring system designed by Marvin McCrory that enabled moving entire sections without dismantling them. (Courtesy of Margaret McCrory Hicks.)

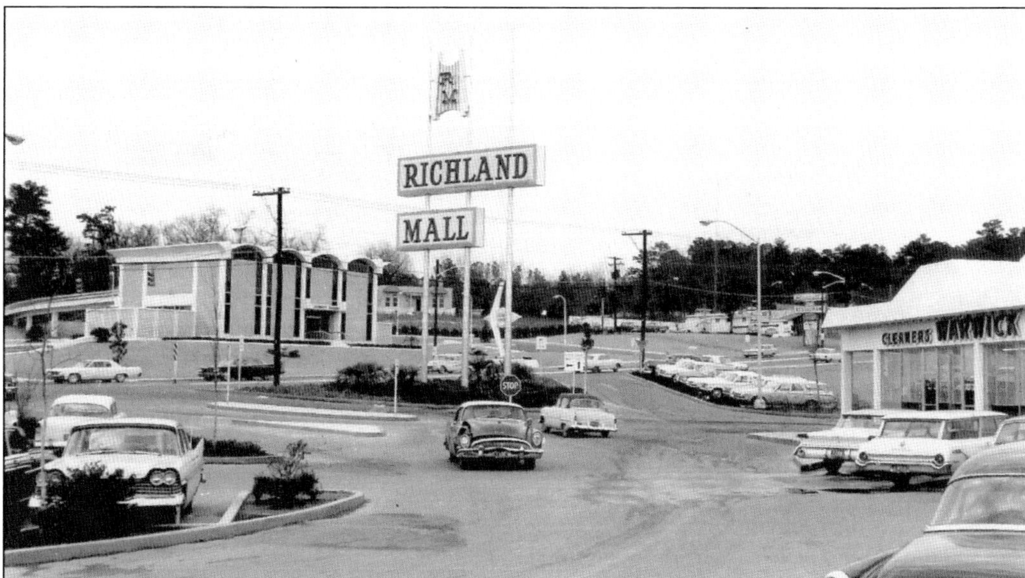

Mayor William J. Stubbs Jr. (1912–1995) and his wife, Bernice (1916–2006), represented Forest Acres at the ribbon cutting for Richland Mall. The major tenants were J. B. White's department store and Winn-Dixie grocery store. Others were Gerald's Shoe Store, Happy Bookseller, Sylvan Jewelers, Meri's Record Shop, Berry's on Main, Eckerd Drugs, F. W. Woolworth, and the Redwood Cafeteria. This was the entrance to Richland Mall from Forest Drive in 1964. (Courtesy of Margaret McCrory Hicks.)

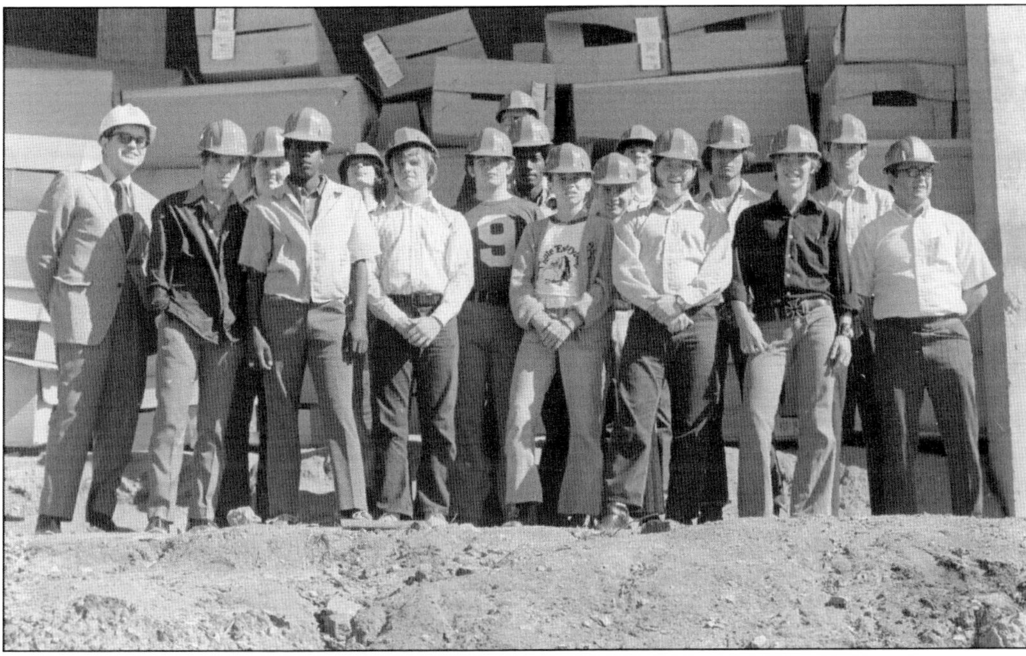

Students from Columbia high schools, including A. C. Flora, were employed by McCrory Construction Company during the building of Richland Mall. (Courtesy of Margaret McCrory Hicks.)

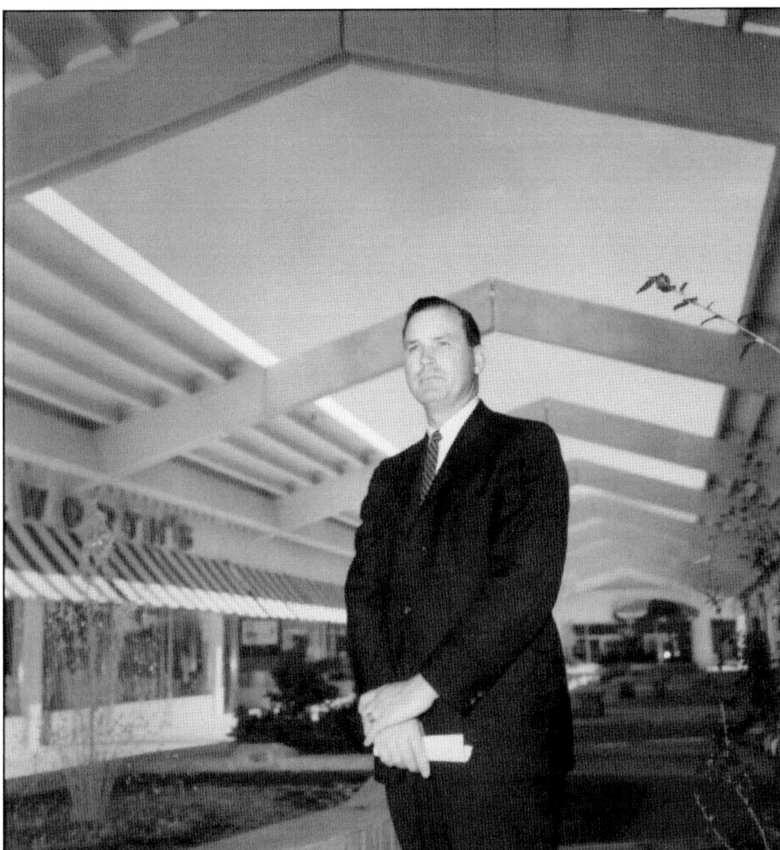

Marvin McCrory, president of McCrory Construction Company, stands in his award-winning Richland Mall in 1962. (Courtesy of Margaret McCrory Hicks.)

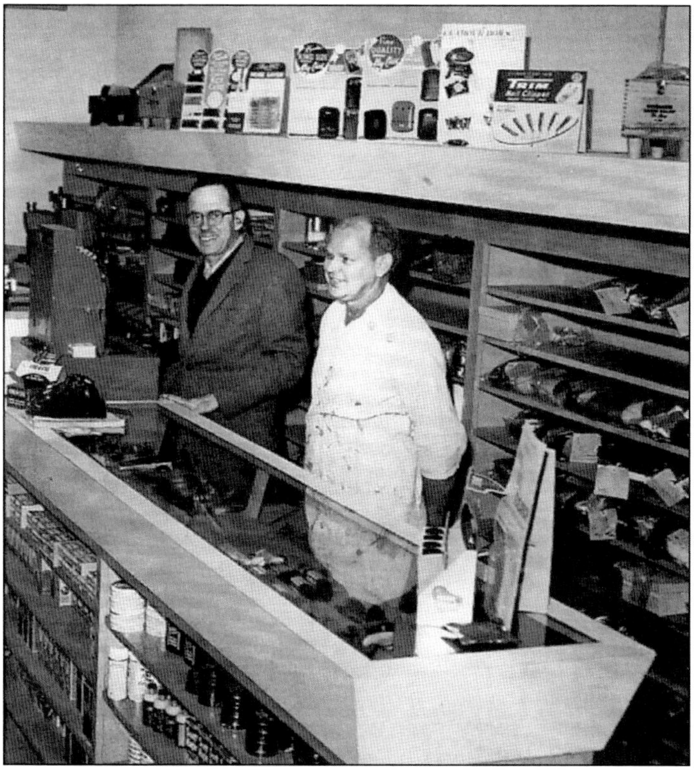

Gerald's Shoe Repair Shop was one of the first tenants of Richland Mall. Avery Gerald (left) was the owner. Herman Hutto was store manager. (Courtesy of Chuck Gerald.)

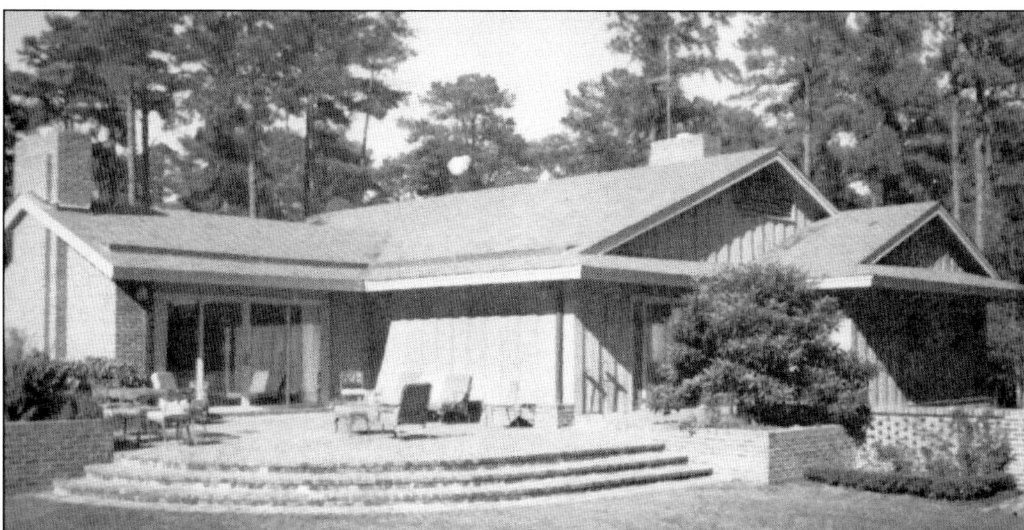

A 287-acre tract south of Forest Drive purchased by David and Hoke Robinson, James A. Reese, Jesse T. Reese, and Alice Johnson for $15,000 after World War II was developed as the Jackson Heights subdivision in the late 1940s. The streets were named for South Carolina colleges—Citadel, Clemson, Coker, Converse, Chicora, Furman, Lander, Limestone, Wofford, and Winthrop. New businesses, schools, and churches sprang up to serve the expanding population. This 1960s photograph shows the home of Marvin McCrory, builder of Richland Mall, on Wittering Drive. (Courtesy of Margaret McCrory Hicks.)

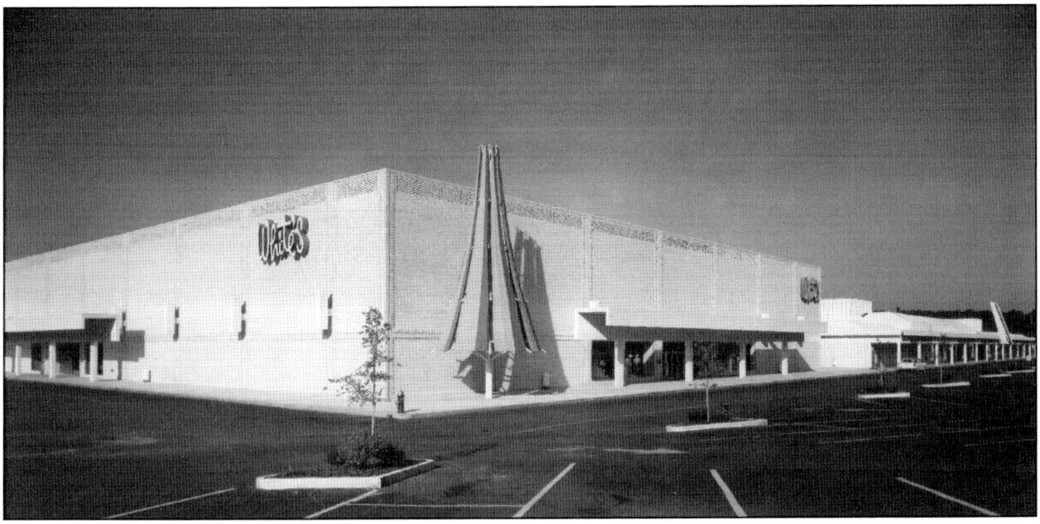

J. B. White's Department Store was the anchor tenant of Richland Mall. (Courtesy of Margaret McCrory Hicks.)

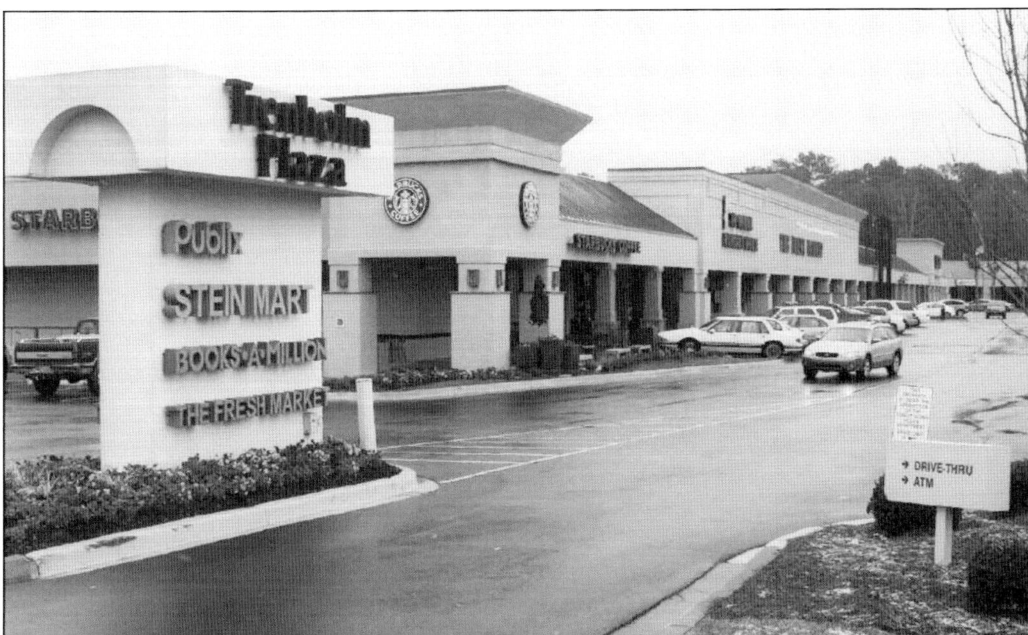

Forest Drive was widened in 1957, clearing the way for new commercial development. The Evans property at Beltline and the Monckton property at Trenholm were rezoned for large shopping centers. Forest Acres began to annex areas north of its original city limits: Willingham Drive (1961), Ponte Vedra Drive (1963), Ravenwood (1967) and Lakeshore and North Trenholm (1974). The Monckton Golf Course closed, and the property was developed as Trenholm Plaza (pictured here in 2010) by Keenan and Company. LBC&W served as architects. The first tenants were Edisto Farms Dairy, Calvert-Brodie School of Dance, Roses 5&10¢ Store, Standard Building and Loan, and A&P Food Stores. (Photograph by Warner M. Montgomery.)

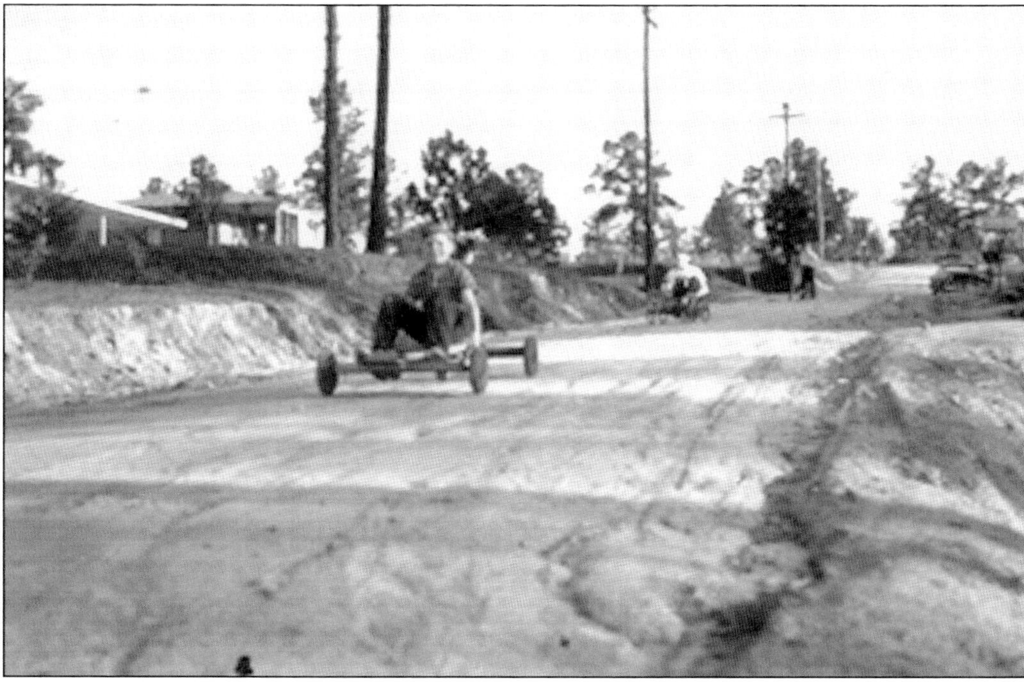

The Heidt boys ride down the hill at Vera Circle on their homemade cars in the early 1950s. (Courtesy of Frankie Garrick.)

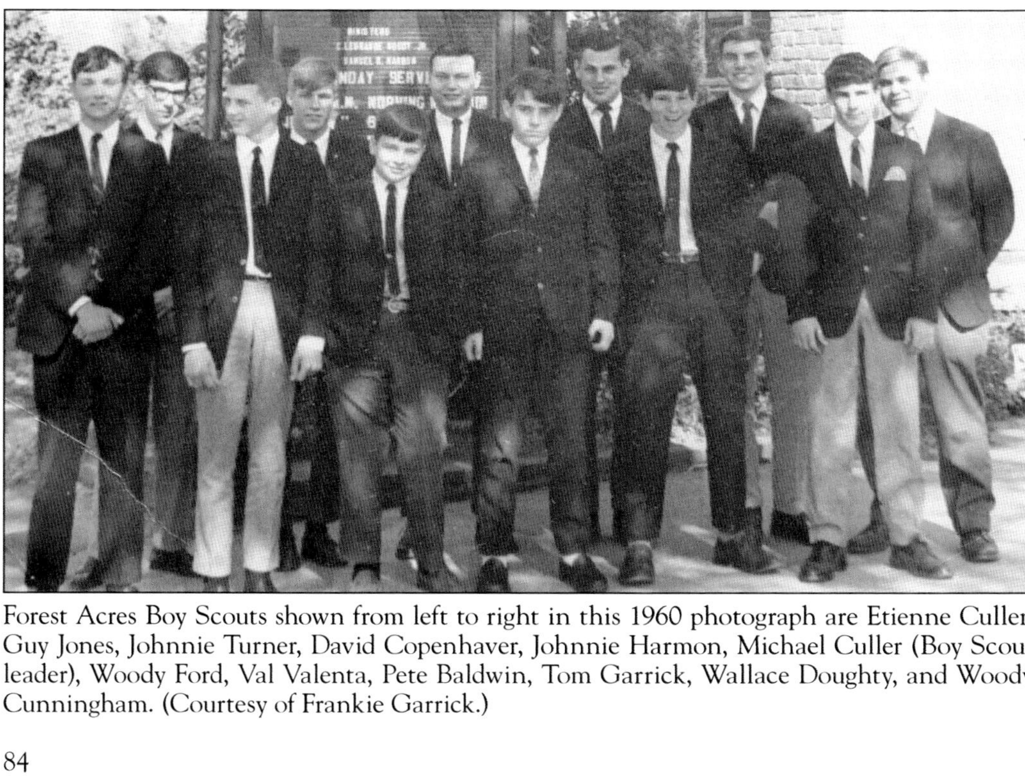

Forest Acres Boy Scouts shown from left to right in this 1960 photograph are Etienne Culler, Guy Jones, Johnnie Turner, David Copenhaver, Johnnie Harmon, Michael Culler (Boy Scout leader), Woody Ford, Val Valenta, Pete Baldwin, Tom Garrick, Wallace Doughty, and Woody Cunningham. (Courtesy of Frankie Garrick.)

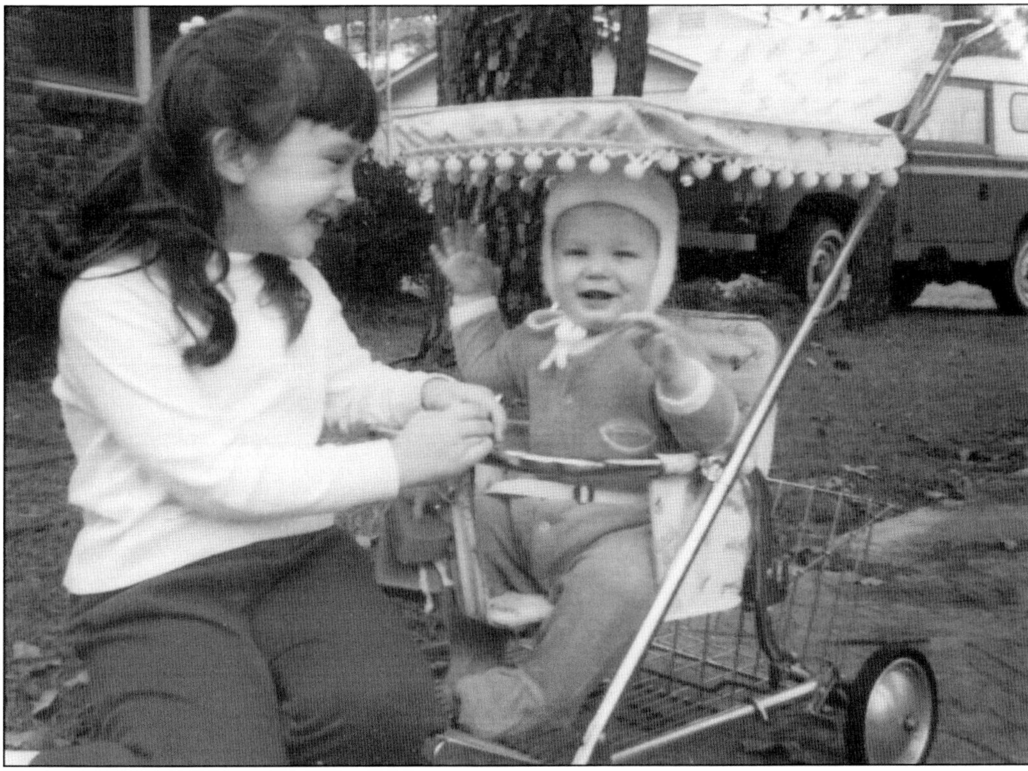

The Sherrer children, Lisa and John, play in their yard on Peachtree Circle in 1969. (Courtesy of John Sherrer.)

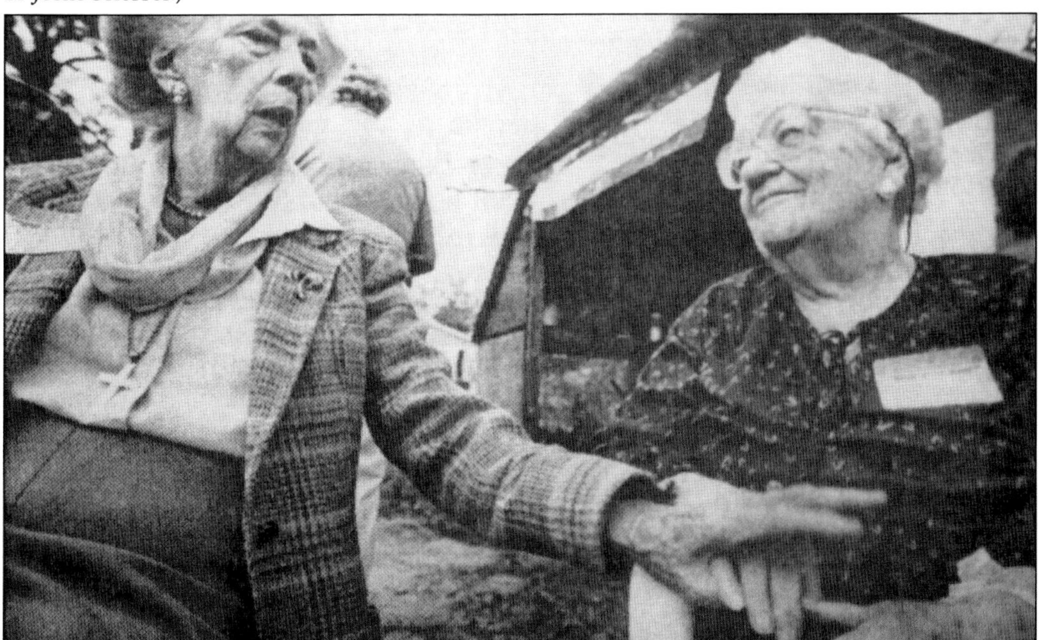

Elise Lamar and Mabel Green enjoy the Quinine Hill reunion in 1991. (Courtesy of Frankie Garrick.)

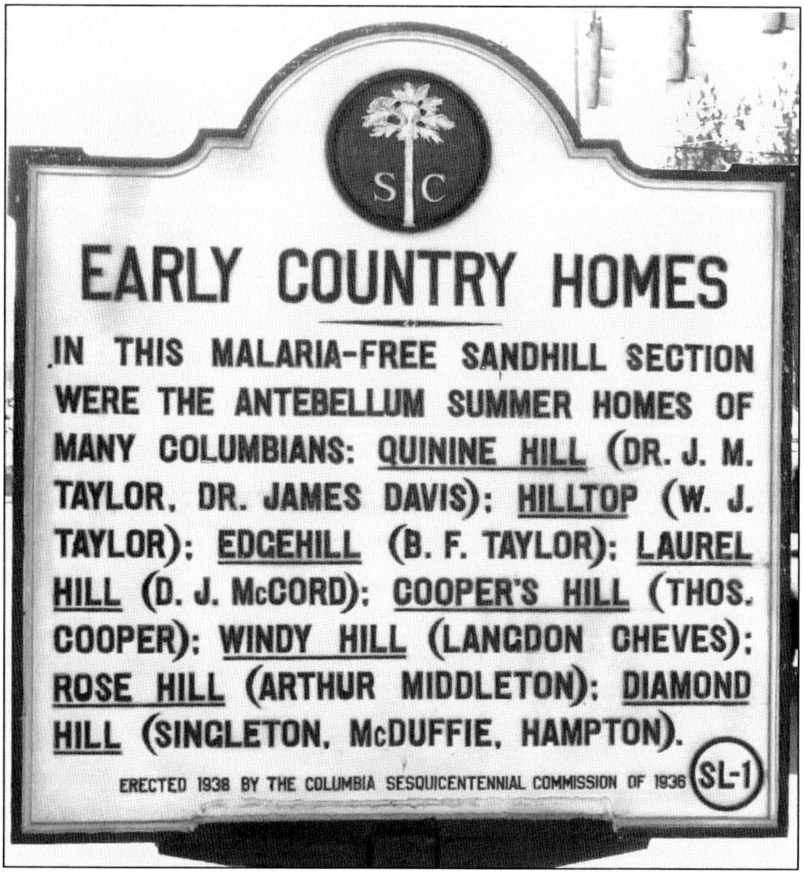

The historical marker at Forest Drive and Beltline Boulevard lists early plantations in the area of Quinine Hill. (Photograph by Warner M. Montgomery.)

Dr. Edmund R. Taylor (b. 1918), the great, great grandson of Col. Thomas Taylor, and his wife, Mary Herbert Taylor, live in this home on Forest Lake. (Photograph by Warner M. Montgomery.)

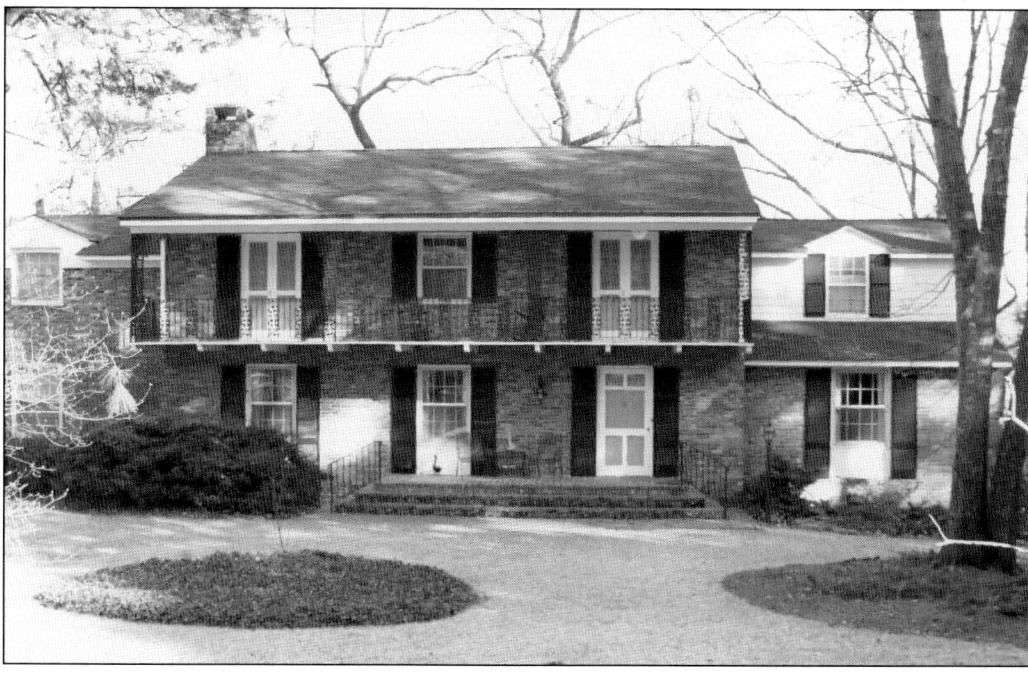

Eight

The Infamous Hi-Hatt Club

In a strange turn of events, the old Bethel School evolved into the most infamous place in Forest Acres, the Hi-Hatt Club. Earl Short bought the two-room schoolhouse soon after it closed in 1935 and converted it into a bar.

Goldie Painter (later Sharpe then Garrett) was proprietress and lived on the property. Given her sometime miniskirt and outrageous reputation, she became a legend in Forest Acres. Goldie's bulldog was quite a character, too. Whenever a coin dropped on the floor, he would dart over and pick it up in his slobbering mouth. Then he would run behind the bar and drop it in a large glass jar. Goldie considered it a tip.

In the days before air-conditioning, noise from the drinking and all-night romping at the Hi-Hatt Club could be heard throughout the neighborhood. Some of the local wives were satisfied for their husbands to spend time drinking there. At least the women knew where their men were.

In the early 1960s, a huge sign was built on top of the club, a tilted top hat with crossed canes and a flashing arrow. City council requested the flashing sign come down, but Short said there was a short circuit in the nailed-shut electrical box and nothing could be done. Irving Belser, the Forest Acres attorney, agreed with Short and the Hi-Hatt prospered in its infamy.

Jim Pinkerton, football coach at A. C. Flora High School, was equally outraged when a few of his players began stopping by Goldie's after practice. He paid her a visit and promised to inform the law unless she made the Hi-Hatt off-limits to his players. His problem disappeared.

The pinnacle of fame for the Hi-Hatt Club was in 1967. Producer Robert Newsom (a USC graduate) brought the actors (Jim Davis, Scott Brady, Andy Devine, Bruce Yarnell, Sue Raney, Robert Dix, and Columbian Jim E. Quick) of his Southern moonshiners movie, *The Road Hustlers*, to Forest Acres to film a segment. The community swarmed around the Hi-Hatt Club during the filming. Jane Garrick (Dyke), a student at Flora High, spent days secretly watching the movie stars.

Due to a renewal of complaints about the Hi-Hatt Club's liquor violations and rumors of prostitution, SLED (State Law Enforcement Division) raided it in 1973. The 38-year reign of Goldie and the Hi-Hatt Club ended. A few years later an insurance company moved into 3830 Forest Drive.

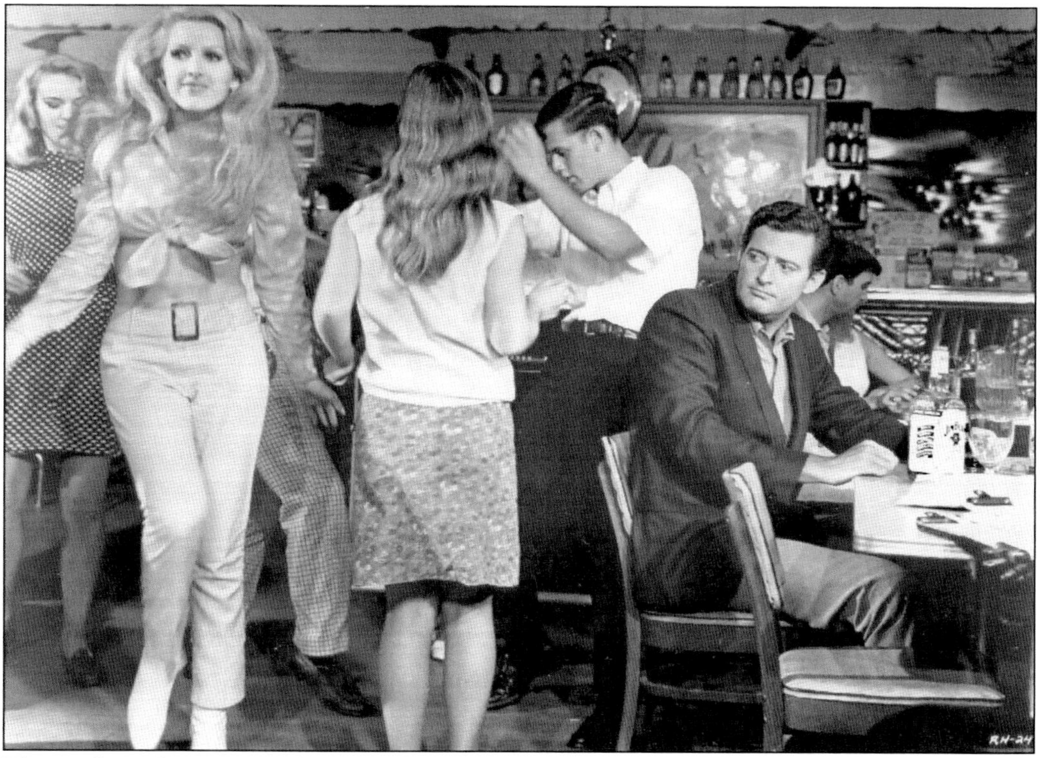

The Road Hustlers premiered in Columbia February 15, 1968, at the Palmetto Theater. Joe Pinner and Audrey Hunt of WIS-TV interviewed the stars as they arrived. Jim E. Quick escorted Mary Arnold Garvin, a teacher at Flora High. Honored guests included the Marshalls of Forest Acres, Mr. and Mrs. Donald Dial, Gertrude Thurmond (Strom's sister), Mr. and Mrs. John A. Montgomery, Mr. and Mrs. Roy V. Lind, Mr. and Mrs. Robert S. Davis, Mr. and Mrs. Arthur St. J. Simons, and Lois Quattlebaum. After the premiere, the stars and guests were honored at a midnight dinner and dance at the Rockbridge Club. (Courtesy of Saturn Productions Inc.)

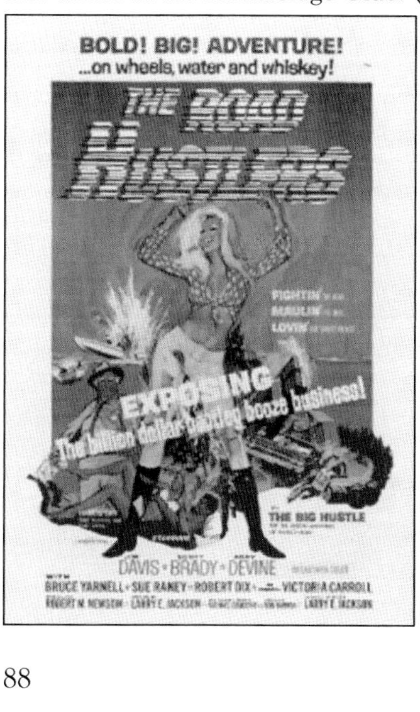

This poster for *The Road Hustlers* was from a scene filmed in the Hi-Hatt Club. (Courtesy of Saturn Productions Inc.)

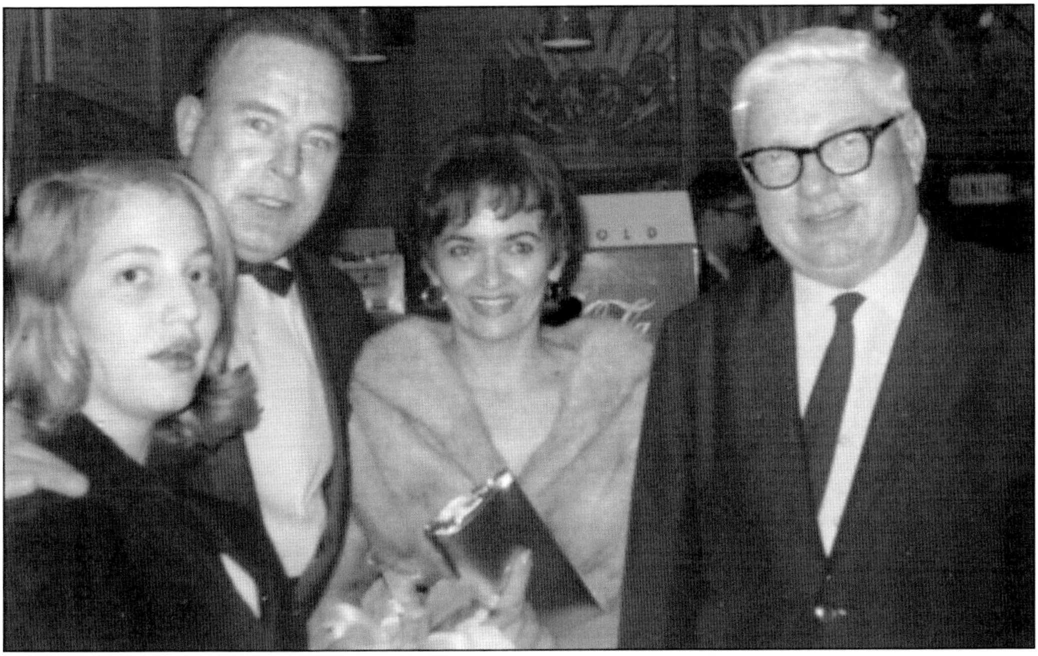

The premiere of *The Road Hustlers*, which was partially filmed at the Hi-Hatt Club, was held at the Palmetto Theater February 15, 1968. Jim Richardson was an extra in the movie and became a lifelong friend of actor Scott Brady. His daughter, 14-year-old Debbie, was Scott Brady's date. Attending the event were, from left to right, Debbie Richardson (Fletcher), actor Scott Brady, Aubrey Hunt of WIS-TV, and Jim Richardson. (Courtesy of Debbie Richardson Fletcher.)

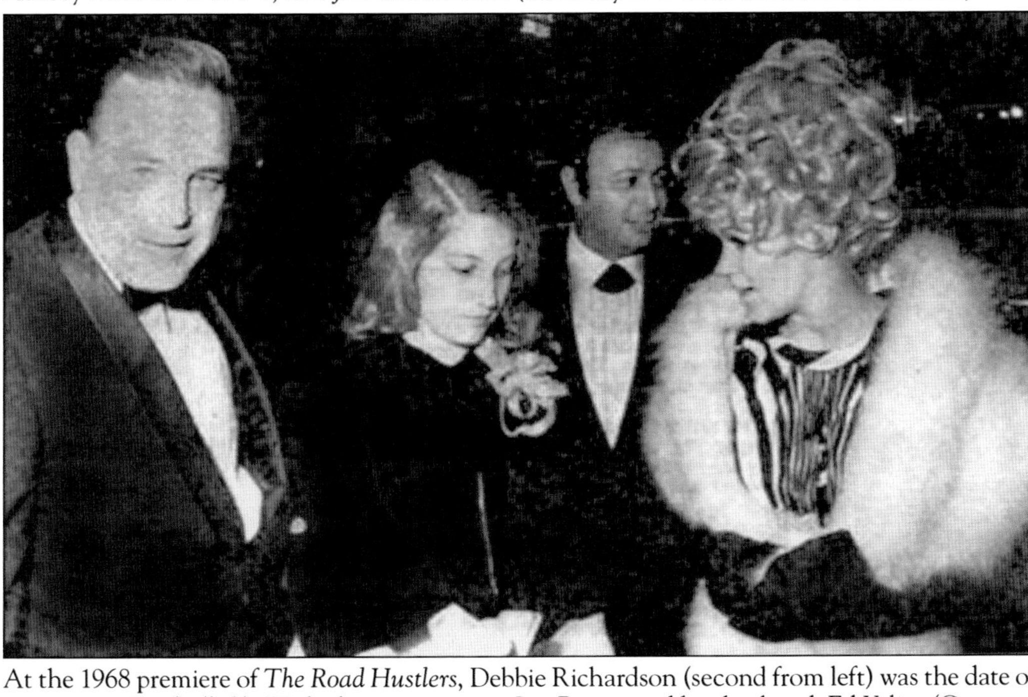

At the 1968 premiere of *The Road Hustlers*, Debbie Richardson (second from left) was the date of actor Scott Brady (left). With them are actress Sue Raney and her husband, Ed Yelin. (Courtesy of Debbie Richardson Fletcher.)

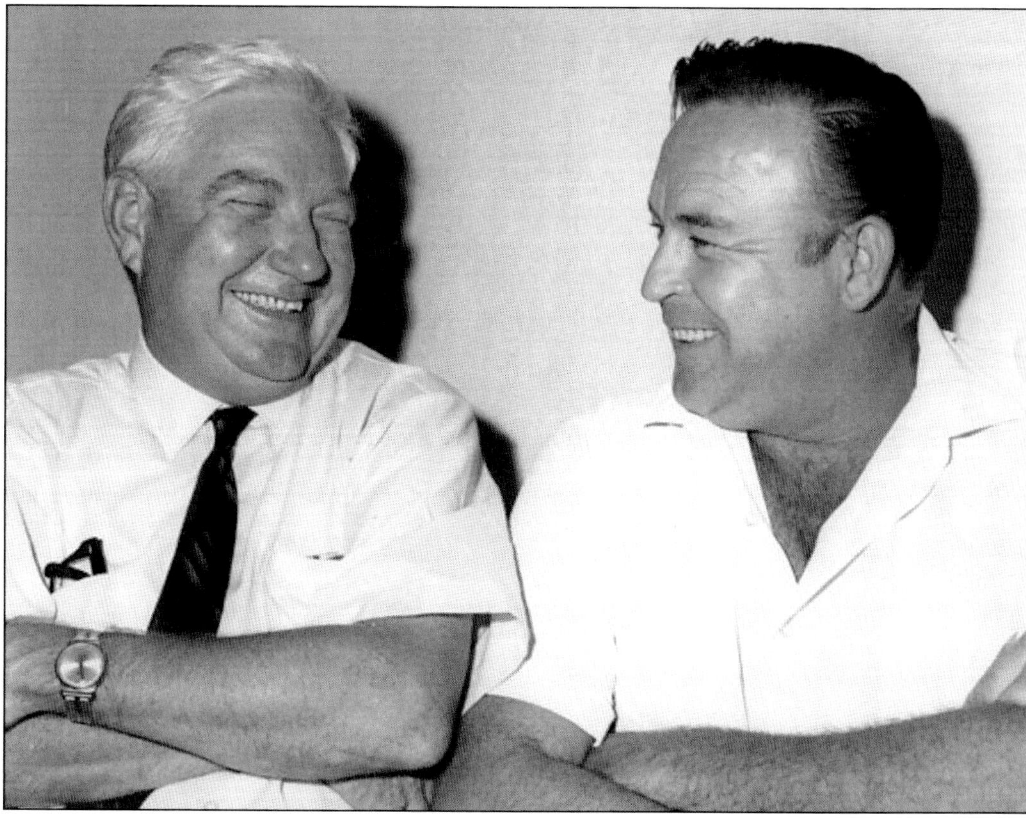

During filming of *The Road Hustlers* in Columbia, Jim Richardson (left) and Brady Scott became best friends. (Courtesy of Debbie Richardson Fletcher.)

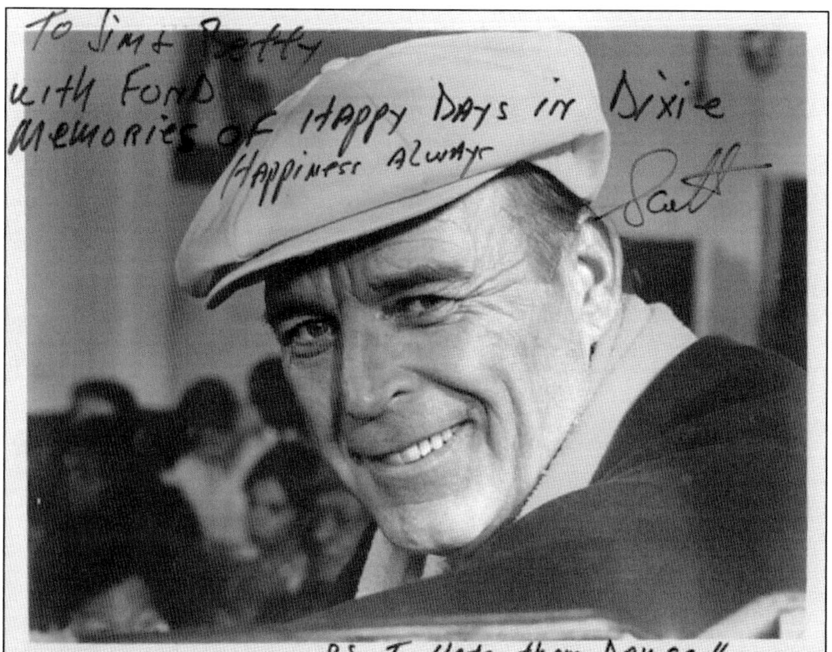

Scott Brady, star of *The Road Hustlers*, gave this autographed photograph to Jim and Betty Richardson. (Courtesy of Debbie Richardson Fletcher.)

Nine

School and Churches Are Founded

Schools followed the increasing business and residential development in Forest Acres. Today Forest Acres has five public schools in Richland School District One (A. C. Flora High School, Brockman Elementary School, Crayton Middle School, Bradley Elementary School, and Satchel Ford Elementary School), two public schools in Richland School District Two (Dent Middle School and Forest Lake Elementary School), and four private schools (Cardinal Newman School, Harmony School, Timmerman School, and Covenant Classical Christian School).

Beginning in the 1940s, religions of all faiths established their houses of worship in the city. By 2010 there were 15 Protestant churches and two Jewish synagogues serving their congregations in Forest Acres. Forest Drive Baptist Church started as a mission in 1943, became a church in 1948, and constructed its first building on Forest Drive at Brentwood Drive in 1949. In 2009, the 4-acre property was sold to Gold's Gym, and the church moved to Longtown Road in northeast Richland County.

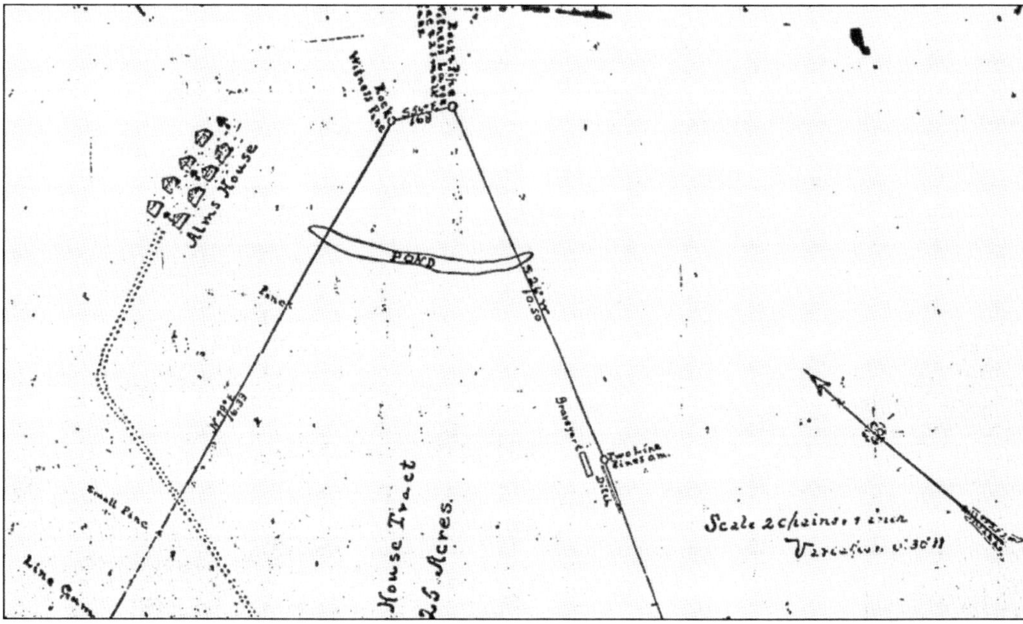

Just north of the original Forest Acres city limits on Bethel Church Road were the Richland County Alms House (public institution for the homeless) and a Richland County Prison (Chain Gang) Camp. John D. Rials (Ryals) Sr. (1838–1914), a Confederate veteran, was the first superintendent of the Alms House. He and his wife, Artie Lovett (1873–1923), are buried in the Rials Cemetery on Satchel Ford Road. This 1901 map by J. McD. Hampton C. E. shows the location of the Richland County Alms House. Trenholm Park is now situated near the same spot. (Courtesy of Richland County Public Library.)

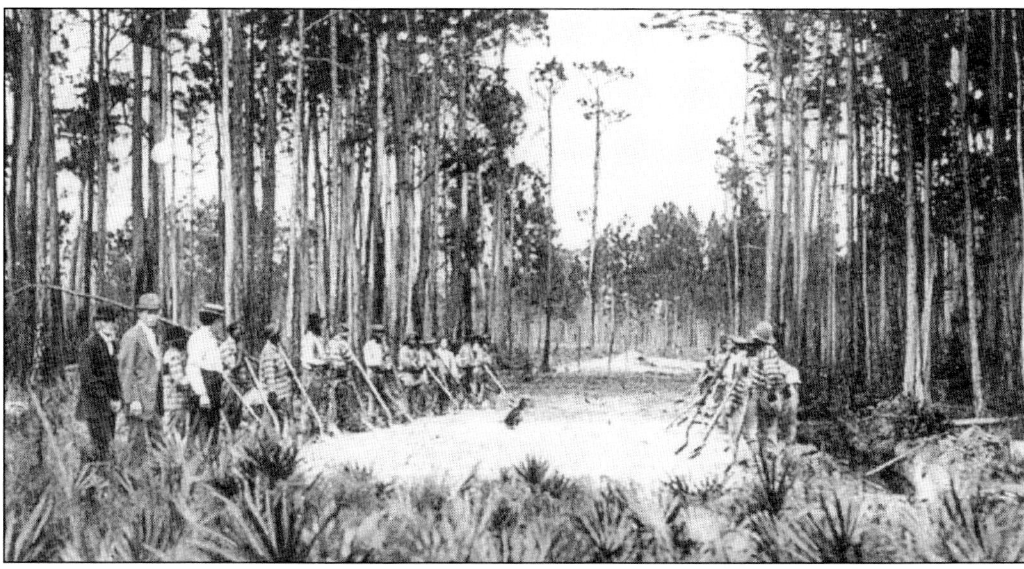

J. C. Turner was foreman of the Chain Gang Camp in 1917. It housed 14 black prisoners, including three trusties who had been referred from the county jail. The camp consisted of prisoner quarters, a kitchen with screens used in the spring and summer, a sewage pit, a mule pen, and a tub for the prisoners to bathe in. This postcard photograph shows the Richland County Chain Gang clearing a road. (Courtesy of David Sennema.)

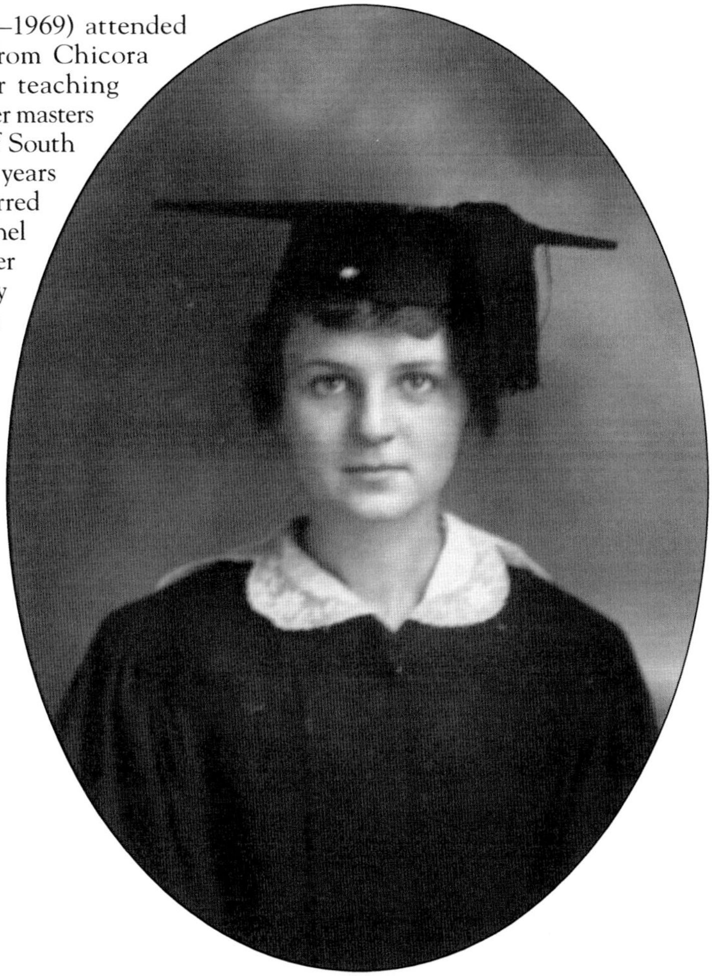

Consuelo "Sue" Dent (1896–1969) attended Bethel School, graduated from Chicora College (1916), received her teaching certificate (1932), and earned her masters degree from the University of South Carolina while teaching four years at Bethel School. She transferred to Dentsville School when Bethel School closed in 1935 then later went to Rosewood Elementary School, where she taught until she retired. (Courtesy of Pete Dent.)

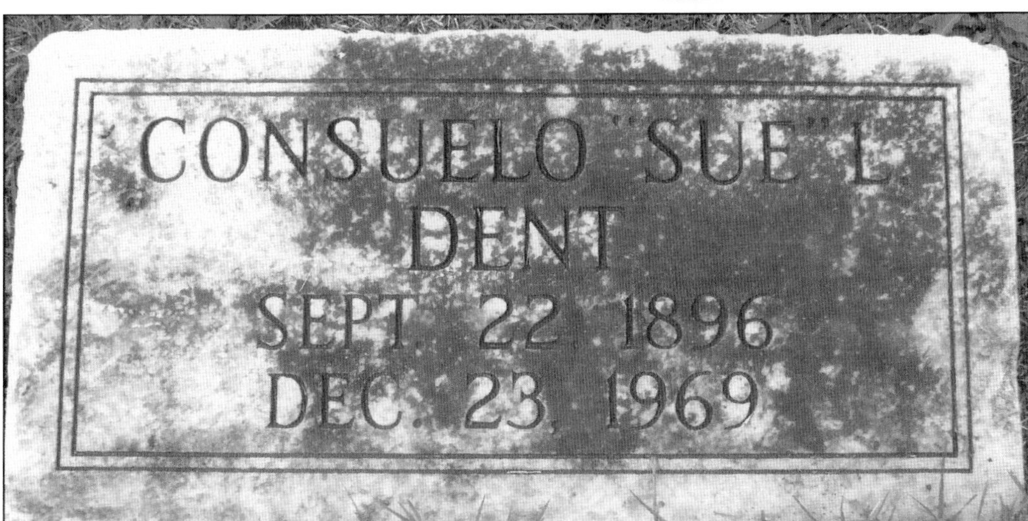

Sue Dent is buried in Elmwood Cemetery. (Photograph by Warner M. Montgomery.)

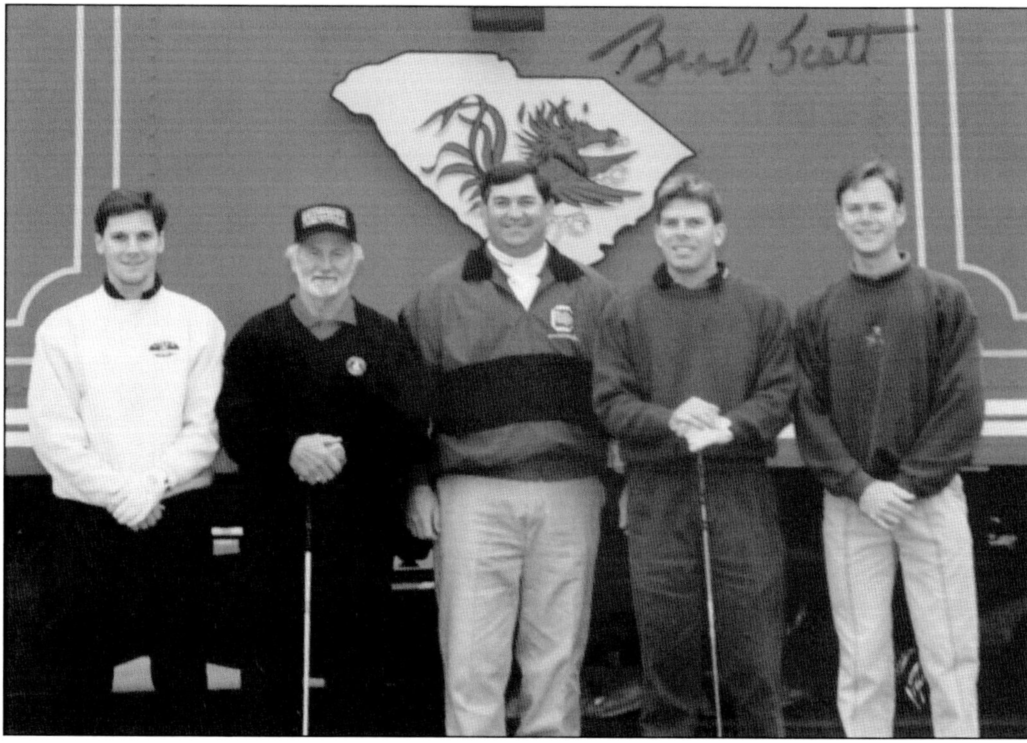

Sue Dent's nephew, Pete Dent, graduated from University High School in 1952. He and his son, Harry, are big Gamecock fans. This 1996 photograph shows, from left to right, Harry and Pete Dent, USC coach Brad Scott, Tony Ramsay, and Durant Southern, and was autographed by Scott. (Courtesy of Pete Dent.)

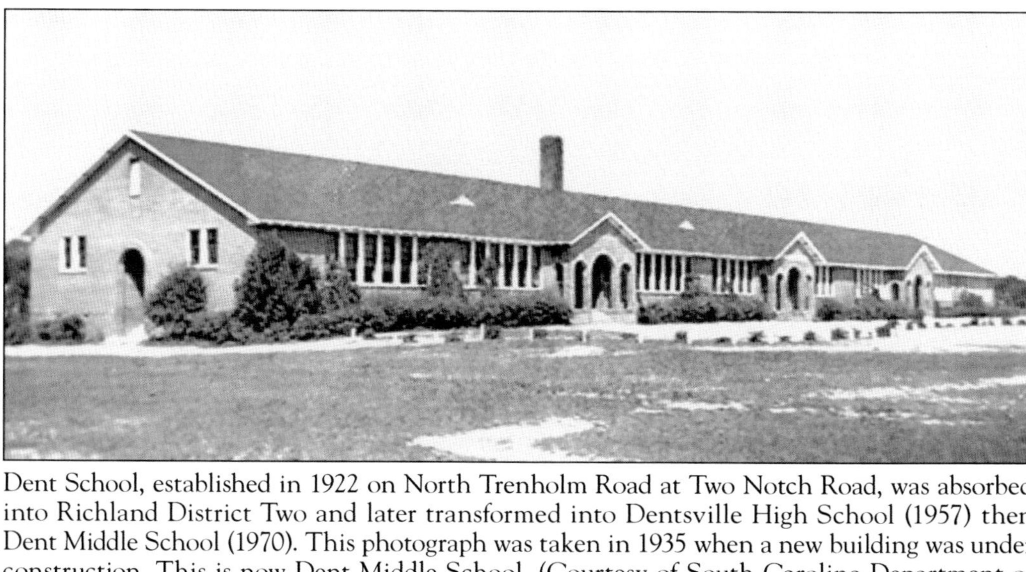

Dent School, established in 1922 on North Trenholm Road at Two Notch Road, was absorbed into Richland District Two and later transformed into Dentsville High School (1957) then Dent Middle School (1970). This photograph was taken in 1935 when a new building was under construction. This is now Dent Middle School. (Courtesy of South Carolina Department of History and Archives.)

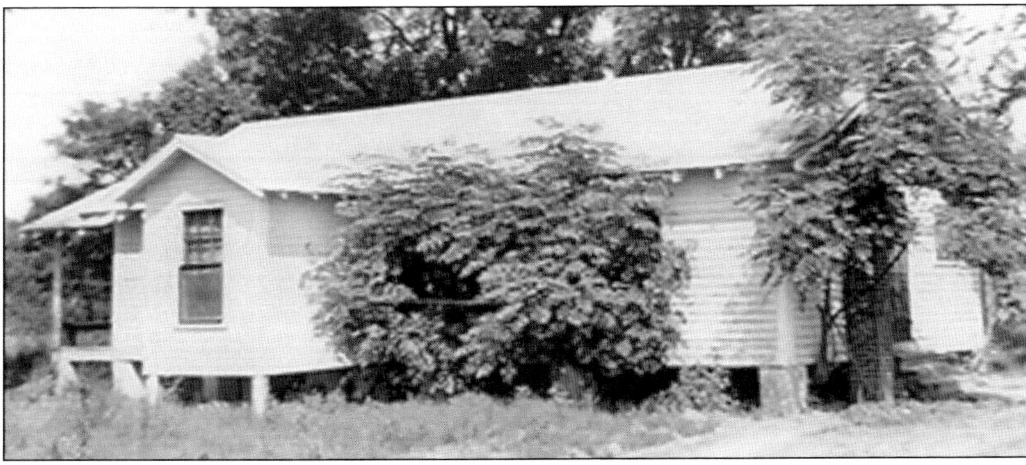

It was the custom in South Carolina prior to 1960 for the school janitor to live on the school grounds. This was the Dent school janitor's home in 1935. (Courtesy of South Carolina Department of History and Archives.)

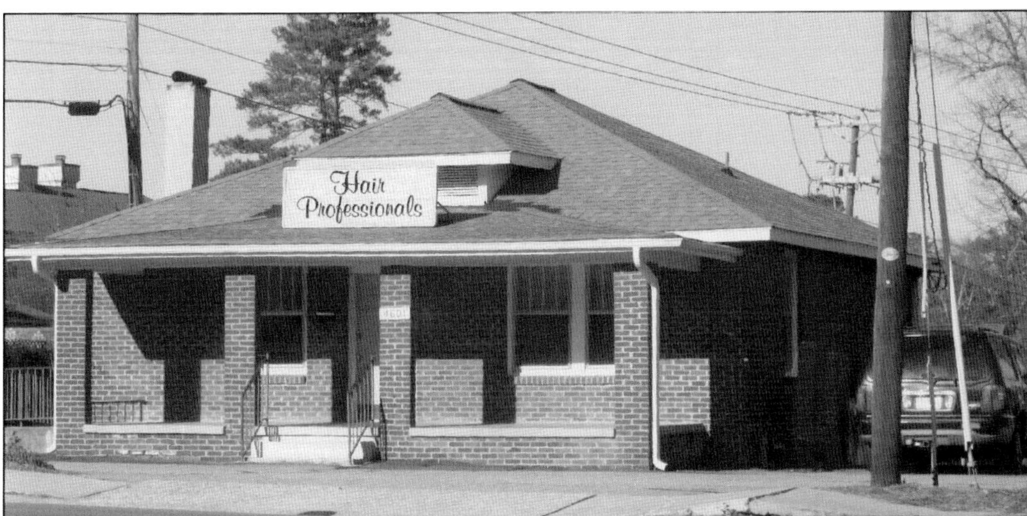

There were four small county schools in Forest Acres in 1935—Bethel School on Forest Drive, Brickyard School on Covenant Road, Lake View School at Willingham and Forest Drive, and Sweet Home School near Fort Jackson. These schools were closed, and the teachers and students were transferred tuition-free to Columbia schools (Taylor Elementary, Wardlaw Junior High, and either Columbia High or University High). The Lake View School was a small two-room school that operated sometime prior to 1935. The building (pictured above) was renovated and is a beauty salon in 2010. (Photograph by Warner M. Montgomery.)

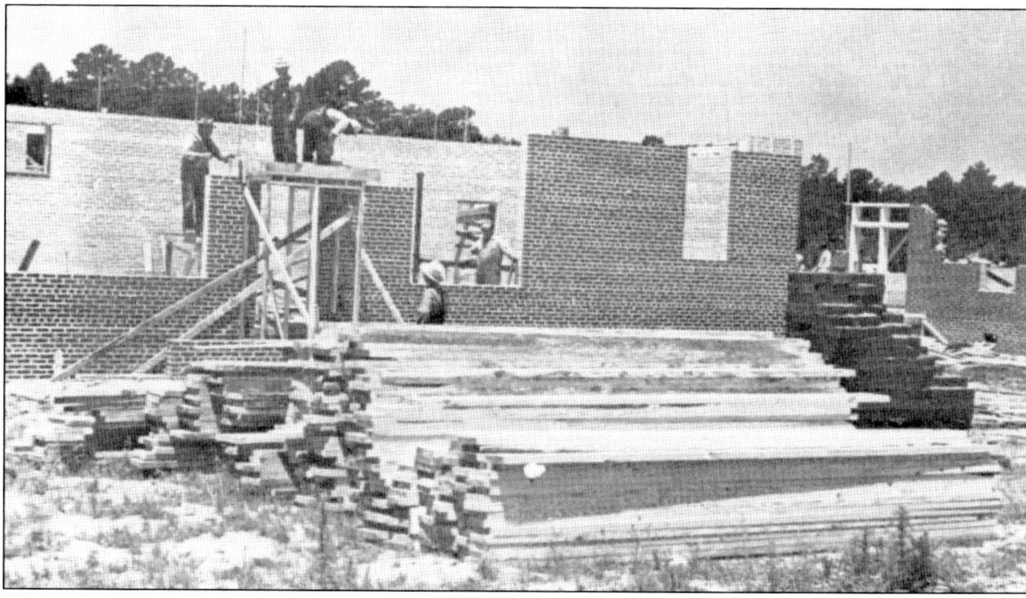

A benefit of the incorporation of Forest Acres and its agreement with the city of Columbia for water service was an agreement with the Columbia public schools that allowed children from Forest Acres to attend Richland School District One schools free of charge. Jackson Heights School was the first Richland School District One school to be built in Forest Acres. The construction contract was awarded to T. E. Moore Construction Company for $263,500. (Courtesy of Richland School District One.)

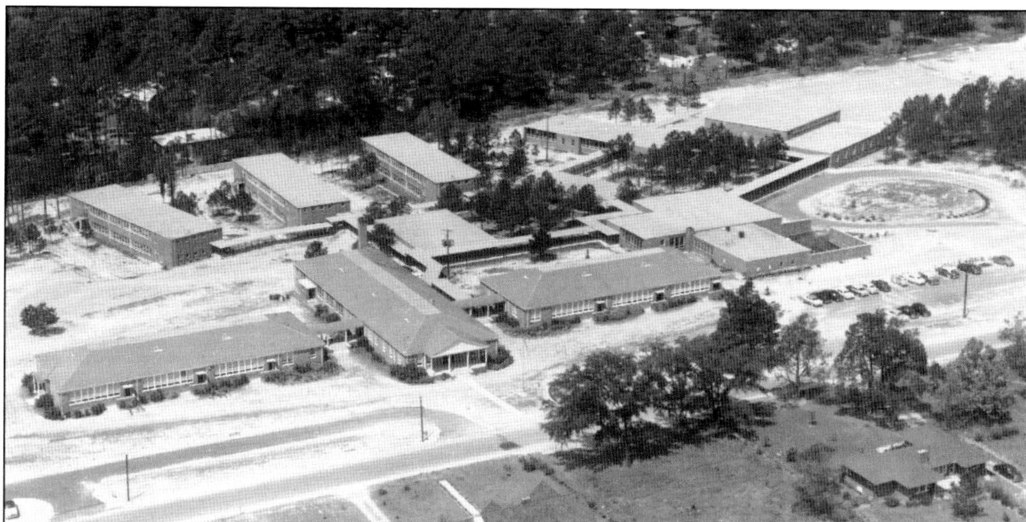

Jackson Heights School opened in 1951 on Clemson Avenue. Some 15 acres had been purchased in 1948 by Richland County School District One, and an additional 10 acres were purchased in 1953. The school was renamed Crayton Junior High in 1953 after Columbia teachers Lizzeve and Nan Crayton. Carol Mundy was the first principal, and Freddie L. McCallum was the second. The first PTO president, Lindsay Odom, was succeeded by Irving F. Belser Jr. The first student body president was Cynthia Anna Durham. Her vice president was Peter P. Leventis. Crayton was converted into a middle school in 1957. R. S. Beckham was the principal and Roger Kirk the assistant principal. (Courtesy of Warner M. Montgomery.)

Carol Mundy was the first principal of Jackson Heights School. (Courtesy of Warner M. Montgomery.)

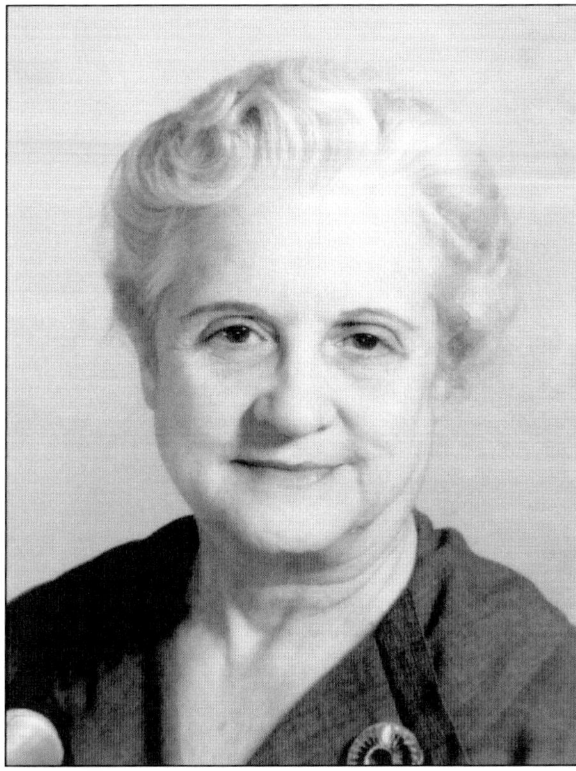

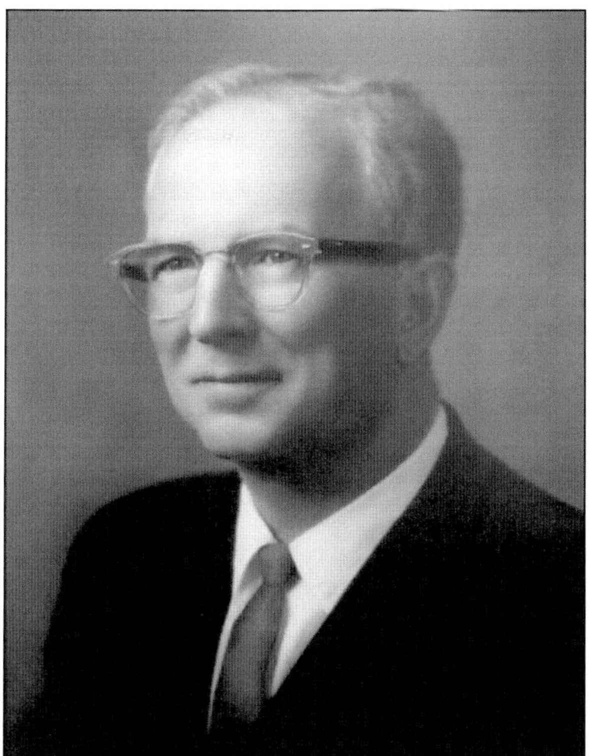

R. S. Beckham served as principal of Crayton School from 1956 to 1965. (Courtesy of Warner M. Montgomery.)

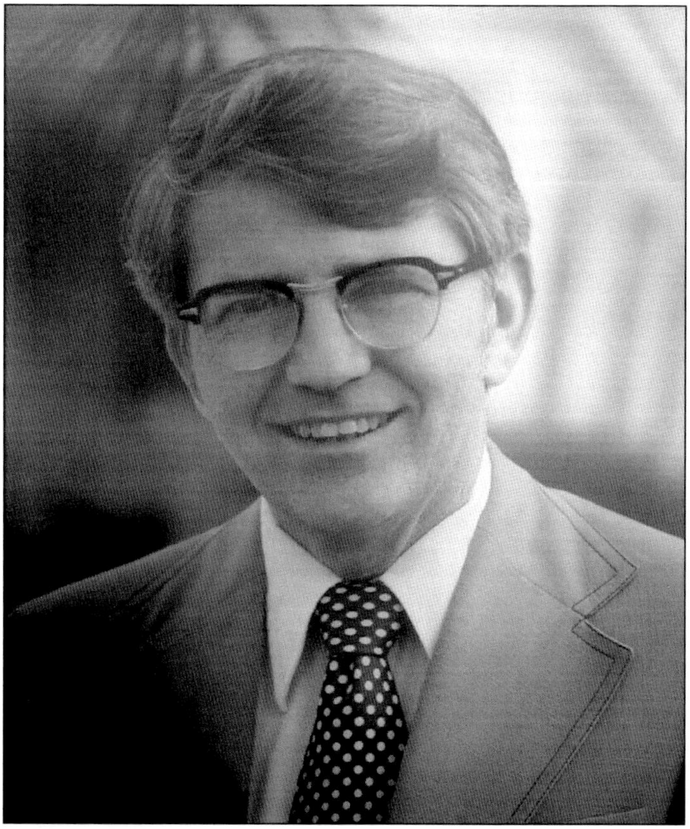

Arthur Taylor was principal of Crayton School from 1965 to 1975. (Courtesy of Warner M. Montgomery.)

Former Crayton administrators attended the school's 25th anniversary in 1976. From left to right are Roger Kirk, Carol Mundy, R. S. Beckham, George Goley, and Matthew Cannon. (Courtesy of Warner M. Montgomery.)

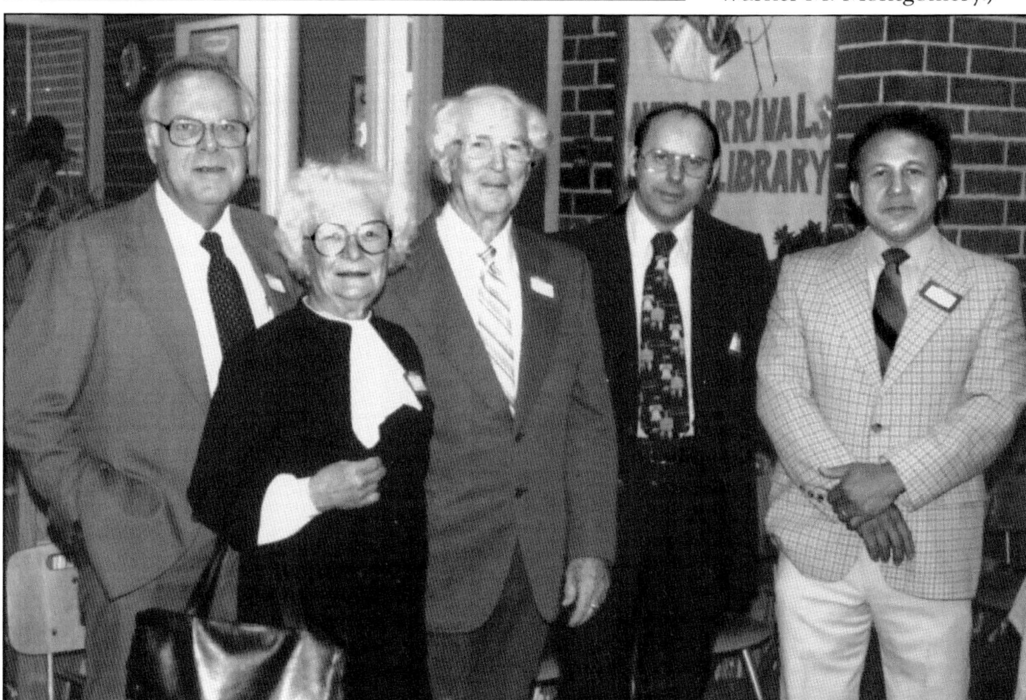

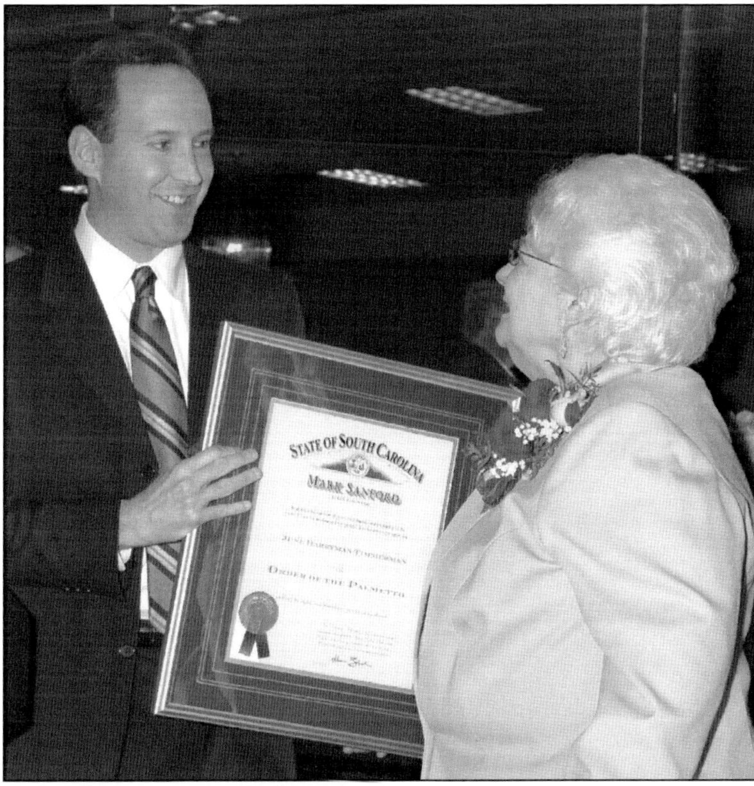

A private K-3 through eighth-grade school, located on 9 acres on Atascadero Drive, was founded by June H. Timmerman on 9 acres on Atascadero Drive in 1954. It began with one classroom of preschool students and grew to an enrollment of over 400 elementary students. June Timmerman, founder of Timmerman School, is shown receiving the Order of the Palmetto from South Carolina representative Joel Lourie in 2005. (Courtesy of Timmerman School.)

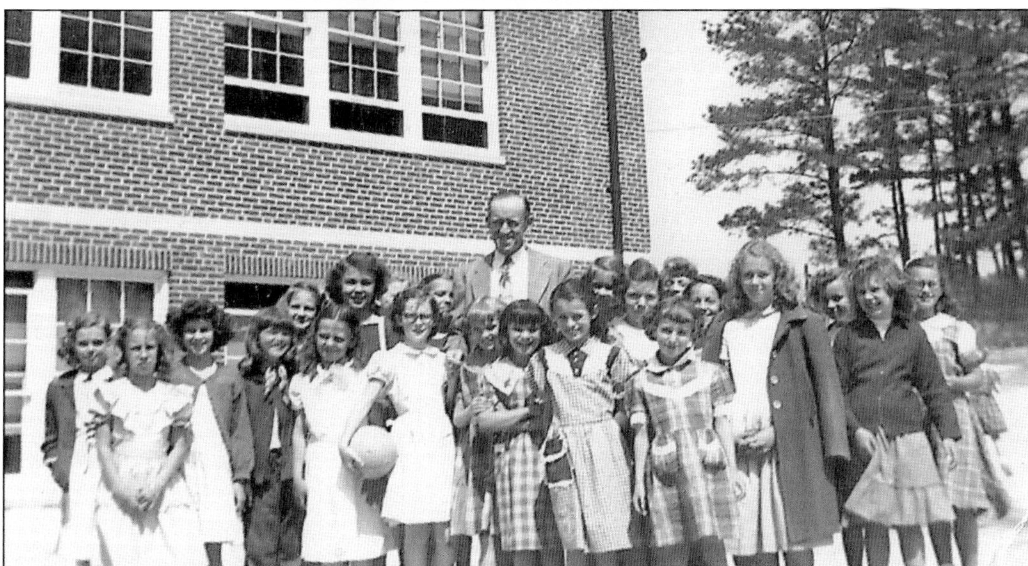

Bradley Elementary School was constructed in 1954 on 9.6 acres of the Keenan estate on Pine Belt Road. The architects were Lyles, Bissett, Carlisle, and Wolfe, who won a design award for the school's "Florida Plan." The school was named for Dr. Francis W. Bradley, who had been acting president of USC and had served on the Richland School District One school board for 24 years from 1928 to 1951. W. J. Castine, the first principal of Bradley Elementary School, gathers with his students in 1955. (Courtesy of Warner M. Montgomery.)

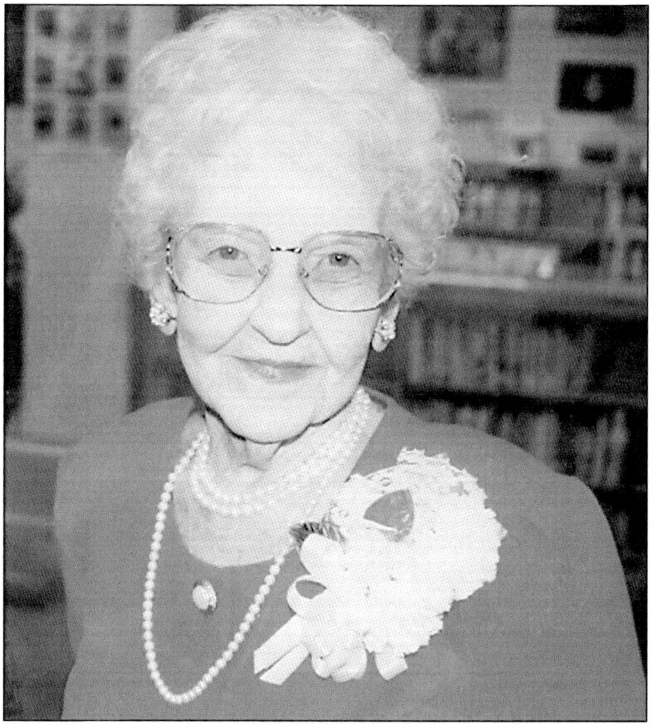

Richland School District One purchased 20 acres of Stork property on Satchel Ford Road in 1950 and 1953. Satchel Ford Elementary School opened with 618 students in 1956. It was the first school in Richland School District One to be constructed with open corridors. Ann Hampton was the first principal of Satchel Ford Elementary School and the first principal of Brockman Elementary School in 1960. (Courtesy of Warner M. Montgomery.)

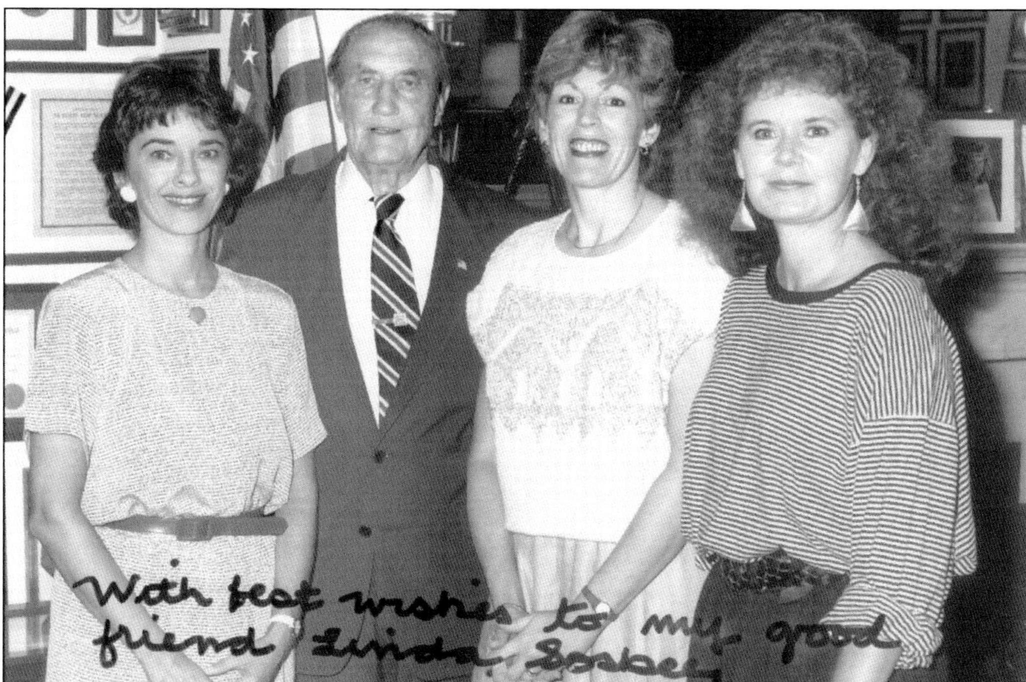

Satchel Ford Elementary School received the U.S. Department of Education Blue Ribbon Excellence in Education Award in 1987 and 2001. Principal Bernadette Scott (left), teacher Cheryl Haltiwanger, and curriculum resource teacher Linda Sosbee (right) are being honored by Sen. Strom Thurmond in this 1988 image. (Courtesy of Warner M. Montgomery.)

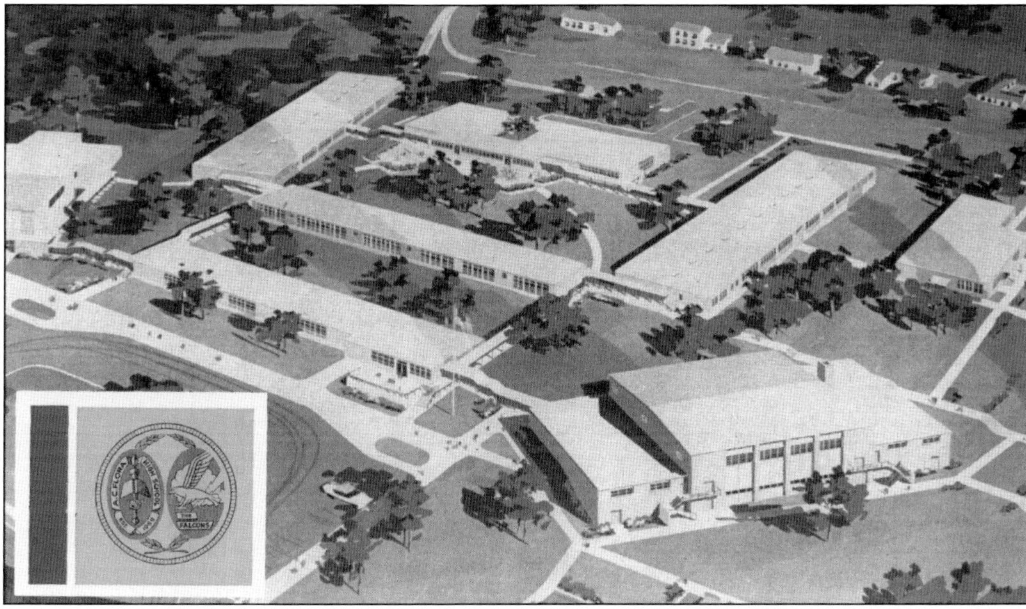

In 1956, Richland School District One authorized the building of a new high school to be named for Dr. A. C. Flora, superintendent from 1928 to 1951. It was constructed on 15 acres on Falcon Drive. The architects were Lafaye, Lafaye, and Fair, and the contractor was Crosland-Roof. The school opened in 1959. J. K. Blum served as principal until 1966. The first student body president was Babcock Fitch, and Charlie Farrell was the second. The Falcon Club, a booster club, was organized in 1960 with Rudy Barnes as the first president. (Courtesy of Warner M. Montgomery.)

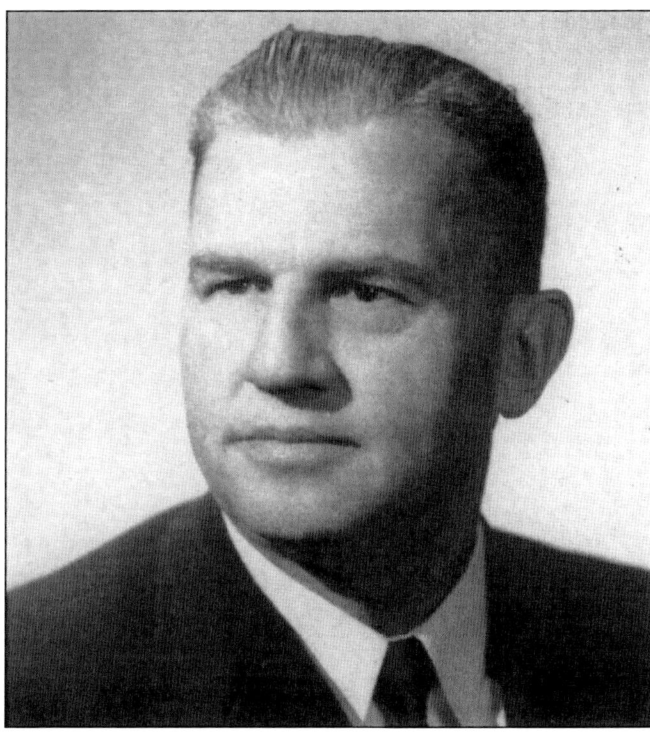

J. K. Blum, the first principal of A. C. Flora High School in 1959, had been principal of Dreher High School since 1947. He retired in 1966. (Courtesy of Warner M. Montgomery.)

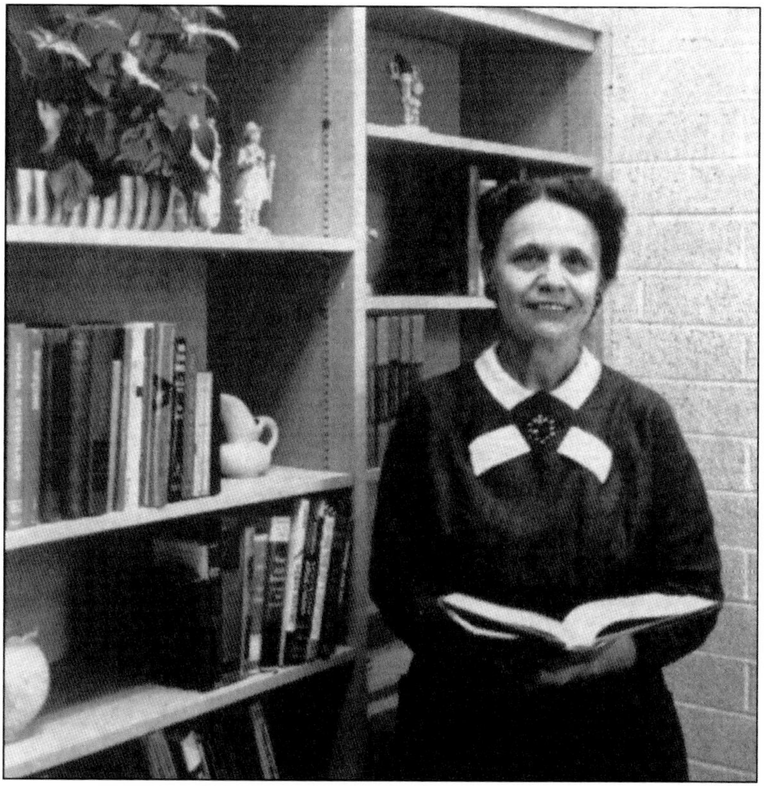

Assistant principal Grace Sease came with J. K. Blum to A. C. Flora High School from Dreher High School in 1959. (Courtesy of Warner M. Montgomery.)

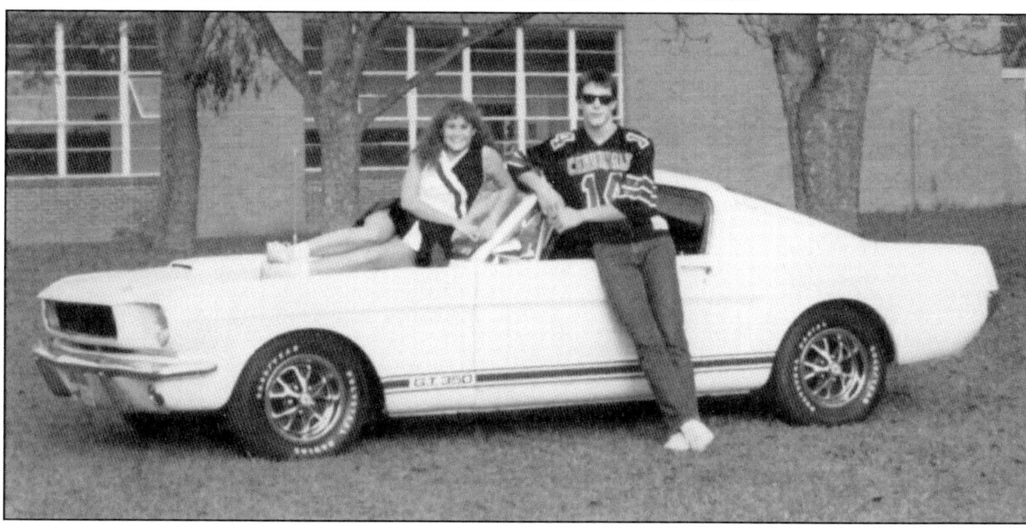

Cardinal Newman High School had its beginnings in 1834 when a group of Ursuline Sisters from Ireland opened Ursuline Convent for young ladies in Columbia. Sherman's army burned the school in 1865. It was reopened as St. Peter's School in 1872. It became Ursuline High School in 1887 then Catholic High School in 1957. The school moved to Forest Drive in 1961 as Cardinal Newman High School. The faculty was composed of Ursuline nuns, with Sister Mary Bernard was principal. A convent was built behind the school on Gamewell Drive. Harold J. Bayerl became principal in 1971. Dawn Lewis and John Sherrer are shown in front of Cardinal Newman in 1985. (Courtesy of John Sherrer.)

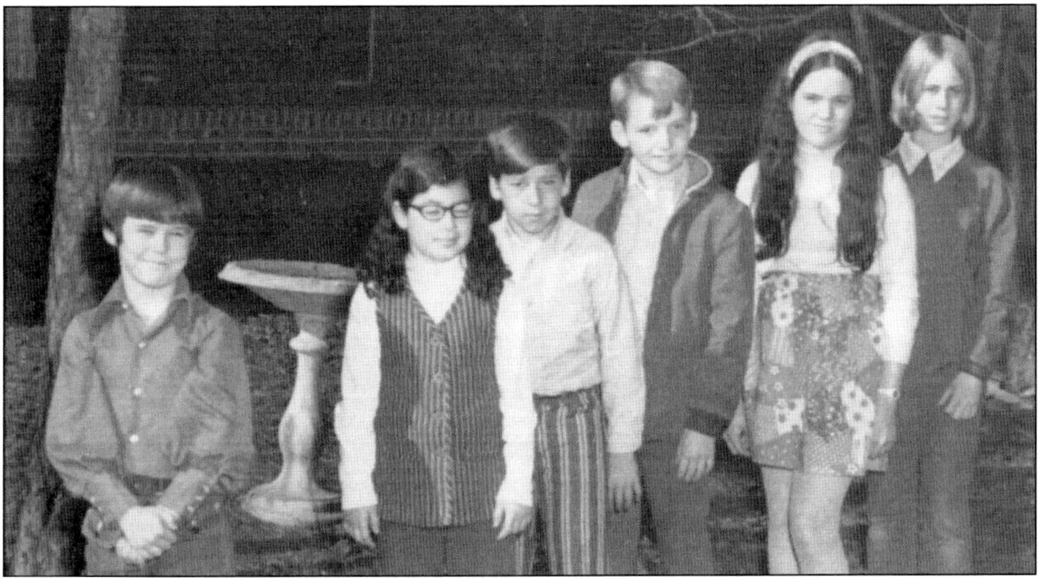

Montclair Drive Elementary School was built on Bethel Church Road during 1959 to relieve overcrowding at Crayton and Satchel Ford Elementary Schools. Ann Hampton was the first principal. Charles Van Patten was the assistant principal. The name was changed to Brockman Elementary School in 1964 to honor W. Clark Brockman, a long-serving Richland School District One administrator. John Cooley became principal in 1980, when it was converted into a school for orthopedically disabled students. Members of the first student council in 1970, pictured from left to right, were Vince Harris, Michelle Bernstein, Bruce Hass, Rick Thain, Janet Wingard, and Caroline Dial. (Courtesy of Warner M. Montgomery.)

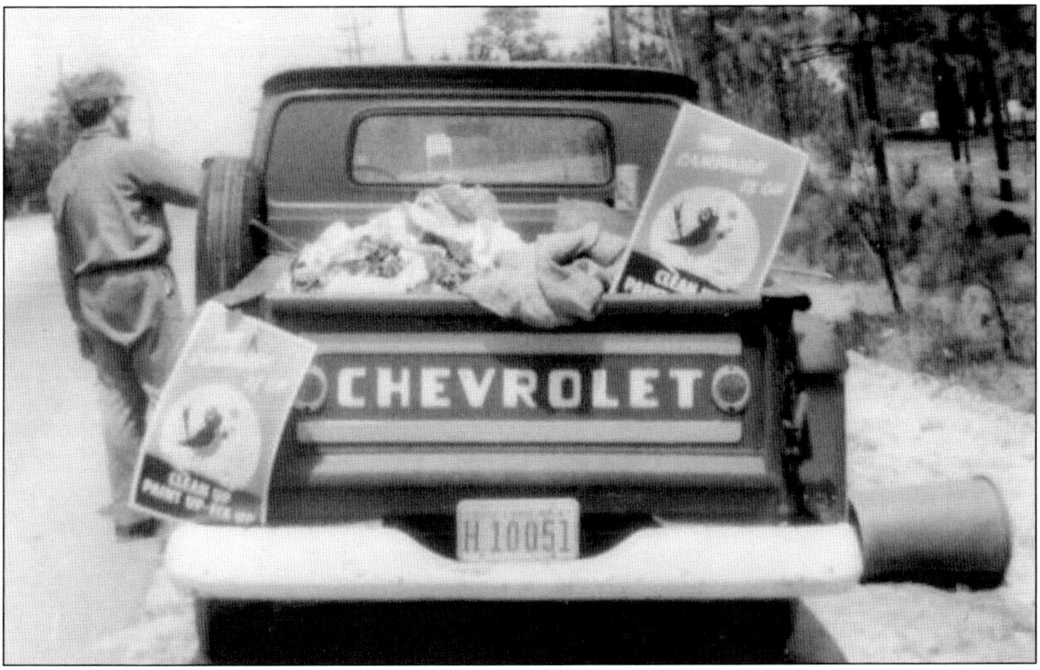

Boy Scouts pick up trash on North Trenholm Road in the clean up campaign of 1967. (Courtesy of City of Forest Acres.)

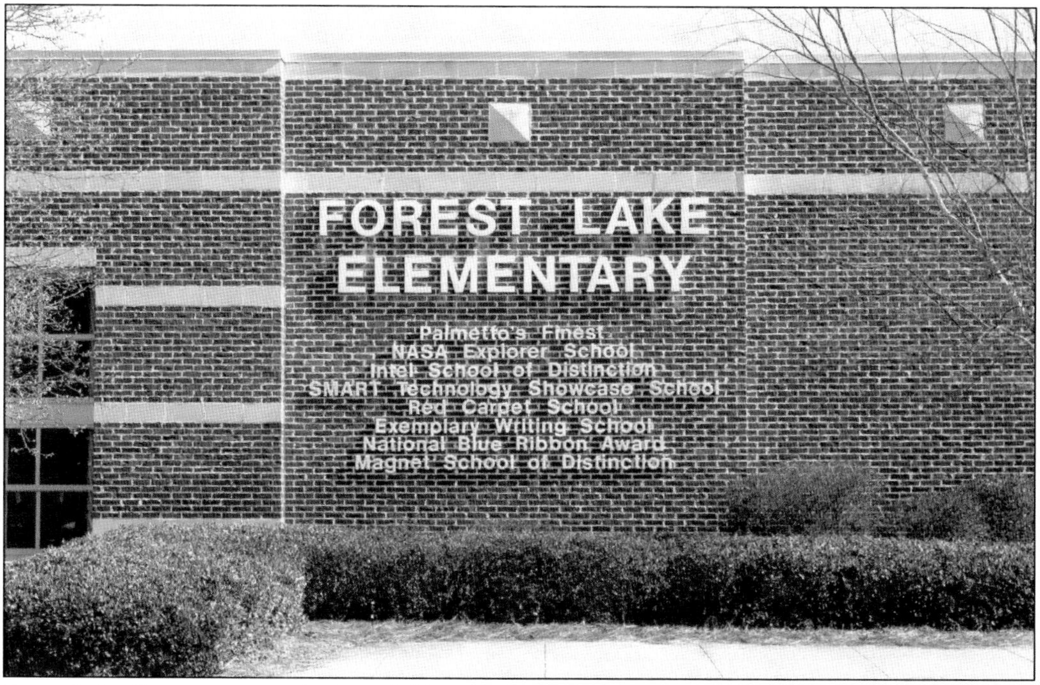

Forest Lake Elementary was built in 1957 on Brookfield Road. It is now a Richland School District Two award-winning technology magnet school. Dr. Kappy Cannon was chosen the 2010 South Carolina elementary principal of the year. (Photograph by Warner M. Montgomery.)

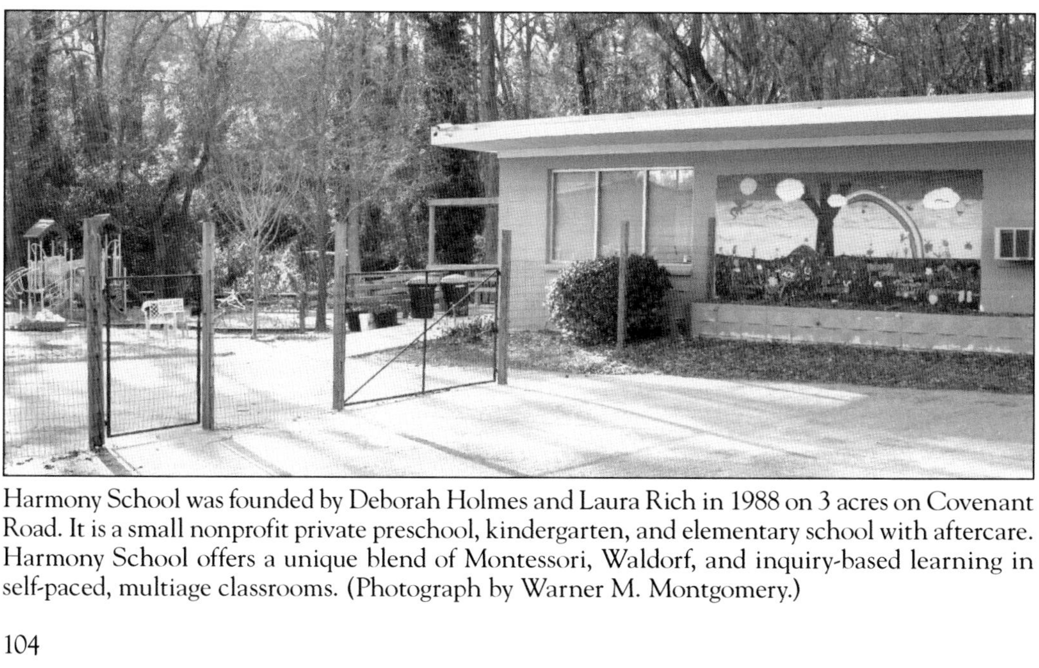

Harmony School was founded by Deborah Holmes and Laura Rich in 1988 on 3 acres on Covenant Road. It is a small nonprofit private preschool, kindergarten, and elementary school with aftercare. Harmony School offers a unique blend of Montessori, Waldorf, and inquiry-based learning in self-paced, multiage classrooms. (Photograph by Warner M. Montgomery.)

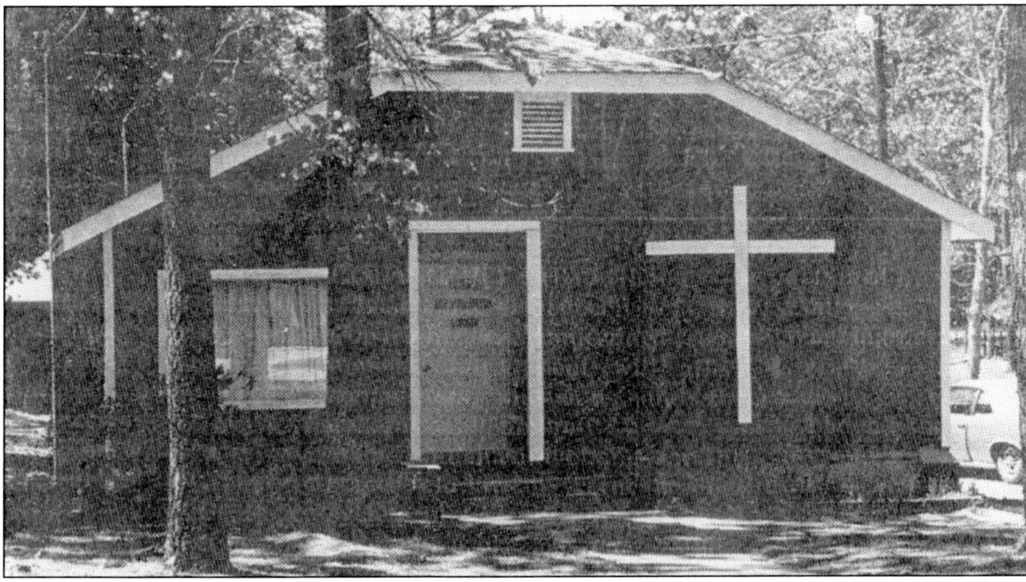

Grace Church of the Nazarene was organized in downtown Columbia in 1948 with 35 members. The first church building was on School House Road. Joseph Finger was the first minister. It moved to Pinestraw Road in Forest Acres in 1977, the year this photograph was taken. (Courtesy of Grace Church.)

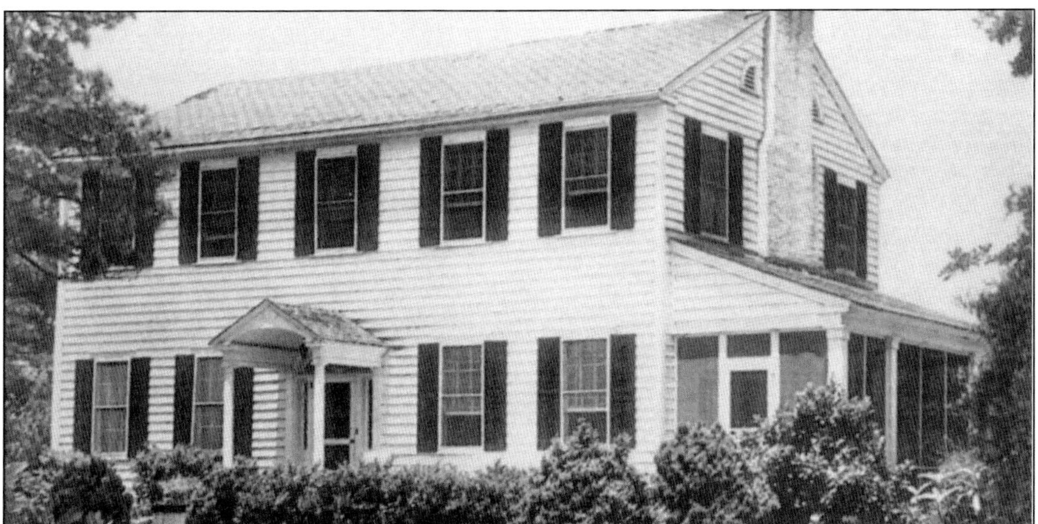

The first formal worship service of the Good Shepherd Lutheran congregation was held in 1949 in the Carolina Children's Home (pictured here). The church was organized in 1950 with 65 charter members. Rev. Harold E. Park was called as first pastor and served until 1958. Services continued to be held there until 3.75 acres and an old house on Forest Drive were secured. The first floor was converted into a worship room. A modern church was constructed in 1955, and a new Zimmer pipe organ was added in 1968. A newly constructed sanctuary was dedicated in 1992. Senior pastors of Good Shepherd Lutheran Church have been Dr. Harold E. Park (1950–1958), Dr. Alton C. Clark (1958–1976), Dr. Larry S. Long (1995–1995), Dr. Herman R. Yoos (1996–2008), and Paul Wollner in 2010. (Courtesy of Good Shepherd Lutheran Church.)

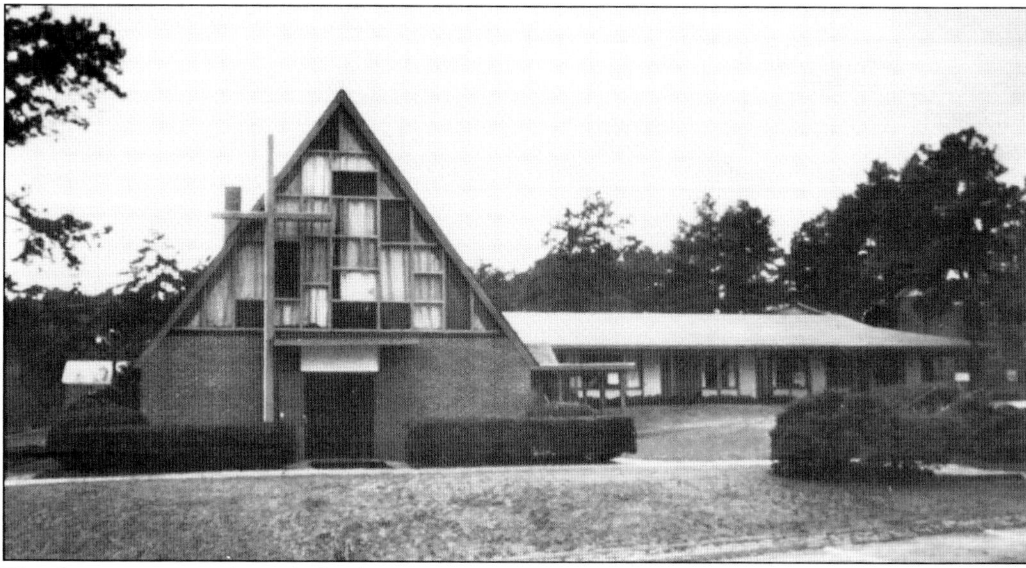

The first sanctuary of Good Shepherd Lutheran Church was completed in 1955 on Forest Drive. (Courtesy of Good Shepherd Lutheran Church.)

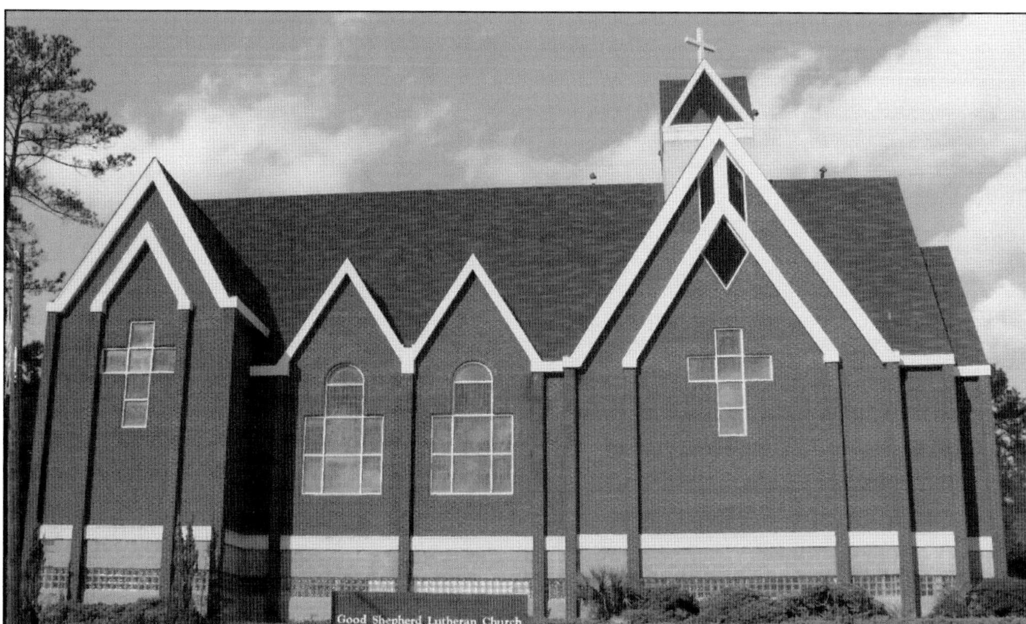

The present Good Shepherd Lutheran Church was dedicated in 1992. (Photograph by Warner M. Montgomery.)

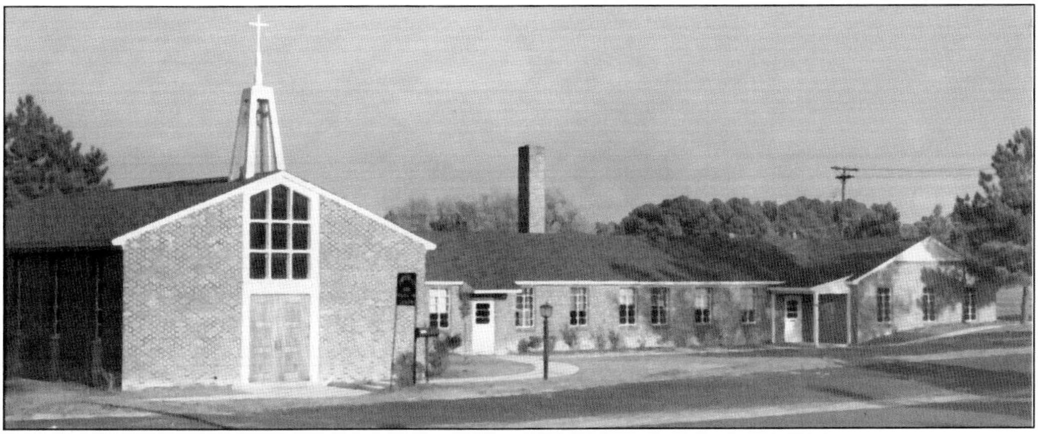

St. Martin's-in-the-Fields Episcopal Church was founded in 1950 when Theodore Jones and Jesse Reese Jr. knelt and prayed at the corner of Clemson Road and Winthrop Avenue. Committees led by Hoke and Bessie Robinson, Dr. Tucker Weston, and Fred Hensley were formed to organize the congregation. The chapel, kitchen, and classrooms were completed in 1951 by McCrory Construction Company. The first rector was Rev. William A. Thompson. He was followed by Rev. Henry C. Barton, Rev. Richard Milner, Rev. S. F. James Abbot, and Rev. Michael A. Bullock. English Morris became the music director in 1987. Rev. Sally Johnston was rector in 2010. (Courtesy of St. Martins-in-the-Fields Episcopal Church.)

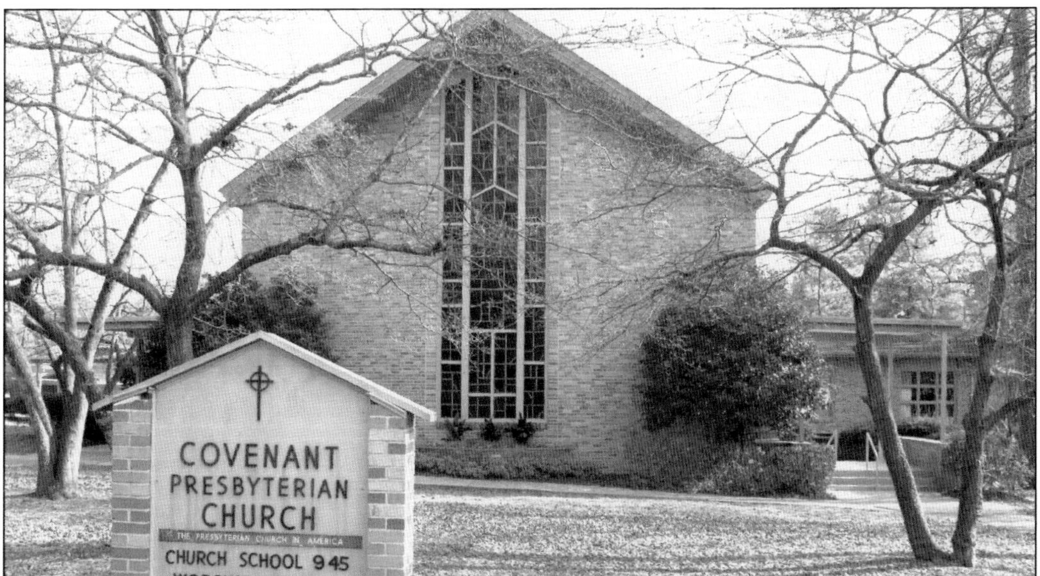

Covenant Presbyterian Church was organized in 1951 and led by Rev. Harry F. Petersen Jr., executive secretary of Congaree Presbytery. The first sanctuary was built on Alms House Road in 1959 and the name of the road was changed to Covenant Road. Pastors have been the Rev. Cecil D. Brearley Jr. (1954–1960), Rev. Harry T. Schutte (1960–1977), Rev. J. Gary Aitken (1977–1990), and Rev. LeRoy H. Ferguson (1991–2001). Rev. Eric R. Dye was pastor in 2010. In 1982, Covenant Presbyterian Church established Covenant Classical Christian School on their property. It now has a full K4–12 curriculum and is an accredited member of Christian Schools International, the South Carolina Independent School Association, and the Association of Classical and Christian Schools. (Photograph by Warner M. Montgomery.)

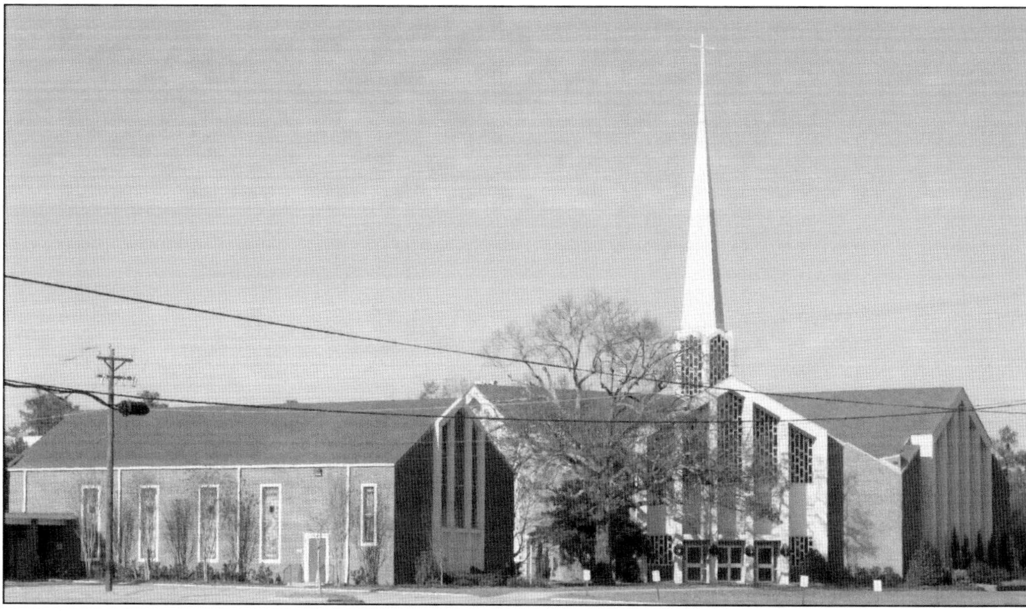

North Trenholm Baptist Church was organized as Tabernacle Baptist Church in Columbia in 1911. The congregation moved to North Trenholm Road in 1955 and changed its name. The present building was completed in 1973, the family life center in 1980, and the education/administration complex in 1993. Paul Ballard was senior pastor in 2010. (Photograph by Warner M. Montgomery.)

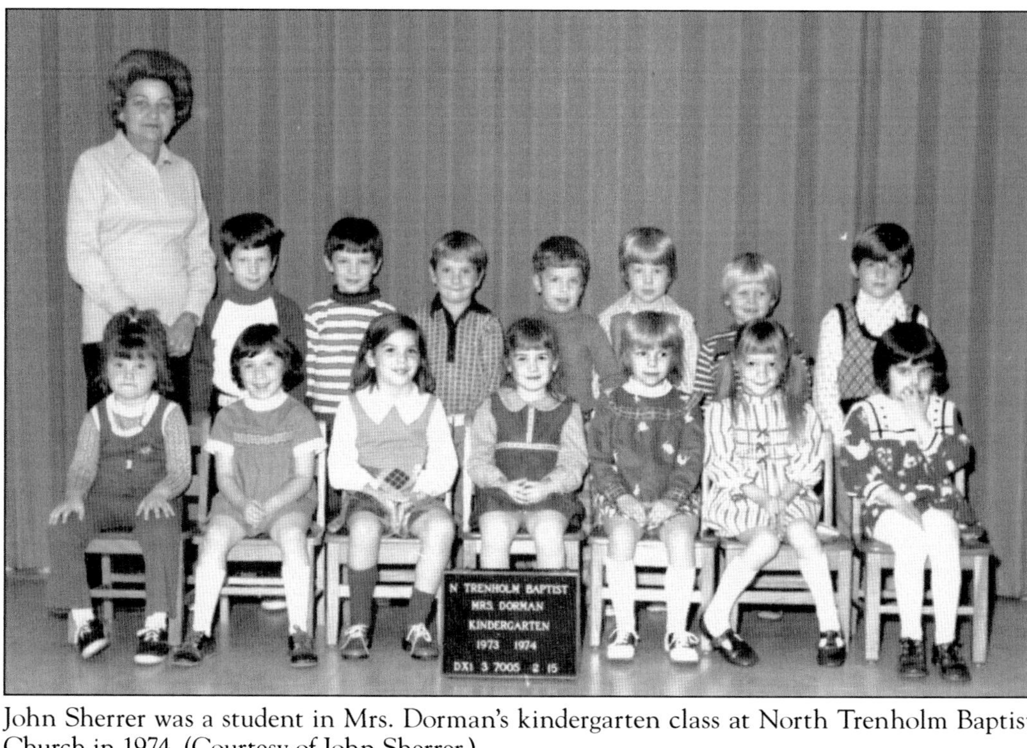

John Sherrer was a student in Mrs. Dorman's kindergarten class at North Trenholm Baptist Church in 1974. (Courtesy of John Sherrer.)

St. Michael and All Angels Episcopal Church was organized in 1957 and met at Satchel Ford Elementary School. The sanctuary was built on North Trenholm Road on property purchased from Forest Land Company, and 200 people attended the first service in the new building in 1958. Rev. James C. Fenhagen was the first rector. He was followed by Rev. Joseph E. Sturtevant (1963–1977) and Rev. Philip D. Whitehead. Rev. Paul E. Stricklin was rector in 2010, and Jack Evans was the senior warden. (Photograph by Warner M. Montgomery.)

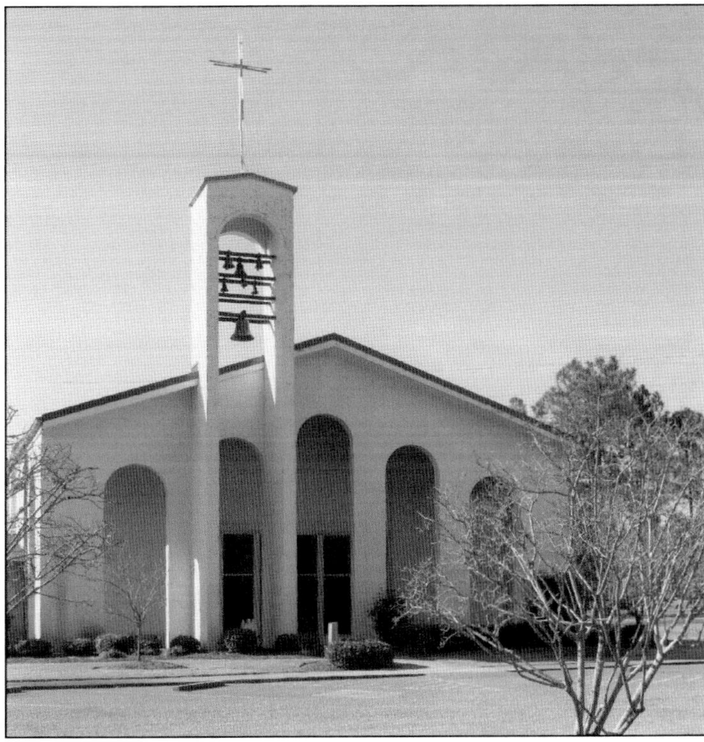

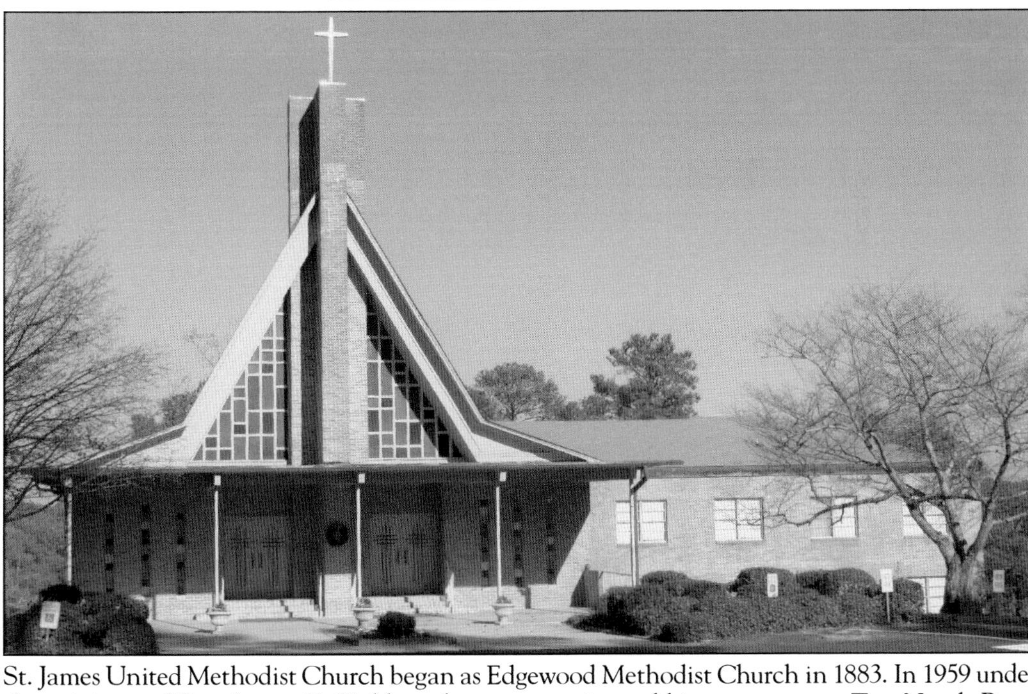

St. James United Methodist Church began as Edgewood Methodist Church in 1883. In 1959 under the ministry of Rev. James C. Holden, the congregation sold its property on Two Notch Road and met at Bradley Elementary School. The current property on Pine Belt Road was purchased and the church built in 1960. Rev. George H. Nichols Jr. was the first pastor. The pastor in 2010 was Rev. Emily Shore Silvola. (Photograph by Warner M. Montgomery.)

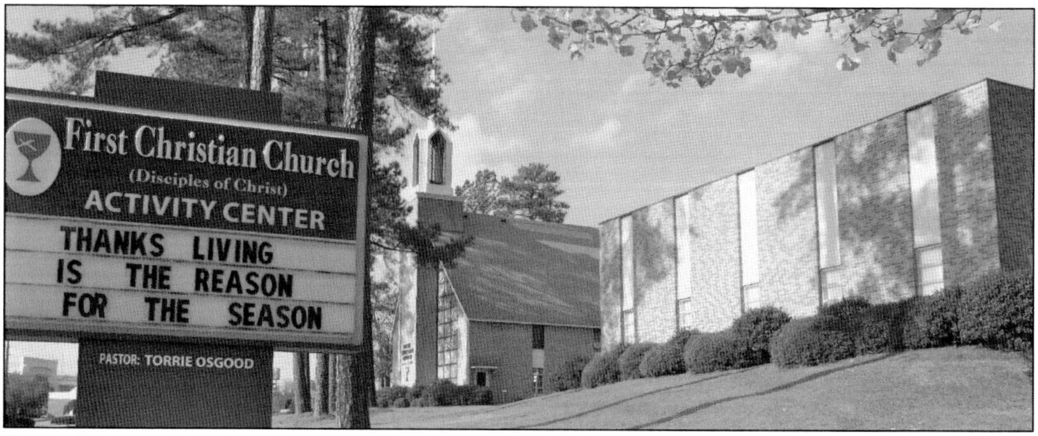

First Christian Church (Disciples of Christ) was organized by B. G. Butler in 1901. They erected a tabernacle in downtown Columbia in 1902. Property on North Beltline was purchased in 1961 and the present church built in 1962. Rev. Torrie Osgood was the minister in 2010. (Photograph by Warner M. Montgomery.)

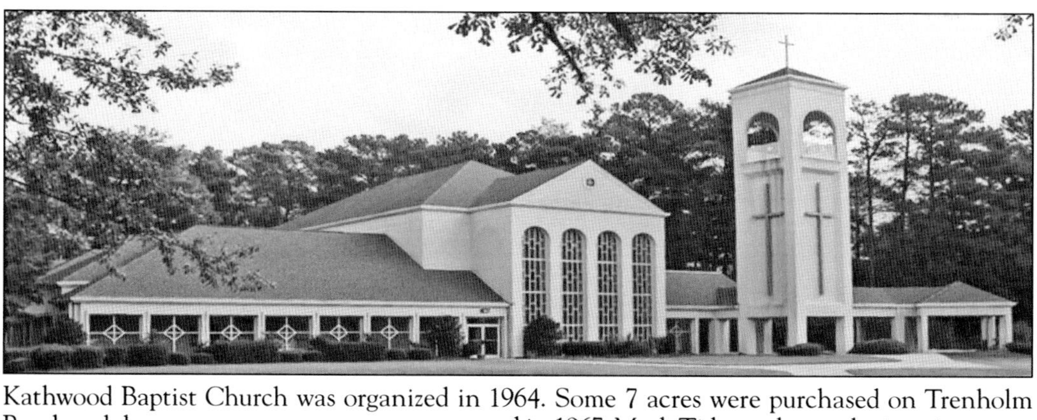

Kathwood Baptist Church was organized in 1964. Some 7 acres were purchased on Trenholm Road, and the current sanctuary was constructed in 1967. Mark Tidsworth was the interim pastor in 2010. (Photograph by Warner M. Montgomery.)

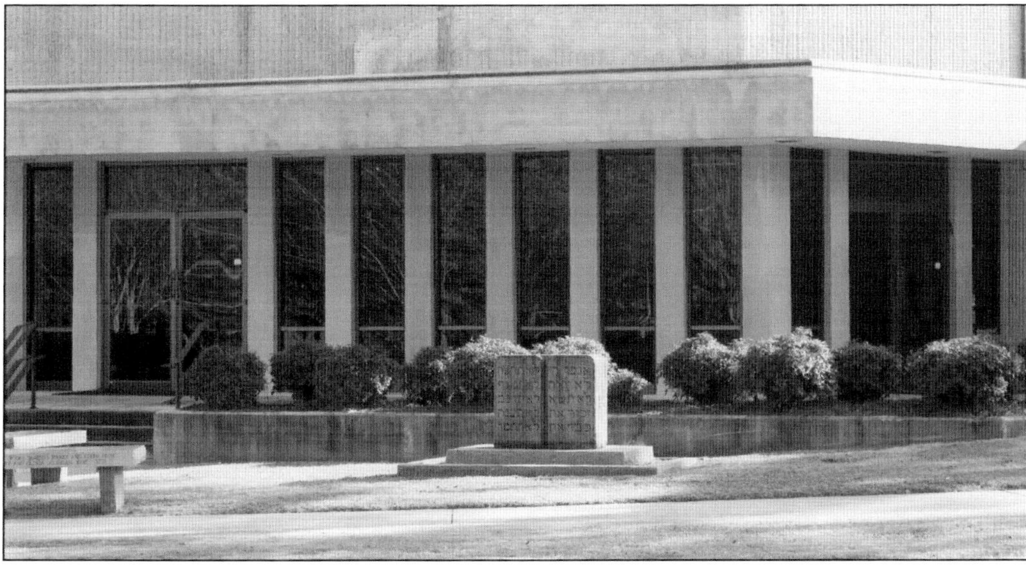

Beth Shalom (House of Peace) Synagogue was organized in downtown Columbia in 1912 under the leadership of Philip Epstein. Land was purchased on Trenholm Road in 1955 and a Jewish community center, education building, and synagogue were built. A new synagogue was constructed on North Trenholm Road in 1973. An education building was added in 1980 and expanded in 1999, along with the addition of a mikvah. The leaders in 2010 were Rabbi Jonathan Case, Dr. Lilly Filler (president), and Rebecca Pinsker (director of education). (Photograph by Warner M. Montgomery.)

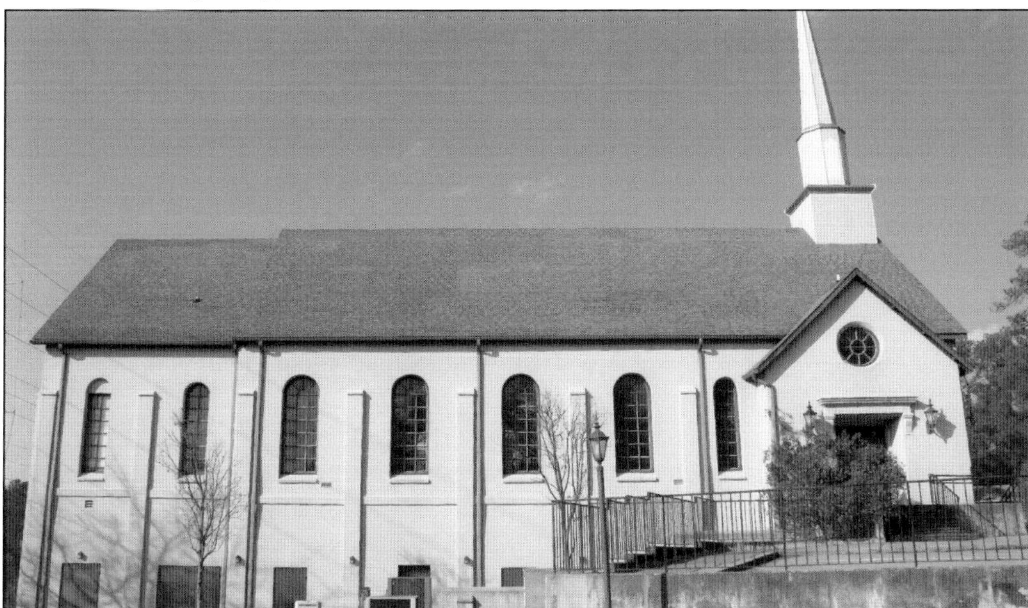

The Anglican Church of the Epiphany was formed by a small congregation of the Church of the Good Shepherd in downtown Columbia in 1977. Rev. L. Samuel Sebring Jr. was called in 1984 and began meeting at the Carolina Children's home. The sanctuary on Beltline at Verner was constructed in 1989. Rev. Canon Craig E. Young was the rector in 2010. (Photograph by Warner M. Montgomery.)

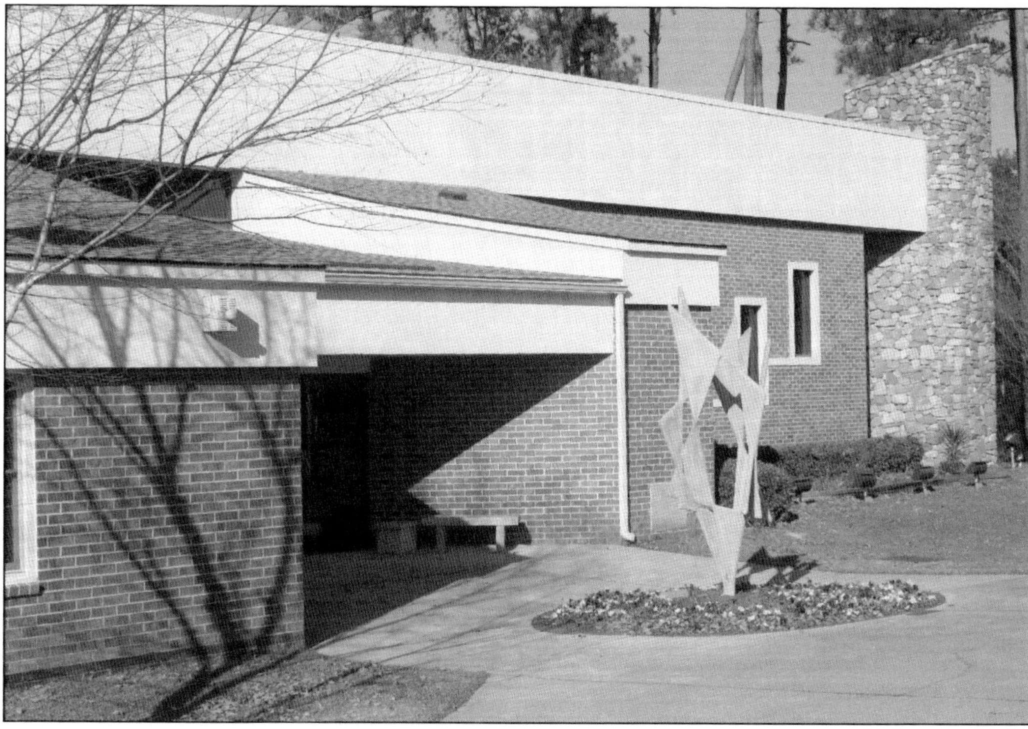

The Tree of Life Congregation was founded in Columbia in 1896. The first synagogue was constructed on Lady Street in Columbia in 1905 under the leadership of Henry Steele. The congregation moved to Heyward Street in 1951 then to North Trenholm Road in 1961. Sanford T. Marcus was called as the Tree of Life's seventh rabbi in 1986. In 2010, Marcus was rabbi emeritus, Daniel Sherman the rabbi, and Jeff Selig the president. (Photograph by Warner M. Montgomery.)

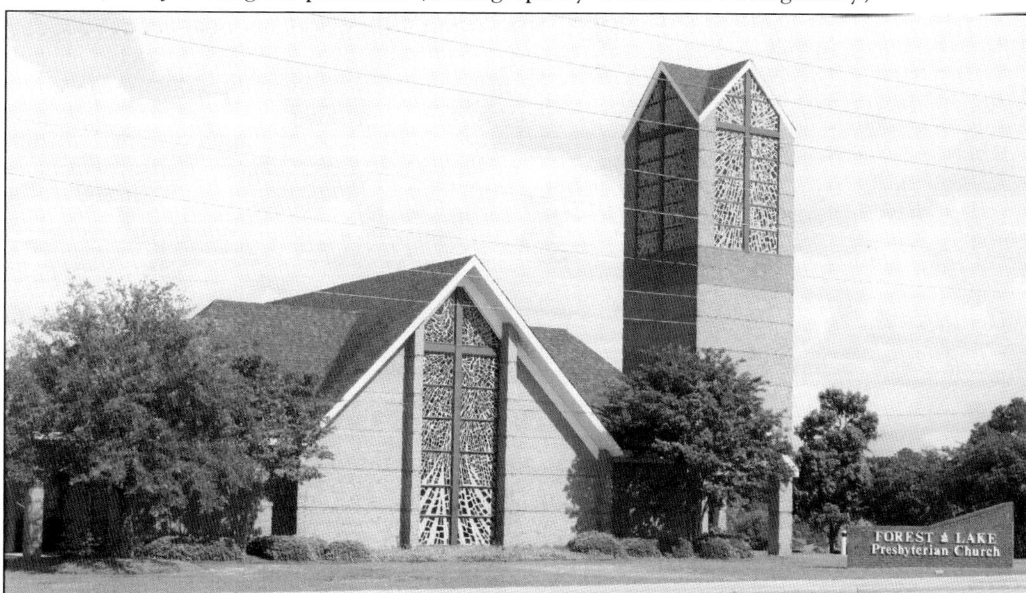

Forest Lake Presbyterian Church on North Trenholm Road was pastored by Dr. Ellen Skidmore in 2010. (Photograph by Warner M. Montgomery.)

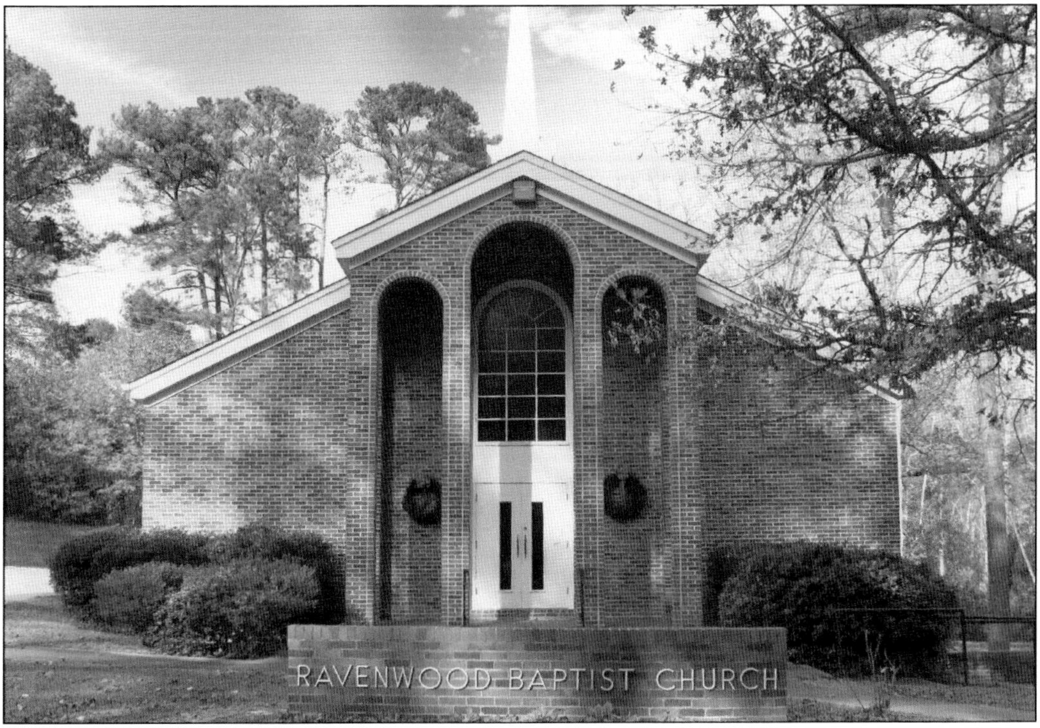

Ravenwood Baptist Church is a small Southern Baptist church on Raven Hill Road in Forest Acres. (Photograph by Warner M. Montgomery.)

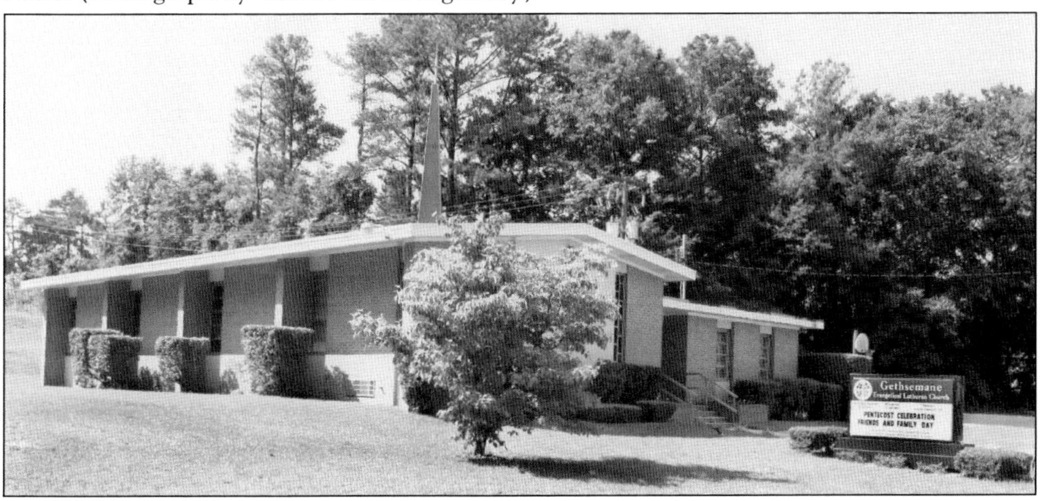

Gethsemane Evangelical Lutheran Church began holding worship services in 1957 at Belvedere Elementary School. The Rev. James R. Connelly Jr. served until 1960. The congregation was officially organized in 1958 and met at a chapel on Bronx Road. A site on Satchel Ford Road was purchased in 1959 and a new building was dedicated in 1964. The pastors have been Rev. Gordon Haigler (1961–1967), Rev. H. Wyndham Burris (1967–1976), Rev. Dermon A. Sox Jr. (1976–1996), Rev. Dr. Phillip Baker (interim 1997–1999), Rev. Christine Parham (1999–2004), and Rev. Louis R. Fawcett III (2005–2010). The 50th anniversary was celebrated in 2008 with Pastor Connelly preaching and Bishop David Donges presiding at Holy Communion. (Photograph by Warner M. Montgomery.)

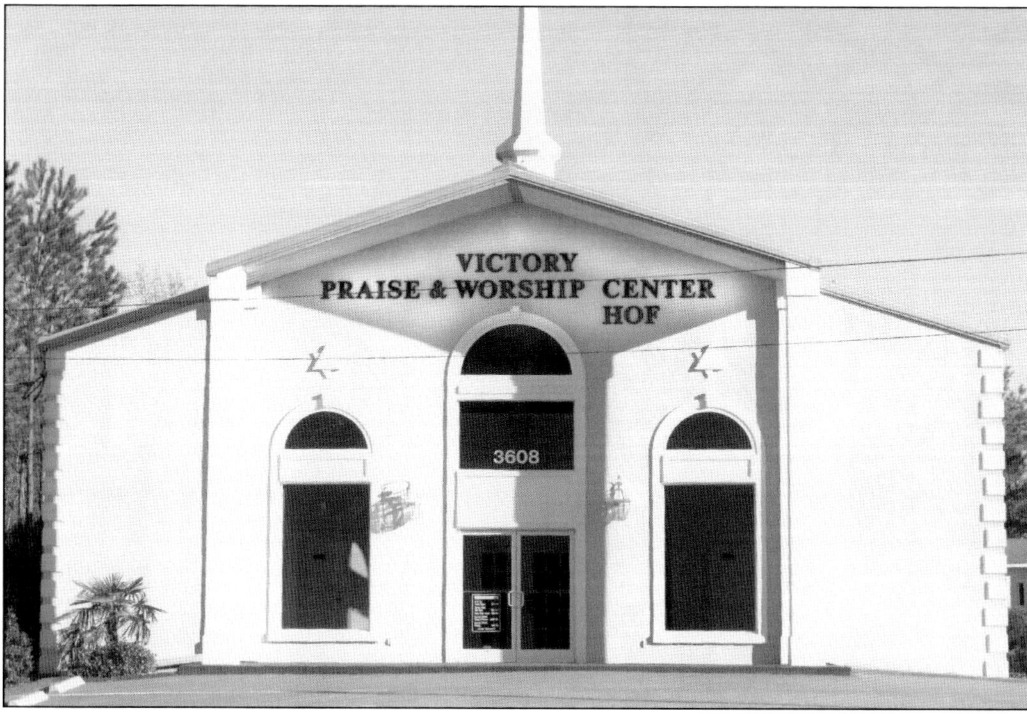

The Victory Praise and Worship Center is located at 3608 Covenant Road. (Photograph by Warner M. Montgomery.)

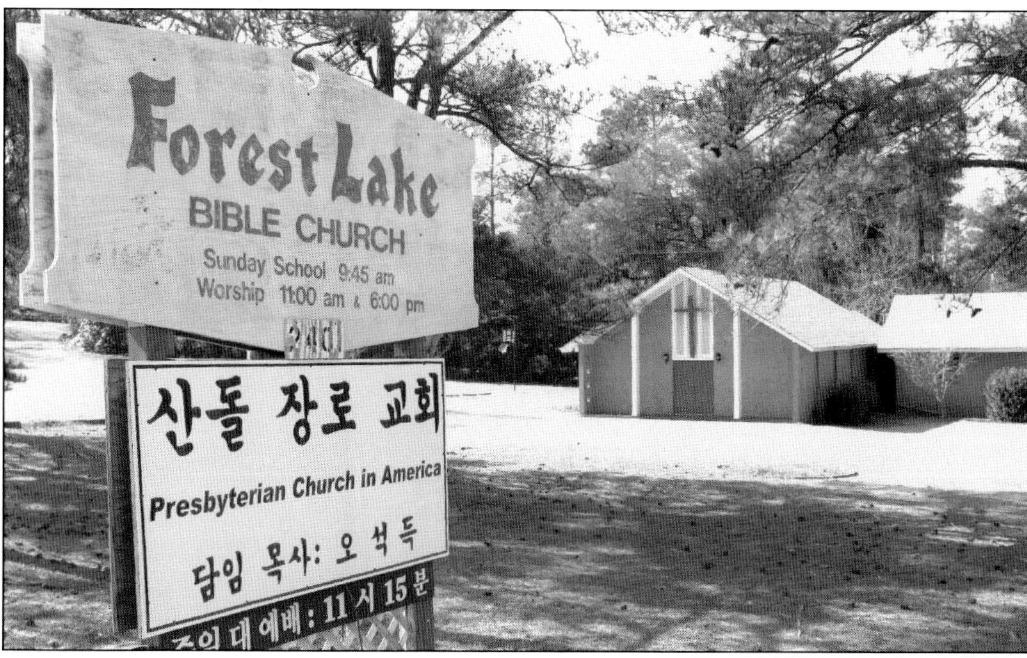

Forest Lake Bible Church was organized in 1959 by people in the Dentsville area. They first met in homes then in the Dentsville High School. Revs. Al Oliver and Rentz Berry were the first ministers. The church is also used by Japanese and Korean congregations. (Photograph by Warner M. Montgomery.)

Ten

Forest Acres Faces the Future

The city of Forest Acres matured as a municipal corporation between 1950 and 1970 during the administrations of mayors Emmette Groover (1949–1957), W. J. Stubbs (1957–1965), and Albert Burts (1965–1971). It took over all water supplies in the city and hired Joe Thomas as city water clerk. Mrs. Curtis Strickland was hired as city clerk in 1959. W. E. Tighe served as the first city recorder. Business licenses were required of all businesses in 1952. Firearms and trailer parks were restricted in 1954. A municipal court was established in 1958, a board of health in 1959, and a planning commission in 1962. Forest Drive was widened and sidewalks added in 1958. Street lights were erected throughout the city in 1961. The same year city council considered building a bomb shelter to protect its citizens from the Red Scare. Sen. Hammond even offered land for the project.

Richland School District One schools were desegregated by court order in 1970 and confusion reigned in the schools. Mayor William "Bill" Y. Edens proposed that Forest Acres establish its own school system. In a 1971 referendum his proposal was accepted 715 to 258, but due to state and national restrictions the idea fizzled away. Edens resigned in 1976 and was succeeded by Earle B. Sligh (one-year interim).

Forest Acres hired Felton C. Benton as its first city administrator in 1975. He was succeeded by Jimmie C. Wright in 1981. Royce G. Waites, a councilman since 1973, was elected mayor in 1977 and served until 1991. Danny Taylor was appointed city administrator in 1988 and served for two years. Ron Garbinsky took over in 1990. Mark Williams became administrator in 2005. Forest Acres city officers settled into a city hall at 5205 North Trenholm Road in 1978. Prior to this they had met in mayor's homes then moved to the Forest Lake Shopping Center and then to a building on Bethel Church Road.

The water system that caused the creation of Forest Acres in 1935 was transferred to the city of Columbia in 1989. This meant lower water rates for residents and no more system maintenance for the city.

The founding fathers of Forest Acres had a vision in 1935. Sen. James Hammond and John Hughes Cooper saw a quiet peaceful rural community outside of Columbia composed of Quinine Hill, Forest Lake, and the land between them along Forest Drive. The city of Forest Acres has grown from 300 to 10,000 people, from 2 square miles to 5 square miles. Forest Acres celebrates its 75th anniversary in 2010 as a progressive, family-friendly city with small town charm, truly, as the motto goes, "A City Apart."

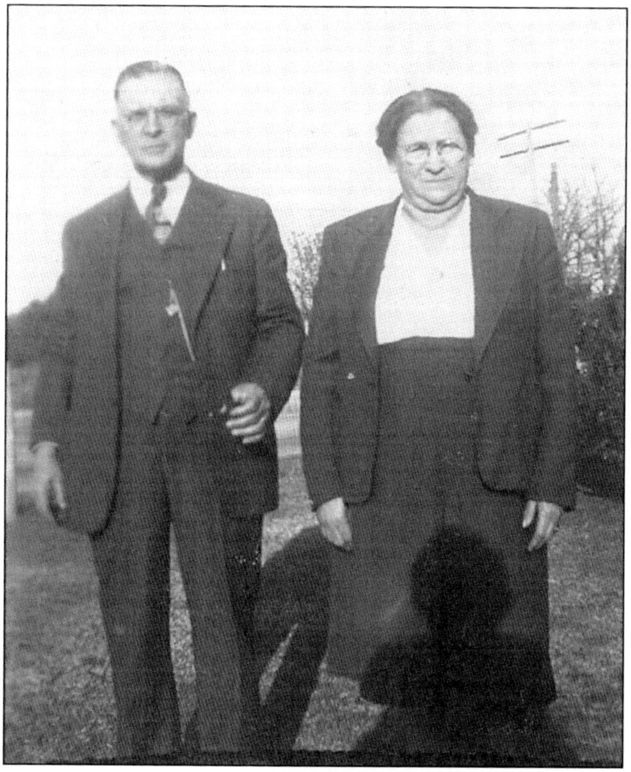

Boykin and Fannie Davis operated the Davis Grocery Store beginning in 1909. It became Forest Acres' de facto city hall and polling place in 1935. (Courtesy of Hammond Edwards III.)

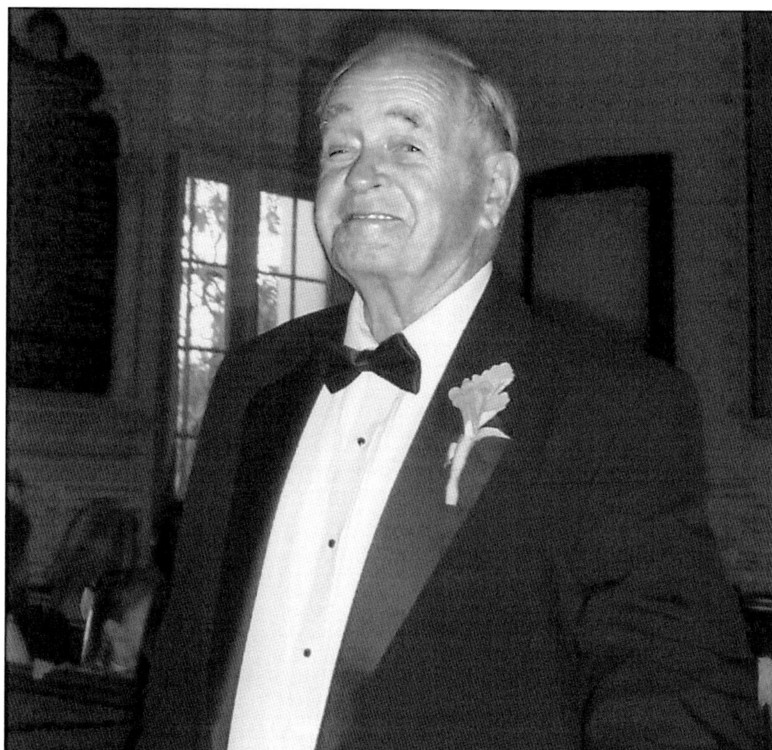

Albert H. Burts served as mayor of Forest Acres from 1965 to 1971. (Courtesy of Richard Burts.)

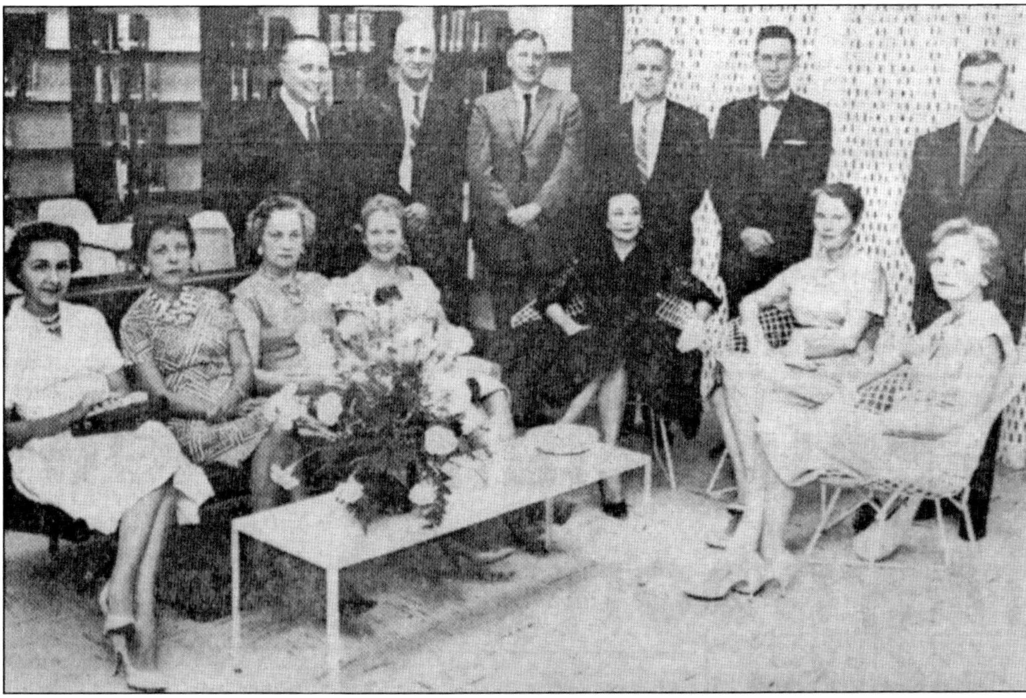

A branch of the Richland County Public Library opened in 1961 in a building given by the Cooper family in memory of John Hughes Cooper, who had died in 1945. Sen. James Hammond spoke at the dedication of the John Hughes Cooper branch and praised his old friend. From left to right in this picture are (first row) Mrs. Paul C. deTreville, Mrs. Charles Cooper, Mrs. Paul Cooper, Mrs. Mary Preston Villwock, Mrs. Sam Preston, Mrs. Edwin Cooper, and Mrs Philip Benton; (second row) Byron Villwock, Philip Benton, Edwin Cooper, Paul deTreville, Sam Preston, and Charles Cooper. (Courtesy of Richland County Public Library.)

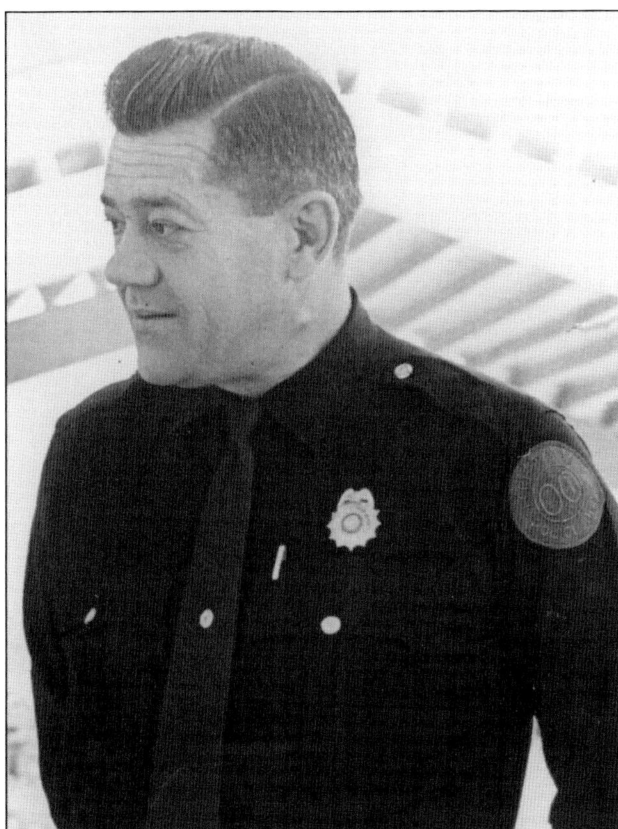

The last resident horse was removed from the city limits in 1962, the same year the police department was formerly organized with John R. Dodenhoff as Forest Acres' first paid chief. He served from 1962 to 1968. (Courtesy of City of Forest Acres.)

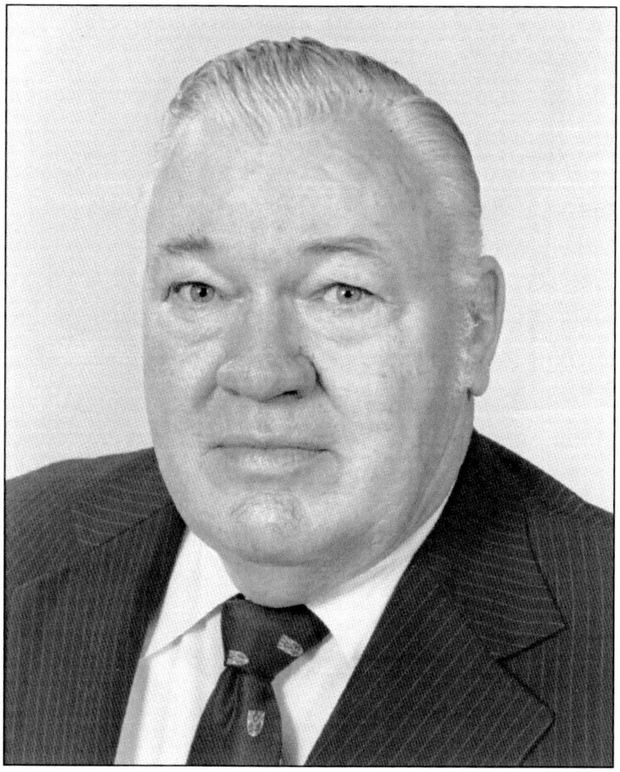

Thomas C. Hyder served as police chief of Forest Acres from 1968 to 1972. (Courtesy of City of Forest Acres.)

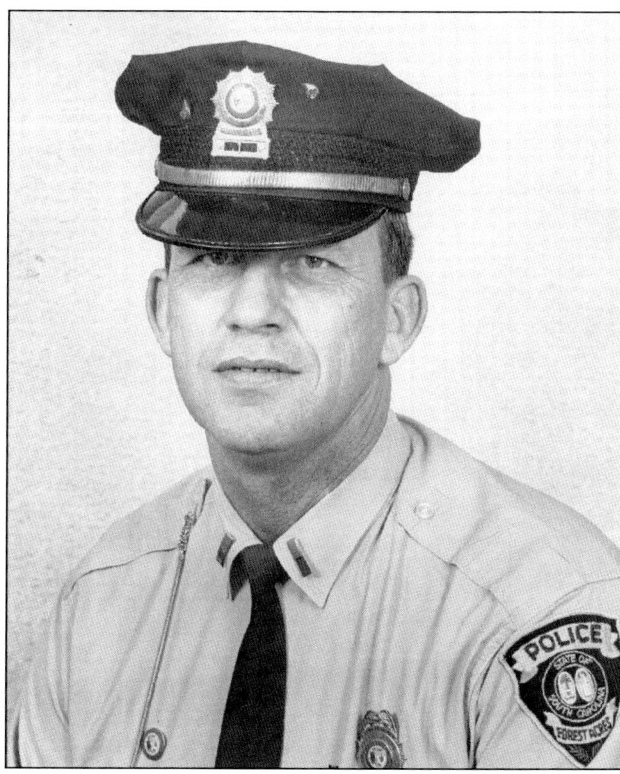

Wesley B. Sexton served briefly, 1976–1977, until J. C. Rowe became chief in 1978. (Courtesy of City of Forest Acres.)

Charles McLean served Forest Acres as police chief from 1972 to 1976 and from 1977 to 1978. (Courtesy of City of Forest Acres.)

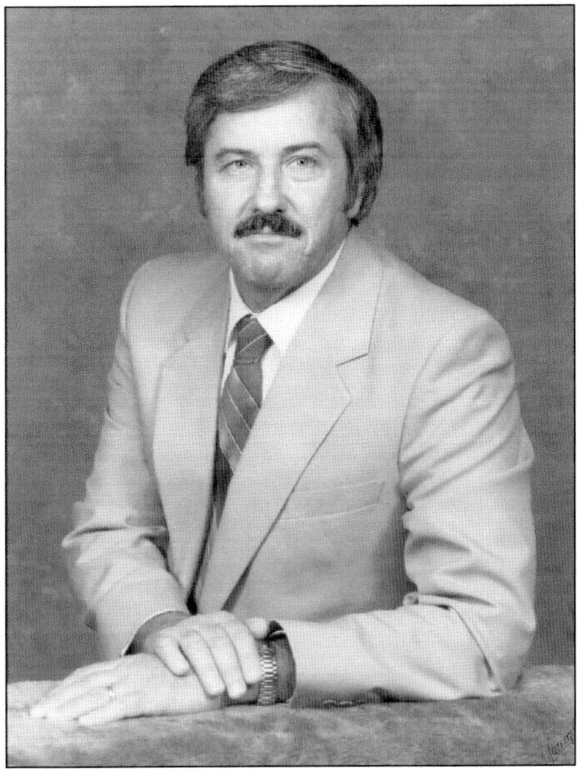

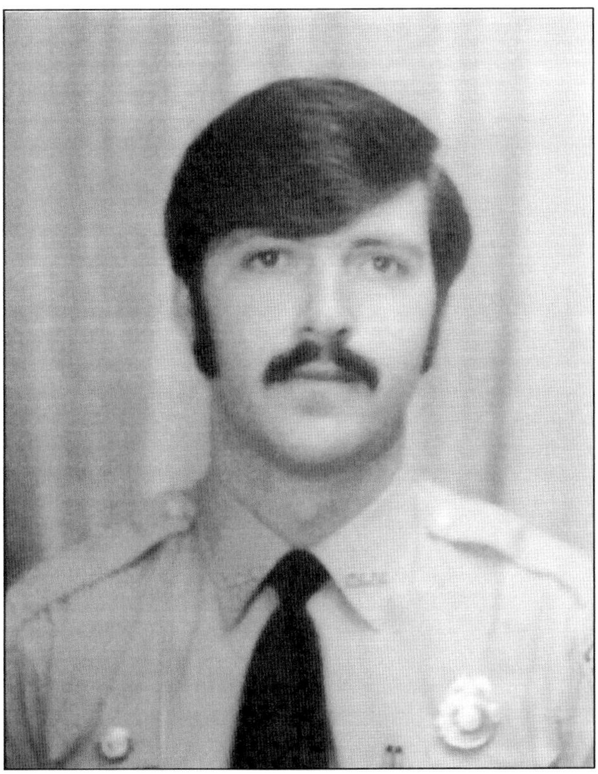

A terrible disaster occurred in Forest Acres in February 1974. Richey O. Finch, a Forest Acres police officer, was killed in the line of duty when he stopped a car on Forest Drive. He was able to give the suspects' license tag number before he died. The three men, who also killed a Kershaw County deputy later that day, were arrested and convicted of murder. (Courtesy of City of Forest Acres.)

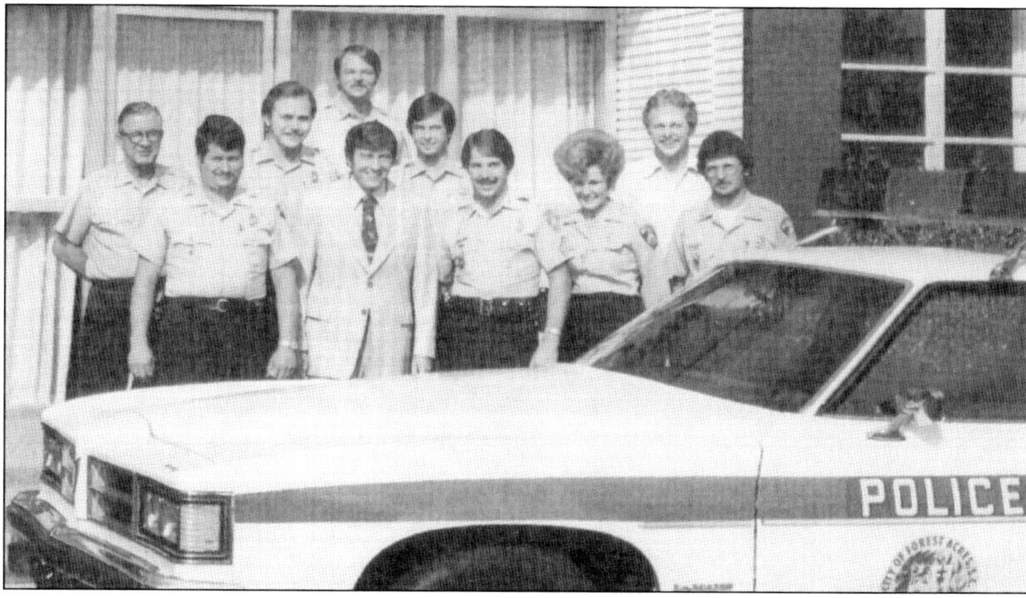

Citizens in Forest Acres demanded stricter law enforcement, tougher zoning restrictions, and increased annexation in the 1960s. In 1965, Alex Sanders was appointed city recorder, Irving Belser appointed city attorney, and three police officers were hired—Jesse R. Barber, Thomas C. Hyder, and William A. Hoefer. Hyder was promoted to chief in 1968. He was followed by Charles McLean (1972–1978) who headed the investigation that led to the arrest and conviction of the infamous psychiatrist-turned-burglar, Dr. Ian Gale. Forest Acres police chief Charles McLean and his officers pose with the new Pontiac police cruiser in 1978. (Courtesy of City of Forest Acres.)

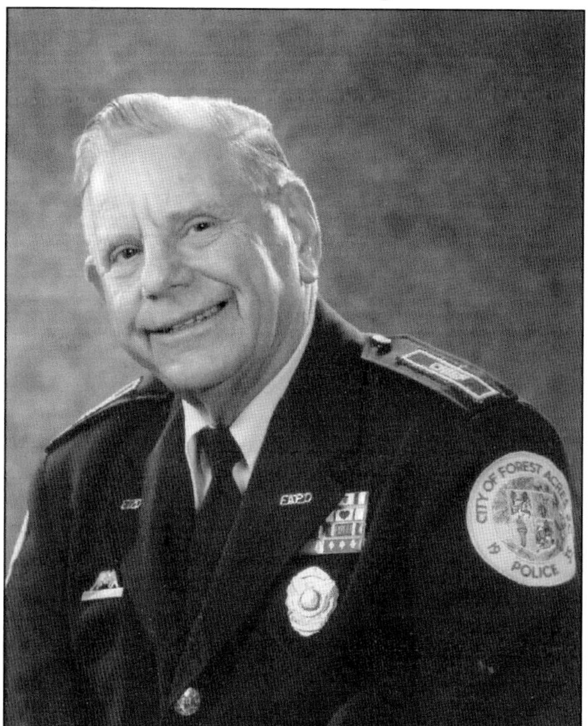

J. C. Rowe served as police chief of Forest Acres from 1978 to 1994 and as mayor from 1995 to 2003. (Courtesy of City of Forest Acres.)

Joseph A. Drawdy served as mayor of Forest Acres from 1991 to 1995. He is shown here with his wife, Sheri, and his son, Adam. (Courtesy of City of Forest Acres.)

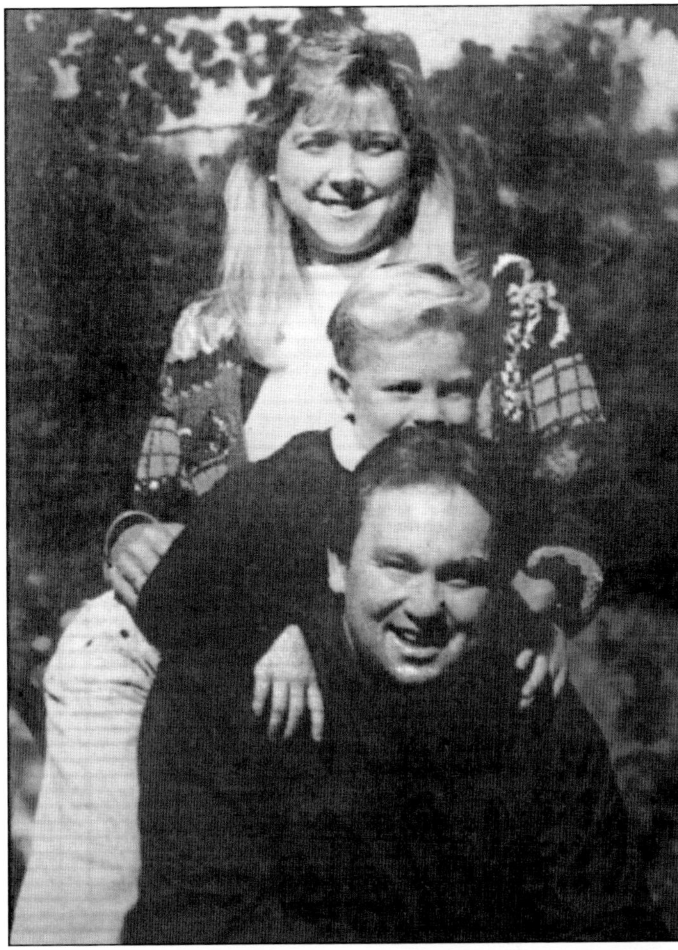

Joe Drawdy was elected mayor of Forest Acres in 1991 along with council members Dorothy Duncan and Robert Galloway. (Courtesy of City of Forest Acres.)

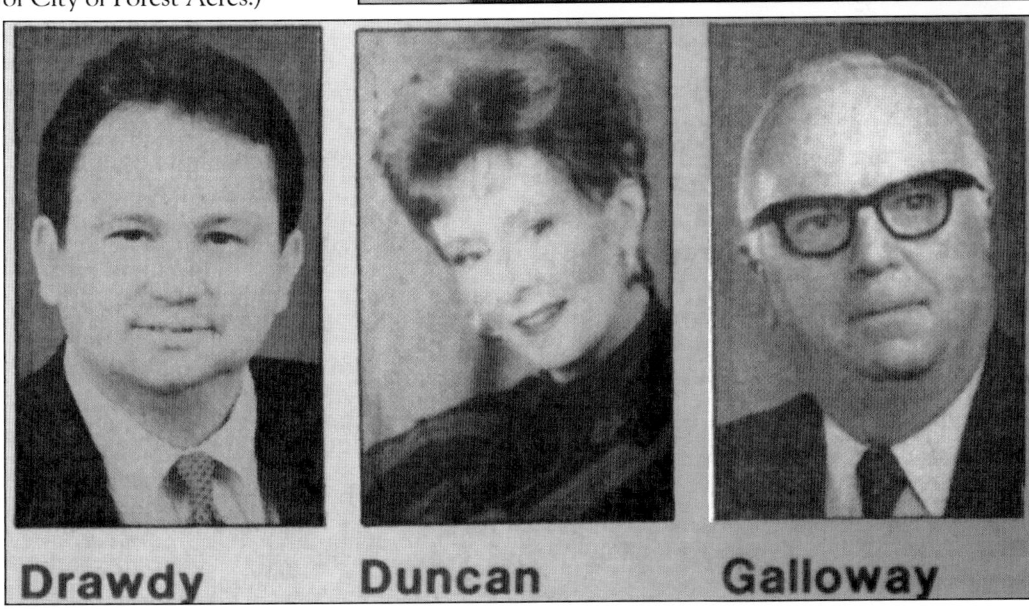

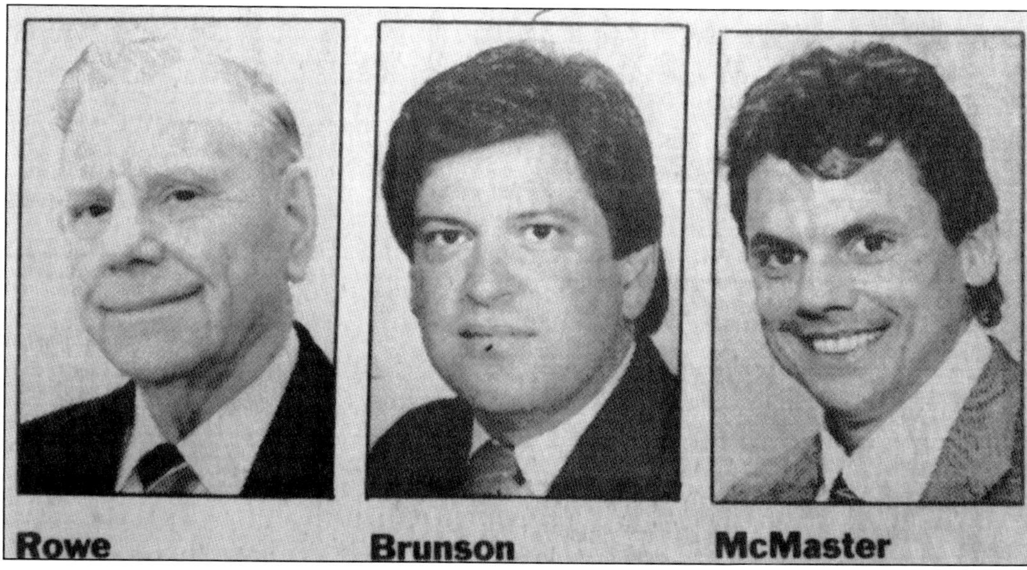

J. C. Rowe was elected mayor of Forest Acres in 1995 along with council members Frank Brunson (who was elected mayor in 2003) and Joe McMaster (who resigned in 1996 when elected to the South Carolina House of Representatives). (Courtesy of City of Forest Acres.)

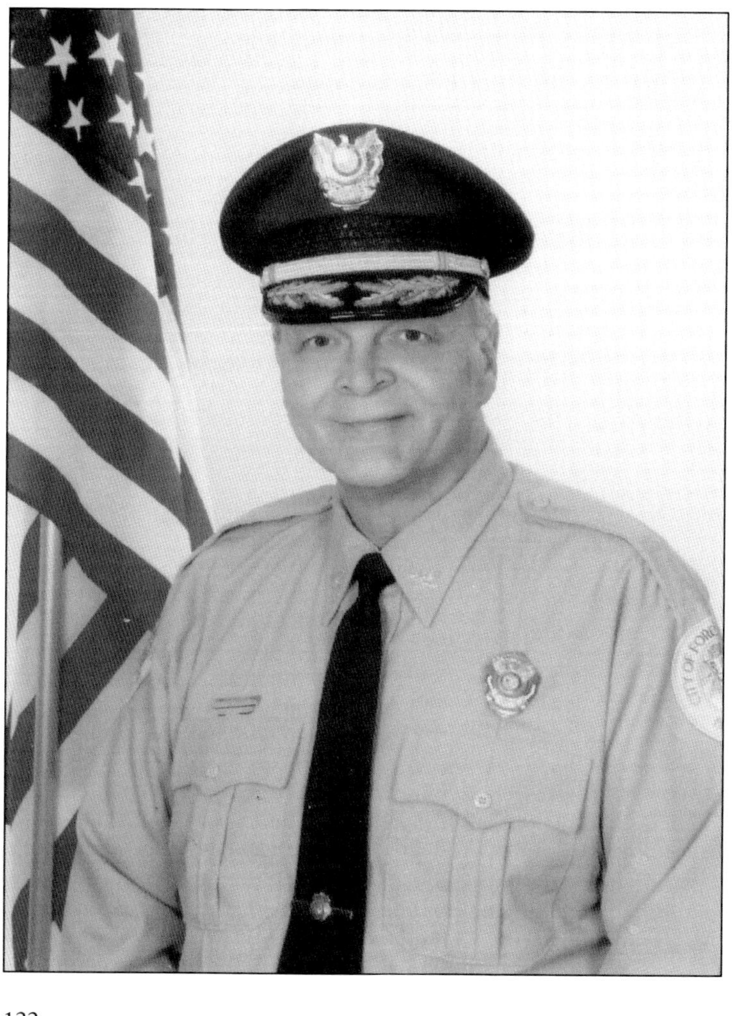

Marion E. "Gene" Sealy was appointed police chief of Forest Acres in 1994. (Courtesy of City of Forest Acres.)

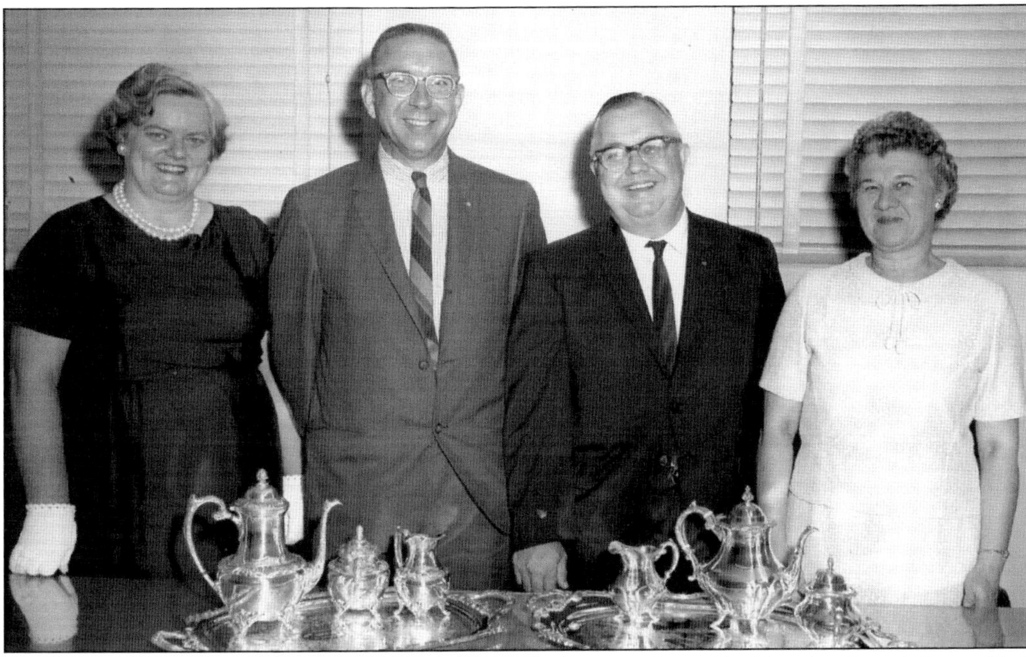

In the early 1950s, William J. Stubbs and his wife, Bernice Dent Stubbs, developed Forest Park on Dent property along Forest Drive. The early tenants were Heilig-Myers Furniture Company, Sunshine Cleaners, South Carolina National Bank, White's Shoe Heel Shop, Powell Liquor Mart, and Constan Car Wash. Stubbs served on city council from 1949 to 1951 and as mayor from 1957 to 1965. Lonnie Garrick served on city council from 1949 to 1965. In 1965, Garrick and Stubbs were honored for their long service to Forest Acres at a reception in their honor. Pictured left to right are Frankie Garrick, Lonnie Garrick, William Stubbs, and Bernice Stubbs. (Courtesy of City of Frankie Garrick.)

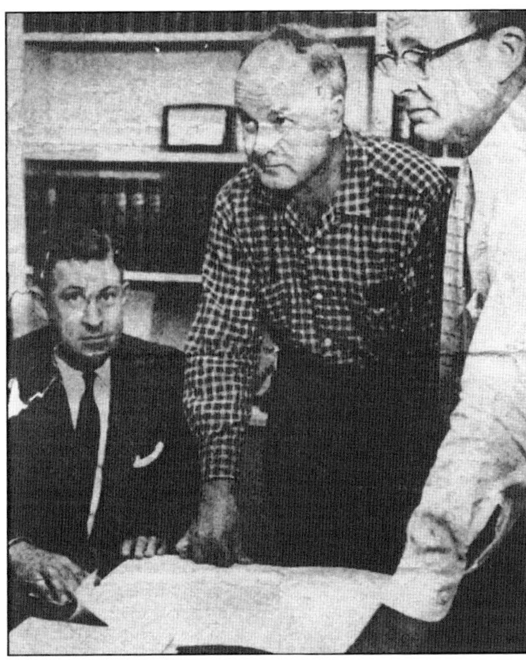

The Forest Land Company developed the intersection of Forest Drive and Trenholm Road as the Forest Lake Shopping Center. In this photograph Sam Preston (left), C. R. Dial (center), and A. S. Thomas review plans for the center. (Courtesy of Rhea Preston.)

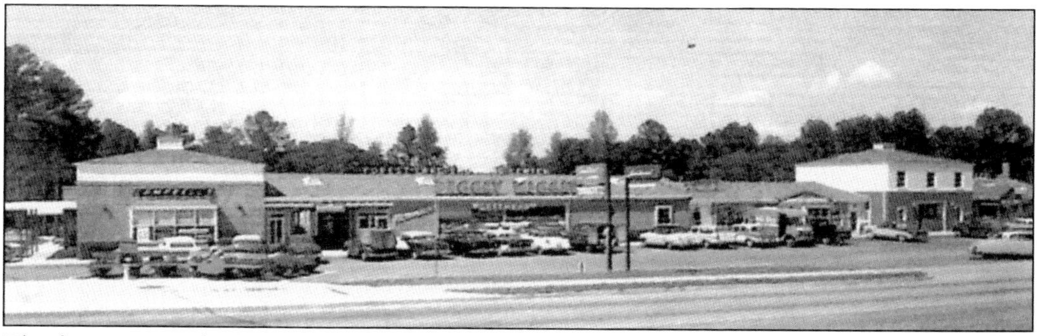

The first store in the Forest Lake Shopping Center was Campbell's Drug Store, run by John T. Campbell, who later became mayor of Columbia. Other early tenants were Forest Lake Pharmacy (Yank Roof, owner), Forest Lake Men's Shop (Bob Moore, owner), James Cooper's Law Office, Keith Schmidt's Liquor Store, Palmetto Hardware, Jack Owen Photography, and Piggly Wiggly. Across the street was Forest Lake Esso Station owned by Ira B. Sowell. (Courtesy of Rhea Preston.)

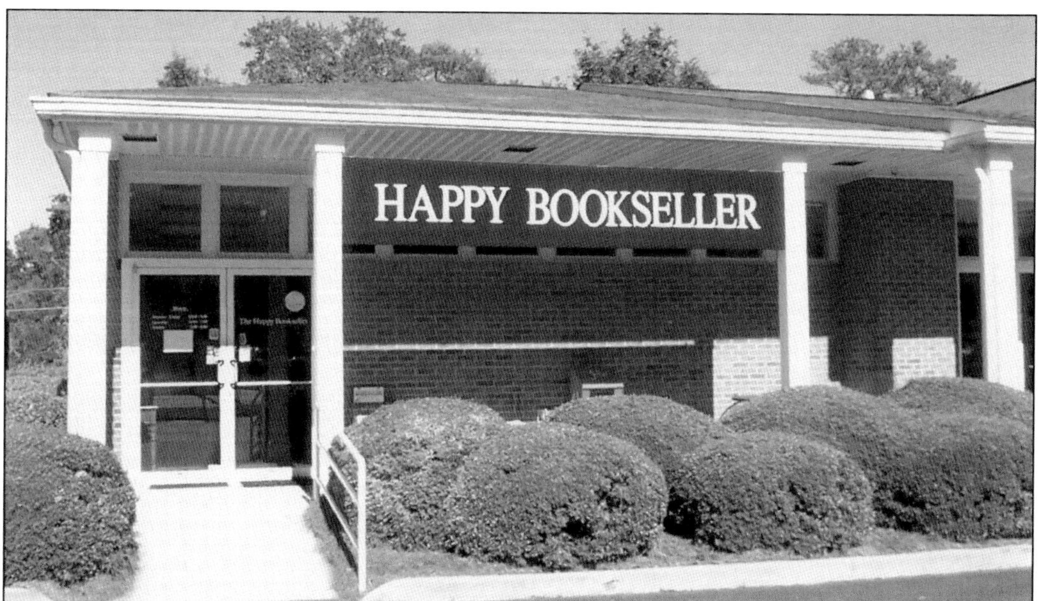

Rhett and Betty Jackson opened the Happy Bookseller in Richland Mall in 1974 and in 1988 moved their independent bookstore to 4525 Forest Drive. They hosted book signings by Alex Haley, Pat Conroy, James Dickey, Janette Turner Hospital, Rosa Parks, Hillary Clinton, and many other famous authors. Jackson sold the store to Andy and Carrie Graves in 1996. The Happy Bookseller closed in 2008. (Courtesy of the *Columbia Star*.)

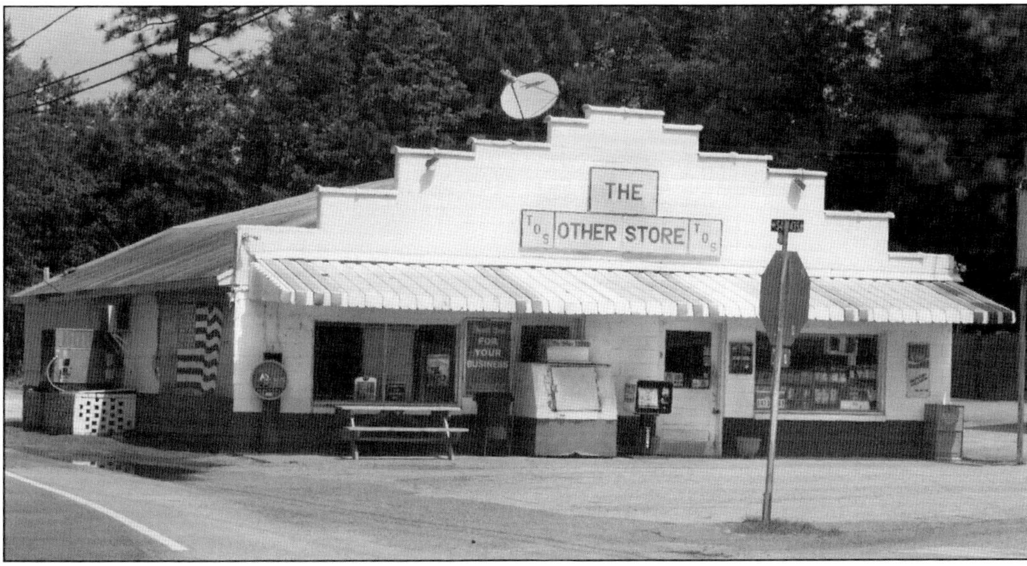

Forest Acres expanded during the 1960s and 1970s. Willingham Drive properties were annexed in 1961, Ponte Vedra Drive properties in 1963 and Ravenwood, the Wheeler property, and northern Satchel Ford Road in 1967. In the 1970s more landowners on Lakeshore Drive and Trenholm Road asked to be annexed into the city. Forest Acres had doubled in area. In the 1980s, 80 acres containing 468 residences were annexed. The Other Store on Bethel Church Road was the de facto town hall of Ravenwood until that community was annexed. It is now a quaint and popular grocery store and restaurant. (Photograph by Warner M. Montgomery.)

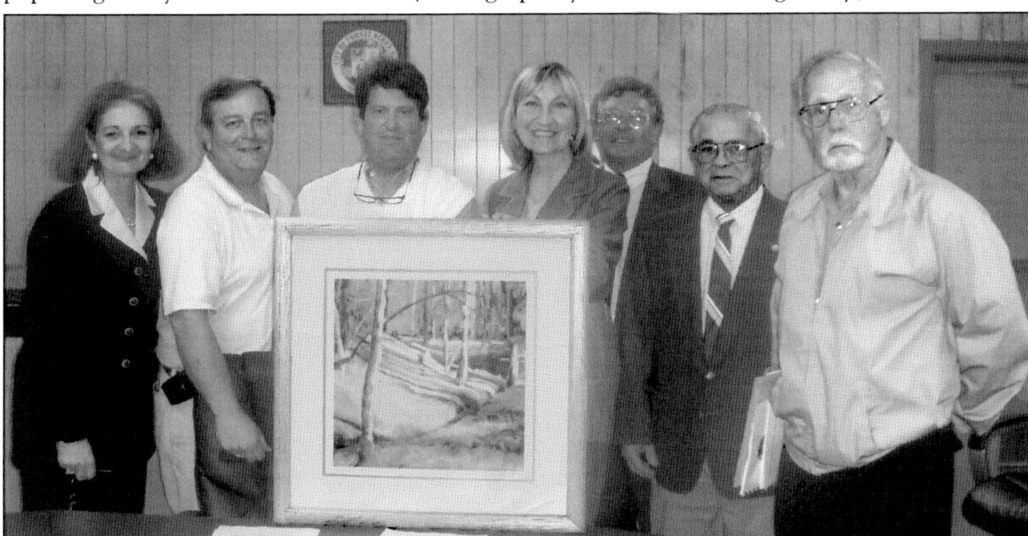

Councilman Frank J. Brunson was elected mayor in 2003. Members of the city council in 2010 were Shell Suber (elected 1973), Charles Fetner (1977), Curtis Rye (1997), and Ginger Dukes (2003). Shown from left to right in this picture are councilwoman Ginger Dukes, mayor pro tem Curtis Rye, mayor Frank Brunson, artist Karen Jamrose, cultural council Director Andy Witt, Councilman Charlie Fetner, and councilman Shell Suber with painting by Jamrose given to Forest Acres by the Trenholm Artist Guild and the Cultural Council of Lexington and Richland Counties in 2009. (Courtesy of the *Columbia Star*.)

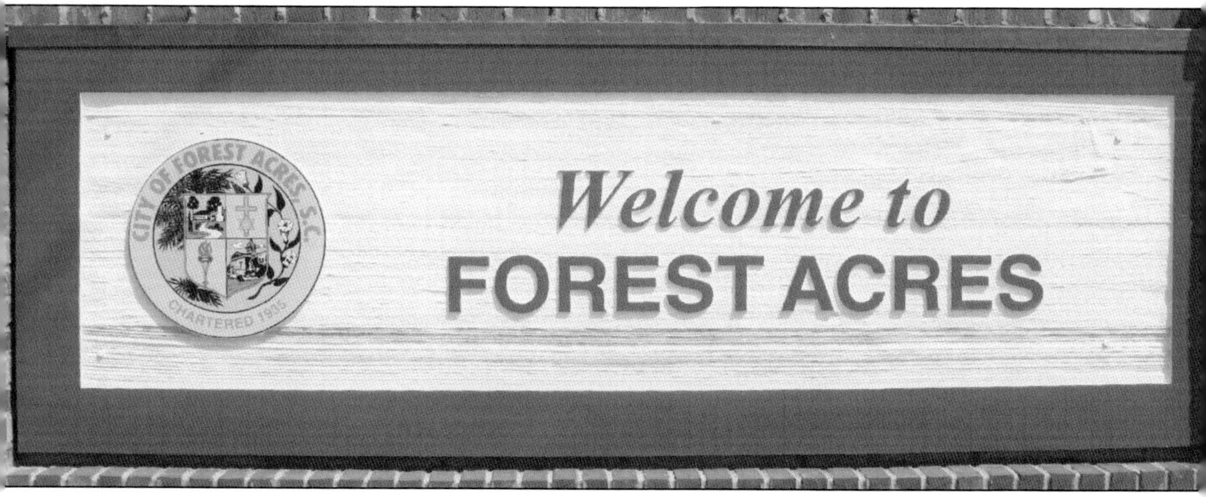

Forest Acres enjoys a rich history, with cultural landmarks that originated before the American Revolution. The community grew from a resort and farming community into a vibrant small town and is now a progressive city. Residents enjoy many parks, walking trails, beautiful lakes, houses of worship, public and private schools, fun festivals, and thriving businesses. Forest Acres is proud of its quality of life, friendliness, and environmental awareness. As the city's motto states, "Forest Acres is a city apart." (Photograph by Warner M. Montgomery.)

BIBLIOGRAPHY

Bowers, Charlton Wells, Jr. *Bowers Beach, A Brief History*. Unpublished manuscript. January 1999.

Forest Acres City Council Minutes. Forest Acres, SC: 1949–2009.

City of Forest Acres Land Development Plan 1987–2007. Columbia, SC: Central Midlands Regional Planning Council, 1987.

Cooper, Edwin H. *From My Point of View, 1907–1945*. Unpublished manuscript, contributed by the Cooper family.

DeMates, Iris. "Columbia Sees Sample Of New York Glamor At Movie Opening Night," The *State*. February 16, 1968.

Duggan, Carol Cook. *A History of the City of Forest Acres*. Forest Acres, SC: City of Forest Acres, 1997.

John Hughes Cooper, A Scrapbook. Columbia, SC: Richland County Public Library, 1961.

Green, Edwin L. *A History of Richland County, Vol. 1, 1732–1805*. Columbia, SC, 1932.

Herbert, R. Beverly. *Forest Lake Club From Its Beginning Through 1964*. Columbia, SC: Forest Lake Club, 1965.

Hennig, Helen Kohn, ed. *Columbia, Capital City of South Carolina, 1786–1936*. Columbia, SC: Columbia Sesqui-Centennial Commission, 1936.

McMaster, Fitz Hugh. "Quinine Hill Harks Back to Ancient Times." The *State*. January 14, 1934.

Montgomery, John A. *Columbia, South Carolina, History of a City*. Woodland Hills, CA: Windsor Publications, 1979.

Montgomery, Warner M. Columbia Schools, *A History of Richland County School District One, 1792–2000*. Columbia, SC: R. L. Bryan Company, 2009.

Moore, John Hammond. *Columbia and Richland County, A South Carolina Community, 1740–1990*. Columbia, SC: University of South Carolina Press. 1993.

Taylor, B. F. "John Taylor and His Taylor Descendants." *Historical and Genealogical Magazine* Vol. VIII, No.1 (January 1907): 95–119.

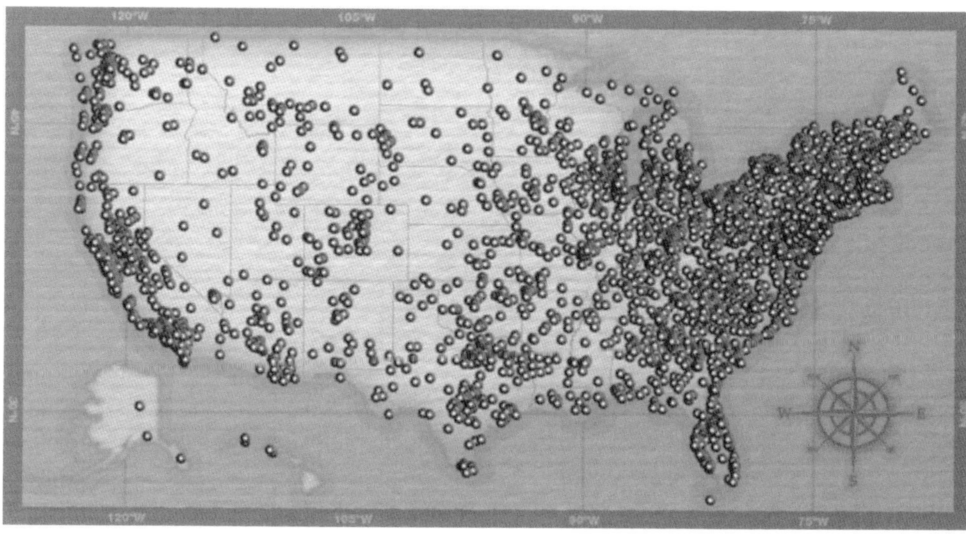